PRAISE FOR *INNOVATIVE B2B MA*

'A long-overdue resource for anyone working in the B2B environment or wishing to enter into it. Simon Hall's development of practical and relevant B2B marketing models make this essential reading for marketers and other professionals.' **Dawn Southgate, Head of Knowledge, The Chartered Institute of Marketing**

'If you read any B2B marketing publication this year, this should be it! Simon Hall provides us with a refreshing view, relevant content and truly practical advice, touching on many areas pertinent in the B2B marketing world right now and for the future. Absolutely fantastic insight.' **Catherine Howard, UK and Ireland Marketing Director, Atos**

'B2B marketers today need to be more dynamic than ever before, but this can be difficult in an environment where the complexity of the tools, technologies, techniques and channels has exploded, leaving many of us floundering. *Innovative B2B Marketing* provides the guidance that all B2B marketers need to help them navigate for success. I will be keeping this book very close to hand.' **Richard Robinson, Chair, B2B Marketing Council, The IDM**

'How do you build best-in-class B2B strategy in today's digital economy? How are great B2B brands built? How do you select the right lead nurturing agency? *Innovative B2B Marketing* is a rich treasure trove of B2B strategic wisdom.' **Shenda Loughnane, Global Chief Strategy Officer, iProspect**

'*Innovative B2B Marketing* is a comprehensive and compelling book that every B2B marketer should read.' **Ashraf Kamel, Head of Technology Vertical EMEA, LinkedIn Marketing Solutions**

Innovative B2B Marketing

New models, processes and theory

Simon Hall

Publisher's note

Every possible effort has been made to ensure that the information contained in this book is accurate at the time of going to press, and the publishers and authors cannot accept responsibility for any errors or omissions, however caused. No responsibility for loss or damage occasioned to any person acting, or refraining from action, as a result of the material in this publication can be accepted by the editor, the publisher or the author.

First published in Great Britain and the United States in 2017 by Kogan Page Limited

2nd Floor, 45 Gee Street
London
EC1V 3RS
United Kingdom

c/o Martin P Hill Consulting
122 W 27th, 10th Floor
New York, NY 10001
USA

4737/23 Ansari Road
Daryaganj
New Delhi 110002
India

www.koganpage.com

ISBN 978 0 7494 8080 6
E-ISBN 978 0 7494 8081 3

British Library Cataloguing-in-Publication Data

A CIP record for this book is available from the British Library.

Library of Congress Cataloging-in-Publication Data

Names: Hall, Simon, 1971- author.
Title: Innovative B2B marketing : new models, processes and theory / Simon Hall.
Other titles: Innovative business-to-business marketing
Description: 1st Edition. | New York, NY : Kogan Page Ltd, [2017]
Identifiers: LCCN 2017023768 (print) | LCCN 2017013828 (ebook) | ISBN 9780749480813 (ebook) | ISBN 9780749480806 (pbk.)
Subjects: LCSH: Industrial marketing. | Telemarketing.
Classification: LCC HF5415.1263 (print) | LCC HF5415.1263 .H36 2017 (ebook) | DDC 658.8/04–dc23
LC record available at https://lccn.loc.gov/2017013828

Typeset by Integra Software Services, Pondicherry
Print production managed by Jellyfish
Printed and bound by Ashford Colour Press Ltd.

This book is dedicated to Laura
for her unwavering support and inspiration

CONTENTS

PART TWO Improve B2B customer-centric marketing 33

LIST OF FIGURES AND TABLES

ABOUT THE AUTHOR

Simon Hall is a marketing innovator with over 20 years' experience in technology and services marketing. In his former career, he served as UK Chief Marketing Officer for Dell, and held senior roles at Acer, Microsoft and Toshiba. In 2016 Simon founded NextGen Marketing Solutions, with the aim to help companies of all sizes capitalize on the latest marketing techniques. He is passionate about pioneering new and exciting initiatives and sharing his knowledge and experience with the current and next generation of marketers, and you can find him regularly speaking at conferences and events, as well as on the board of several associations.

Simon is a course director with the Chartered Institute of Marketing (CIM), where he runs public courses as well as in-company training, a B2B council member with the Institute of Direct and Digital Marketing (IDM), the Internal Consulting Group's (ICG) Global Thought Leader for B2B Marketing and a member of both the CMO Council and European CMO Council.

PREFACE

Undeniably, the B2B environment has undergone huge change in the last decade, probably more so than in the 30 years preceding. Business customers are demonstrating new buying habits, the digital era has brought about new ways of marketing, the industry landscape has produced an enormous range of digital applications which impact, support and enable the full spectrum of B2B marketing disciplines, eg content, marketing performance marketing, brand building and channel partner marketing.

This change has meant that a number of the marketing models and approaches developed 20 to 30 years ago for B2B marketers have become less relevant and applicable; these models needed to be adapted, updated or even replaced.

For B2B business and marketing professionals, it may seem overwhelming to try to understand and grasp what is going on across all the different areas of B2B marketing, assuming they have the time to read and interpret literally hundreds of articles. *Innovative B2B Marketing* is a clear, practical guide that demystifies modern aspects of B2B marketing, including new marketing models, processes and thought leadership pieces. This book divides these multiple themes and areas into five core sections: marketing strategy creation, customer-centric marketing, content and digital marketing, channel partner marketing, and marketing related to marketing execution.

You will also find several case studies throughout the book. A good percentage of these come from the information and technology sector, because IT has been the home of digital applications and digital technology, and is therefore one of the first sectors to pilot and implement digital marketing practices.

Innovative B2B Marketing is perfect for any marketer working in, or with an interest in, the B2B space. It is also suitable for non-marketers wanting to get a grasp of the core elements of modern B2B marketing. In short, this book is great for marketers at any stage in their career.

ABOUT THIS BOOK

Part One: Developing your marketing strategy

The newly evolved business landscape has impacted the traditional marketing mix over the past decades driving a shift away from product-centric approaches to customer-centric and more recently towards a more dynamic marketing mix including social and offline communities. Associated with the changing business, marketing strategy and planning activities have needed to be adapted; this part looks at how to deal with this new landscape and provides a framework for a new marketing mix as well as guidance on how to create and plan strategies.

Part Two: Improve B2B customer-centric marketing

Customer-centric marketing is about putting the customer at the forefront of any marketing initiative; it's about viewing customers as valued entities. A customer-centric marketing approach can help a business add value and identify ways to differentiate through leveraging customer relationships and insights.

In this part we look at different stages of the customer lifecycle from customer acquisition through to retention and loyalty. Also included is a section on C-suite marketing; the ability to market to senior business executives is also becoming more important for vendors' future success and profitability. Customer solutions marketing is about how vendors can market solutions and offerings as opposed to product marketing where the focus is on providing solutions according to customers' needs. Finally, you can learn about how influencers can be capitalized on for B2B.

Part Three: Transform through content and digital marketing

With shifts in buyers' journeys, in media consumption, offline and online channels, and in technologies, it's more important than ever before for marketers to think strategically and embrace different tactics that support business goals. In this part we'll cover the main aspects of B2B digital and content marketing, from digital channels to B2B brand building.

Part Four: Collaborating with channel partners

The channel plays a critical role in supporting businesses in providing solutions, in growth across geographies, as well as many other business goals. Marketing to or through channel partners is an area all B2B marketers still wrestle with. What are the techniques, are there technologies making our lives easier? This and many other questions are addressed in this part.

Part Five: Optimizing marketing execution

With new digital applications such as marketing automation, CRM, etc, B2B marketers can and need to engage sales better and maximize marketing performance. This part spans topics such as how to engage and market to accounts, how to engage customers better through events, and how to improve lead generation and lead nurturing. Across all these areas B2B marketers need to understand the new role of sales and of marketing and work more effectively as one sales and marketing unit.

> Supporting online resources for *Innovative B2B Marketing* can be downloaded from koganpage.com/Innovative-B2B.

Introduction to business marketing 01

The changing business landscape

In less than 100 years we've moved through multiple eras of business and industry, from the production age through to the marketing age and recently from the globalization era to the era of digital and applications.

Various factors have affected a shift away from internationalization and globalization in the 21st century; businesses during this period moved from a model of focusing on globalizing to a more balanced model where businesses benefited from globalization but reverted to a more localized business approach; sometimes called the 'Glocal' model.

Business today looks and feels very different even compared to 10 years ago; they need to deal with increased data and information; to understand and capitalize on digital technologies; to operate with rapidly shifting business models and new working behaviours where location becomes less relevant.

As a result of this dynamically changing business environment, business-to-business marketing has needed to change, new models have needed to be developed and old models adapted. This book looks at the core areas of marketing where change has occurred and provides up-to-date tools for B2B marketers to deal with this challenging new business environment.

What is B2B marketing?

B2B marketing, sometimes referred to as 'business marketing' or 'industrial marketing', is the practice of individuals or organizations marketing products or services to other companies or organizations. The customer in this case is an organization rather than an individual customer or consumer, though the products, services and solutions they purchase may sometimes be the same or similar.

Table 1.1 The changing shape of industry

Business era (20th and 21st centuries)	Description	Period
Production era	Emphasis on goods production, innovation in production techniques enabling faster manufacturing	1900–1930
Marketing era	Focus on consumer and satisfying their needs and preferences	Since 1950s
Relationship era	Deepening engagement with customers, employees and suppliers	Since 1990s
Globalization	Greater focus on internationalisation of business, going global	Since 1990s
Internet age	Greater use of the internet for information, for commerce	Since mid-1990s
Digital (or Application) age	Characterized by digital applications	Since late 2000s

B2B vs B2C marketing

B2B marketing differs from consumer (or B2C) marketing in several ways, such as time to purchase, number of stakeholders involved, complexity of offerings, and the buying process. For example, the buying period for a consumer to purchase a new mobile phone could involve a few days: the buyer is influenced by a positive review of a mobile phone and the next day decides to purchase it. In business this can be very different: a business buying new mobile phones for its salesforce may want to understand more about the technology, capability and business-related services before deciding to purchase. The stakeholder involved in a consumer purchase is typically one person; in a large business there may be multiple departments involved, such as operations, finance, sales and procurement before deciding to purchase.

A B2B marketing audience expects more detailed and richer information as well as different forms of content to help guide them in their decision process. A B2C marketing audience may expect content to be simpler, more engaging and stimulating rather than informative.

Channel

Despite the many differences there are points of cross-over where B2B is like B2C marketing. For example, businesses targeting small businesses or home offices may use similar distribution channels and retailers as those for consumers; small business owners may use retailers or other consumer channels to purchase goods in small quantities.

The emotional factor

Consumer purchases are often regarded as being emotionally based, as opposed to being purely rational. In business this may also be the case as those buying for themselves may be small business owners. Even in large organizations an individual who has the ultimate responsibility for procuring for the business may be emotionally influenced as the purchase decision, if it goes wrong, could negatively impact the business and its performance.

Large audiences to target

Consumer marketing tends to be aimed at large groups of consumers through mass media and retailers; likewise, small businesses and small office users may also fall into large audience groups. For example, a business selling to a small business community needs to send messages to thousands or millions of businesses, if not segmented.

Segmentation

Another difference between B2C and B2B marketing can occur with segmentation. In B2C segmentation can occur across life stage and life style, eg families, teens, parents, to make marketing and budgets work better. In business the segmentation can be based on organizational factors such as industrial sector, size of business or buying behaviour.

B2B marketing types

Within B2B marketing there are clear distinctions between marketing to small businesses or small office customers and medium or large enterprises. This distinction is transactional marketing for small business and relationship or enterprise marketing for medium and large businesses. The main differences are summarized in Table 1.2. The core factors are: the type of product or solution involved, which is typically more elaborate and requires more scrutiny; the number of buyers or departments involved; and the drivers of the buying process.

Table 1.2 B2B marketing types

Transactional B2B marketing – SOHO/small business	Relationship B2B marketing – scaling business/medium/large
Product driven	Trust-based relationships
Large target audience = small businesses (>4m in UK)	Small, focused audience (<100k in UK)
Simpler buying process	More complex process
Small size of purchase; more quantity	Large size of purchase and bids
Single stakeholder in buying process	Multi-stakeholder buying process
Emotional buying decisions	Emotions invested + rational buying decisions
Increasing and generating revenue	Increasing and generating leads Increasing pipeline and revenue

B2B insights

According to the latest B2B buyer research published by DemandGen Report (Demandbase, 2015), the world of B2B marketing is continuing to get more complex and buyers more sophisticated. Some of the findings of the survey are:

- 53 per cent of buyers say their time to purchase has increased with 80 per cent of those saying they are taking more time to research and 82 per cent saying they are viewing more sources.
- 43 per cent stated there is an increase in the number of people who are part of the buying committee with 48 per cent saying there are one to three people involved and 35 per cent stating there are four to six.
- Buyers are increasingly using the internet as a source with 53 per cent saying that social media played a role in their purchase decision.
- 52 per cent of B2B buyers stated they viewed two to four pieces of content before making a decision and 28 per cent stated they viewed five to seven.
- 85 per cent stated they wanted a vendor with knowledge of their industry.

All these statistics point to the fact that marketers need to embrace different marketing vehicles and better tailor their messages and content to the customer. Marketing has the challenging role of influencing buyers more than before so that when customers are about to purchase they're already considering the vendors' products or services.

Business market segmentation and size

There are many ways a vendor can segment its business audience; the most typical being by number of employees a company employs. Table 1.3 shows how the UK Department of Business, Innovation and Skills splits the UK business market into four categories: micro, small, medium and large.

In 2015, within the UK, the medium and large enterprise segment accounted for less than 1 per cent of the total business population; organizations with fewer than 50 employees accounted for over 99 per cent. According to these figures the medium and large business segment has grown about 20 per cent over the past 10 years (Department for Business Innovation and Skills, 2015).

Business market segmentation

Segmenting a business market means dividing the market into different homogeneous groups of companies. Some ways to segment business markets are by demographics, buyer behaviour, situational behaviours, industry classifications, by region and operations variables.

The aim of segmentation in B2B is to gather businesses that have similarities into groupings. These groupings help a business' effectiveness in targeting, engaging and selling to them. Businesses classify and segment audiences not only for marketing reasons but for business reasons such as how they go to market, for structuring sales or entire divisions and for better tracking business performance.

Marketing departments can help with buyer behaviour segmentation by understanding the customer's likelihood of purchasing a product or service based on sector, previous purchase history, size of business, etc. This is sometimes called 'propensity modelling' – the customer's propensity to purchase

Table 1.3 Estimated number of businesses, UK private sector (thousands)

Size	2012	2013	2014	2015
All private sector business	4,818	4,914	5,243	5,389
All SME (1–249)	4,811	4,907	5,236	5,382
Micro (1–9)	1,023	987	1,044	1,069
Small (10–49)	178	187	195	204
Medium (50–249)	30	31	31	33
Large (250+)	6	7	7	7

certain products is determined by a set of common identified factors or criteria. Arming the business with key information about a customer's propensity to purchase goods helps sales and marketing be more effective in delivering customer leads.

Behavioural segmentation looks at knowledge, attitudes, usage rate, response rates or readiness stage for a product or service. Marketers can also segment according to multiple geographic sub-segmentations, eg regions, countries, cities, neighbourhoods, or postal codes. A small business providing services may target only local businesses rather than national or international organizations.

SIC classification system

Businesses can be segmented according to the sector they operate in, using Standard Industrial Classification or SIC codes. Established in the United States in 1937, this is a system for classifying industries by a four-digit code, and is used by government agencies to classify industry areas. The SIC system is used for classifying business activities in the United Kingdom, and it correlates the European Union's industrial classification system, NACE (Nomenclature Générale des Activités Économiques dans les Communautés Européennes).

Business clusters are important for business marketers and can influence the use of locations and communication channels:

- *Business clusters*: geographical concentrations of interconnected businesses or suppliers in a field that can exist on a local, national or even global scale.
- *High-tech clusters*: technology-oriented groupings, often built around universities or research centres. Examples are Silicon Valley and the South West and Thames Valley areas in the United Kingdom.
- *Know-how-based clusters*: more traditional in their nature and have built up over many years. In London one can find a concentration of financial companies in the City.
- *Government-incentivized clusters*: some countries use economic incentives to attract companies or industries. An example is the software industries and call-centres in India.
- *Low-cost manufacturing clusters*: these clusters have typically emerged in developing countries within particular industries, such as automotive production, electronics, or textiles. Examples include electronics clusters in Mexico (eg Guadalajara) and Argentina (eg Córdoba).

The digital economy

The digital application economy has been one of the strongest forces of change in the business world. It has brought about multiple new business models, new business growth perspectives and helped shift economies and economic status for some countries. Some examples of these new business models are e-commerce, the cloud and online advertising.

E-commerce in the form of online transactions has impacted almost all traditional business forms; some businesses have made a move to a full e-commerce approach while others have opted for a hybrid approach. One example is buying flight tickets, where purchasing and checking-in have almost fully moved online.

Cloud business, where services are provided via the internet, has the key benefits of lower set-up costs, fewer operational resources requirements, flexibility, ability to grow and scale, and ease of collaboration. Examples of cloud date back to the 1990s where free e-mail services in the cloud were provided by Hotmail, Yahoo, Google and so on.

Online advertising has also arrived and grown as a result of the digital economy. New advertising-based models include free or subsidized services and new payment methods such as cost-per-mille (CPM), cost-per-action (CPA) and cost-per-click (CPC).

Core trends and this book

The past 10 years have been characterized by several specific trends in B2B marketing (see Figure 1.1); this book takes into consideration those core trends as well as essential topics to support B2B marketers in developing more innovative marketing plans and strategies and optimizing their execution:

Core trend 1: Increased customer-centricity

With changing business behaviours and changing organization dynamics B2B marketers need to have a better grasp of organizational influences, and to better engage and communicate with businesses and stakeholders through more targeted and tailored communication and content. C-suite marketing and influencer marketing have become hot topics in B2B as they are about leveraging different relationships and influencers all to be found in Chapters 4 to 9.

Core trend 2: Rise of digital and content marketing

There has been a shift in marketing communications to include a greater emphasis on content; in turn content formats have diversified, and generally become richer. There has also been a move away from interruptive marketing towards inbound marketing. Interruptive marketing is promoting a product or service through continued advertising, promotions, public relations and sales; sometimes it is regarded as an annoyance rather than a help for customers. With inbound marketing customers are receptive to your marketing messages and it is marketing that attracts and pulls customers, rather than marketing pushing messages. Ten years ago marketers didn't have the capability to track customer buying behaviour or media consumption across multiple marketing vehicles; also customers didn't use such a variety of marketing vehicles in one purchase. Digital and associated technologies have changed all that: businesses today are able to track customer media consumption and journey in a more connected manner. Digital applications allow companies to understand how customers engage across digital channels such as mobile, blogging and social, how many pieces of content they use, and how they engage with such content. Chapters 10 to 15 shed light on how to leverage new B2B digital and content marketing to support the business.

Core trend 3: From single routes to market to multi-channel marketing

Businesses and marketers were once constrained to think about singular physical routes to market, directly or indirectly. With the growth of digital technologies and applications companies today need to embrace digital and physical distribution channels and integrate them in their plans, to support and accelerate their growth. Chapters 16 to 19 outline key B2B channels as well as different forms of marketing through and with channel partners.

Core trend 4: Increased pressure to optimize marketing execution

With new digital applications such as marketing automation, CRM, etc, marketers today can and need to engage sales better and maximize marketing performance. With the changing nature of buying decisions, the tactics marketers use to generate leads have become richer, and new technologies and digital applications have increased the ability to track customers' behaviours across different communication channels. You'll find more about this in Chapters 20 to 24.

Figure 1.1 Innovative B2B marketing

References and further reading

AT&T, Cisco, Citi, PwC and SAP (2011) The new digital economy: how it will transform business, Oxford Economics, Oxford, available at: http://www.pwc.com/mt/en/publications/assets/the-new-digital-economy.pdf (accessed 8 February 2017)

Demandbase (2015) B2B buyers survey report, available at: http://www.demandgenreport.com/resources/reports/the-2015-b2b-buyer-s-survey (accessed 8 February 2017)

Department for Business Innovation and Skills (2015) *Business Population Estimated for the UK and Regions 2015*, DBIS, London

Rayna, T (2008) *Understanding the Challenges of the Digital Economy: The nature of digital goods*, Imperial College, London

PART ONE
Developing your marketing strategy

The new marketing mix 02

This chapter will give you an understanding of:

- the benefits of the marketing mix
- the new marketing mix
- the marketing mix process
- how to trade-off on marketing mix elements

The marketing mix defined

The marketing mix is a framework for marketers to strategize, plan and execute their marketing activities. The marketing mix was originally defined as putting the right product (or combination thereof) in the right place at the right time and at the right price, sometimes called the 4Ps. Some of the original work on the 4Ps has evolved to be more customer-centric.

The purpose of the marketing mix is to capture all the key variables that need to be considered in marketing strategy, planning and implementation, and to reach an optimum balance between the marketing variables. One focus of the marketing mix has remained core to all recent marketing mix approaches: that the needs of the target customers are met. The challenges in defining the marketing mix are many, such as market forces and changes in business environments and customers' needs.

Is the marketing mix still relevant?

The marketing mix provides multiple benefits for marketers; it is a framework for assessing resource allocation within the team. For example, where the marketing department is required to put greater emphasis on social media or digital marketing, the marketing head of department may need to consider allocating more resources.

The marketing mix also serves as a checklist for marketers, whether in creating strategy, planning, implementing or reviewing activities. It's a steer for responsibilities: each mix element can have accountable owners or one owner, for example some can be accountable for channel marketing, others for pricing, others for solutions marketing. It also facilitates better internal communication due to assigned SPOCs (sales point of contacts), so sales understand who to go to for what; in turn clearer communication reduces confusion or conflict between sales and marketing departments.

The shift away from the four Ps

The original marketing mix was associated with the four Ps: price, product, promotion, and place. It assumed little difference existed between B2B marketing and B2C marketing, marketing of products in volume or marketing of complex solutions, and marketing supporting a simple sales process compared to marketing to customers requiring higher sales touches.

After the 1980s it was felt the original four Ps were centred on the business rather than the customers and an adapted set of mix variables or descriptors was required to become more customer-centric. The four Ps were adapted as follows:

- *Product* was originally about tangible goods or intangible services a customer requires. Most products under the original 4Ps were considered subject to a product lifecycle, from launch to end of life. The changed focus was centred on customer solutions.
- *Place* was originally about where the product was found and its associated distribution channel; this has evolved into channel and accessibility to the product or service and how convenient it is for customers to receive or access products and services.
- *Price*: the focus on the amount the customer pays for the product shifted to cost; cost became the new determining factor behind pricing where marketers help businesses correctly price products or service according to needs or buying capabilities.
- *Promotion* represented different communication vehicles; 'communication' or channels of communication became the new elements, where they allow for customers wanting two-way communication with the companies that make the products or services.

Since 2000 there has been a greater move to the internet as a buying channel, which has given customers a greater ease in purchasing. The ability to access data through more powerful mobile devices means customers and business customers could use different types of content. There has been a greater richness in the content customers use, which has placed more demands on business to align through content marketing. Additionally, with more sophistication in social platforms and more real-time usage, business customers can engage quicker, better and with more people than even five years ago.

The new B2B marketing mix

These influences have brought about a new B2B marketing mix (see Figure 2.1) and the five Cs to help marketers deal with the new B2B situation:

Channels of communication

Since the 1990s communication channels have changed to reflect a higher mix of digital communication. Existing digital channels have also evolved and new channels have emerged such as social, digital PR, and webinars.

Content

Tied to communication channels, content has increased in importance. B2B marketers are now dealing with more diversified and richer content formats and more content overall. Businesses also have more possibilities to create content.

Customer solutions marketing

This has evolved due to commoditization of products in areas such as telecommunications and IT, as well as customers who expect more than simply products. This trend has influenced companies to think of true solutions as well as end-to-end solutions. Social listening and digital monitoring tools have allowed companies to track and listen to customers and come up with solutions that are more relevant and targeted.

Channels to market

This area has changed to include a digital channel mix. Some companies will offer multiple options for customers to purchase products, potentially with different customer experiences. Companies can face the challenge of managing an omnichannel approach due to the transparency brought about by digital and customers demanding greater consistency between channel offerings.

Figure 2.1 The new marketing mix (updated)

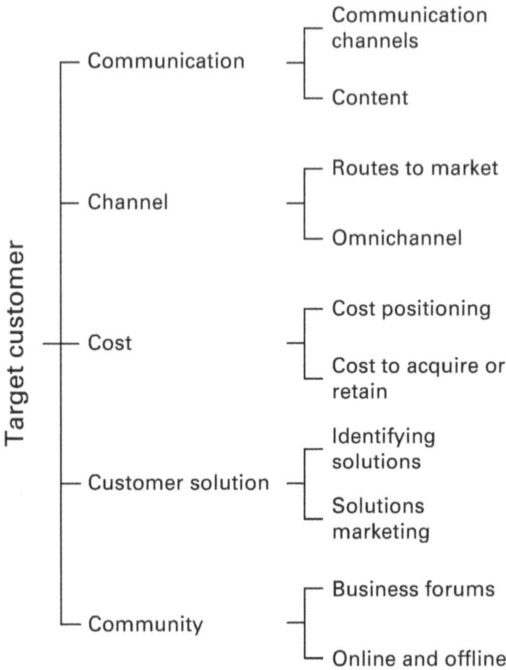

Communities

These are groups or grouping of people, mainly centred on common interests or themes. Social has played a big part in bringing these communities together and in reinforcing offline communities. Due to the impact communities have on businesses it's important for marketers to adopt communities as part of their mix, whether centred on associations, offline groups, memberships or social forums.

With the need for businesses and marketers to meet the needs of business customers through combined partner approaches, whether alliances, channel partners or marketing partners, collaborative marketing has become even more important.

How to determine the marketing mix

Marketers need to determine the optimum mix of the different marketing Cs to satisfy the needs and wants of the customer and create maximum impact from their activities. With customers' needs and environmental factors in constant flux this is not always an easy task. In the words of Philip Kotler, 'Marketing mix represents the setting of the firm's marketing decision variables at a particular point of time' (Chand, 2016).

TIP The marketing mix process

1. Target customer identification: this first step is about defining the target customer; the more detailed the description the better the plan and quality of marketing mix elements.
2. Needs and requirement analysis: once the target customer is identified a needs/requirement analysis should be carried out; this can use in-house resources and knowledge such as customer service feedback, sales account plans, customer input and forums where customer insights can be collected directly. Marketers should use the analysis to define buying power, motives of customers, and key current and future needs associated with the business offerings.
3. Once customer research is complete the next step is to look at product offerings and solutions aligned to the customer and their needs.
4. The next stage is to determine the channel to the customer; for some customers the organization may need to offer alternative routes to purchase, eg online and by phone.
5. This step is about selecting the communication channel and content formats according to the previous steps.
6. Next is aligning communities, and cost as well as price structure; for example, depending on channel the price and cost structure will be different.
7. Before finalizing the mix the elements are reviewed in light of constraints or parameters defined by the business or marketing departments. For example, the route to market may require adjustment through business strategy plans; the price, pricing policy and cost may need operations and sales buy-in or may need market testing; and channels of communication and content may be determined by the marketing budget.
8. Implementation – in this phase the marketing mix is implemented and reviewed on a regular basis to assess the need for adjustment.

In general, parameters can come in the form of budget limitations, salesforce limitations, business growth stage and channel development.

Marketing mix and trade-offs

In defining the marketing mix the most difficult task for marketers is to incorporate trade-offs. For example, if marketing decides on a low price then it is likely there will be less budget to advertise; if marketing decides on a heavily tiered route to market the budget will need to be able to support this approach.

Deciding on the trade-offs

Where to trade-off and how needs to be decided according to the target customer segment. The first step in the marketing mix could be to look at customer solutions to fulfil customers' current or future needs (see Figure 2.2). Following that, the optimum route to deliver the solution to the customer can be decided upon, depending on the cost and the price the customer is prepared to pay, or according to market forces. With this knowledge, the content and its forms can be built according to the communication mix; eg where it's a more complex solution a webinar, slideshow and face-to-face events may form part of the mix. If the customer is a large enterprise, the trade-offs may be between richer and tailored content to reach specific target stakeholders, or multiple formats of less rich content that support a corporate reseller and engage the same customer on the vendors' behalf.

Figure 2.2 Marketing mix process

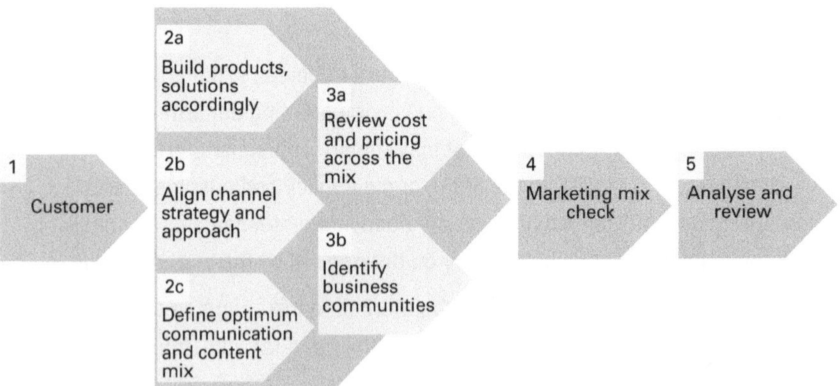

The channels of communication will depend on how much marketing budget there is, how many resellers the business is considering and the bandwidth to provide and promote directly or indirectly. If the strategy is to reach and influence an executive set of decision makers via social media at the customer side, the trade-off on content and channels may be to over-index content for social platforms rather than advertise through other digital channels or even offline channels. Such trade-off decisions can be mapped against parameters and interdependencies can be called out or highlighted on a grid like the one shown in Table 2.1.

Other external factors affecting marketing mix decisions can include the following:

- Shift in customers' buying behaviour – where customers make a shift to buy through a channel rather than directly. Customers' change to using more social or less TV will influence media/vehicle mix.
- Technologies changing the game, for example where customers move from booking a flight via travel operators to buying directly from the airline online.
- Trade behaviour, where customers find they can benefit from easier purchasing across borders.
- Competitor consolidation – where a consolidation of providers leads to the remaining vendors having to market harder to highlight their benefits.
- One organization leaving a market provides an opportunity for others, through aggressive acquisition, to sweep up customers left adrift.
- Government legislation such as placing a ceiling on prices or restricting price dumping will affect a company's approach to price setting.

ACTIVITIES

Review your recent marketing plan for the new marketing mix and the five Cs. Where do you see opportunities to adapt in terms of collaborative partnerships or in taking advantage of customer communities?

Choose one marketing mix element and look at decision making and dependencies between that one and the other marketing mix elements.

Table 2.1 Marketing mix: mix/trade-off review

Trade-off review	Communication and content	Channels	Customer solution	Cost	Community	Collaborative partnership
Communication and content	X					
Channels		X				
Customer solution			X			
Cost				X		
Community					X	
Collaborative partnerships						X

FOCUS Communications and content	Channels	Customer solution	Cost	Community	Collaborative partnership
VARIABLE A: Number of content formats					
VARIABLE B: Content mix					
VARIABLE C: Digital channel mix					

Reference

Chand, S (2016) Marketing-mix: definition, nature and determining the marketing-mix, available at: http://www.yourarticlelibrary.com/marketing/marketing-management/marketing-mix-definition-nature-and-determining-the-marketing-mix/27951 (accessed 10 February 2017)

B2B marketing strategy and planning 03

This chapter will give you an understanding of:

- B2B marketing strategy and planning
- the marketing planning process
- market audits and key aspects
- how to formulate marketing strategy
- how to develop effective B2B strategies

Introduction

A marketing plan outlines a company's marketing activities for a coming period whether three months, a year or longer. It describes the business activities involved in achieving specific marketing objectives within a given period. Typically, those using marketing plans are marketing departments to ensure key elements are implemented and reviewed. Other departments such as sales and finance will need to view marketing plans to understand what marketing delivers to the business.

The planning process entails two core activity areas: marketing research to understand the market, competition, environment and customers; and planning the marketing mix. In this chapter we look at marketing planning in a B2B context, which has undergone many new influences, meaning that some of the more traditional marketing planning models need adapting to address such changes.

The traditional and new B2B marketing planning process

The process of marketing planning usually follows a number of stages from the development of objectives, through to strategy setting, the implementation of activities to achieve the strategic objectives, and the control and review of how the marketing implementation occurred. Figure 3.1 outlines the main steps and some adaptations based on changes in B2B marketing that have occurred in the past 10 to 15 years.

Goal setting

Within this stage, goals are clarified that align to the business overall mission and business purpose. Marketing alongside other departments needs to work to support the business and corporate goals and marketing need to understand and appreciate corporate objectives. Goal setting in the 21st century needs to allow for more flexibility due to the rapid shifts in technologies, customer behaviour, B2B social marketing potential and digital technologies.

The audit – situation analysis

The next main stage is situation analysis and during this phase a marketing audit is carried out. The marketing audit helps marketers analyse and

Figure 3.1 Traditional vs new B2B marketing planning

Traditional	New + Adaptations	
Goal setting	Adaptable goal setting	Adaptable goals based on faster evolving business ecosystem
Situation analysis	Modern situation analysis	Customer buying cycle review Market technology landscape
Strategy	Strategy	Flex or tolerance to include
Marketing planning	Marketing planning	New marketing mix to incorporate
Implementation	Digital enabled implementation	Marketing technology enabled
Review	Digital enabled monitor and review	Marketing technology enabled

evaluate the marketing strategies, current activities, goals and how marketing is performing against those marketing and business metrics.

New aspects that B2B marketers need to invest in are a situation analysis of business customers in terms of needs, behaviours, buying process and other related aspects; with the rapidly evolving changes in customers and their context, existing assumptions from marketing departments can quickly become out of date. Also new to the audit should be technology landscape and audits associated with the business type and marketing type.

Marketing strategy

The next main phase is the development of the marketing strategy, which involves developing objectives and addressing the outcomes of a SWOT analysis (strengths, weaknesses, opportunities and threats). During this phase weaknesses and threats are defined which the business should address, and opportunities are incorporated into the plan, leveraging existing strengths. The marketing objectives reflect what the business is wanting to achieve in the coming period. Marketing goals usually follow a SMART approach (specific, measurable, achievable, results based and timed). After identification of opportunities and challenges, the next step is to develop marketing objectives that indicate the end state to achieve.

Marketing planning

Following the strategy formulation, the next stage is to define the marketing plan for the new marketing mix; based on mix definition the plan is created, which includes overall goals, timings and customers to target.

Implementation and evaluation

During this phase the marketing activities are allocated resources, and activities implemented and evaluated. Marketing budget is determined and reviewed based on defined outcomes and therefore return on investment (ROI). The marketing team implements plans by launching programmes and campaigns, and spends budgets on various activities. During this phase evaluation takes place; evaluation can be an informal review.

New digital technologies as well as changes in business customers using more digital applications means marketers can more easily track and monitor customers and behaviours. Digital applications such as marketing automation and CRM support marketing departments in implementing and monitoring activities as well as tracking spend.

B2B marketing audits

Comprehensive marketing audits include the following.

SWOT analysis

The SWOT analysis (strengths, weaknesses, opportunities and threats) should answer key questions such as what strengths customers believe your business has, what it could do better, what weaknesses it needs to address, and what opportunities it needs to exploit. Conducting this analysis helps the business understand how it performs in the eyes of the customer.

> **TIP** Use the SWOT to build customer relationships
>
> The questions related to the SWOT can be a way to build better relationships with customers as the business is seen to be listening to its customers; of course, it is important for the business to subsequently address those concerns from a customer's perspective. Opportunities and threats need to be understood so companies can deal with threats and go after opportunities.

Competitor analysis

During this part of the audit competitors are also reviewed using SWOT. The outcome from competitor analysis can be defensive as well as offensive. This analysis should include a strategic as well as tactical component as this helps your business incorporate short-term tactics as well as longer-term turn-around activities. The objective here is to identify strengths to match, weaknesses to exploit and to predict potential opportunities that the competitor may capitalize on, and to prevent this through offensive and defensive tactics.

Defensive tactics may be short term in dealing with price, promotion or other competitive tactics that impact current business performance. Offensive approaches are usually longer term and strategic in nature.

External market factor review

Of course, competitor analyses are part of an external audit; there are several other factors that need to be included, distilled into the PESTEL model, ie political, economic, social, technological, environmental and legal aspects. For example, political factors such as elections can impact business confidence; new technologies coming to market may lead to a downturn in purchases of current technology or, where business stability is key and staying with older technology deemed to be stable and reliable, current technology could be seen as a more attractive purchase. Economic factors such as a recession may impact the business overall; new legislation such as laws about the use of cookies or storage of contact details and privacy can impact how businesses market to customers.

Customer research

During this part of the audit a business directly or indirectly researches into customers' needs; their decision criteria; why, when and how frequently they buy; and why they buy certain products and not others. In defining the customers' needs it's prudent to understand those of both current and future potential customers. Often the tendency is to focus on today's customers and their needs rather than define future potential customers and future needs. Incorporating this into customer research will help businesses position themselves for the future.

Internal marketing review

The current marketing plan, activities and performance are reviewed. In a B2B marketing context this can be carried out via a digital review of online clicks and conversion through to deals, or through a relationship marketing approach reviewing how leads or outbound activities convert to opportunities, pipeline and revenue. Sub-segmenting activities according to the marketing source can help marketing assess the performance at a tactical level as well as support marketing in addressing those performance gaps.

Marketing strategy formulation

The formulating of the marketing strategy starts with competitive advantage and differentiation review (see Figure 3.2).

Competitive advantage can be identified by conducting a SWOT and a competitor analysis. Differentiators can be identified by conducting a differentiator review, ie a gap analysis of major competitors. Traditionally B2B organizations differentiated themselves through new technologies or new

Figure 3.2 Marketing strategy formulation

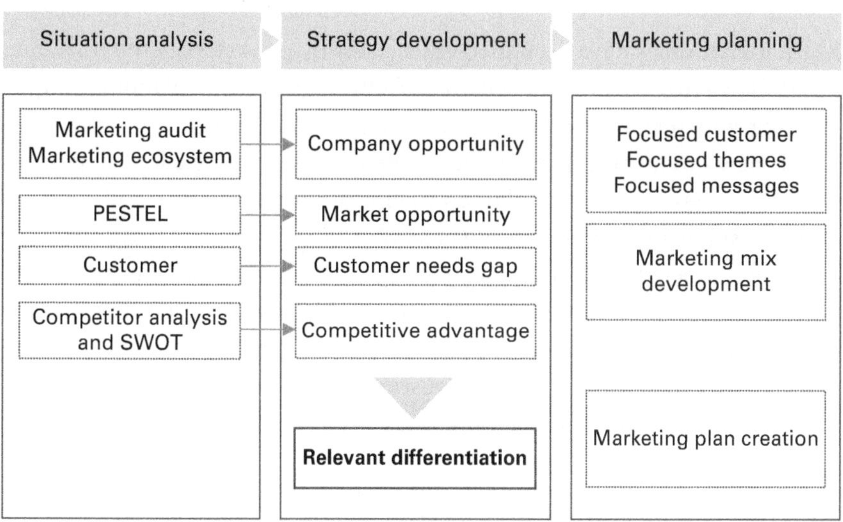

product offerings, or better cost or price and/or geographical presence. With increased globalization and commoditization of products and technologies, differentiation now tends to arise from digital applications, organizational reputation, and omnichannel purchase possibilities.

Much has been written about competitive advantage or unique value propositions; B2B marketers need to think about 'relevant' differentiation. This is not only about having an advantage over competitors that is unique, it is vital that it is aligned to customers' needs.

Table 3.1 Relevant differentiation source

Channel mix	Customer targeting	Perception and CSR	Customer engagement	New digital applications
Mix of online/offline Change routes to market Offer online possibilities	1) Target niche customers 2) Leverage account-based marketing	Invest in perception building and corporate social responsibility	1) Offer possibilities to engage before purchase 2) New educational material and formats Social engagement CLC marketing	New service and application offering

The marketing funnel and beyond

Marketing funnels have been used extensively by marketers in the consumer and B2B environments and have been effective tools in planning, implementing and reviewing. Using funnels can be misleading as it assumes a linear view of customers' behaviour in marketing activities; it also assumes that a business starts with a large target customer set and steadily shrinks down to smaller customers to engage.

While funnels can be useful as ways to track media, activities and leads, marketers should consider that customers' behaviour is less linear, their decision process is more organic and receptive to multiple stimuli from the market and other customers. Also, customers tend to follow a cyclical path in purchasing and deciding on purchases; see Figure 3.3.

Applying the customer cycle

Essentially the marketing funnel is there to help marketers plan from one end of the customer journey to the next. For planning purposes marketers still need to consider that those who are aware of or are becoming aware of needs will be a larger group than those exploring options or purchases. Where things differ is the ability of companies to better target customers and prospects and in being able to re-engage customers through new approaches in marketing and new technologies. Businesses are potentially more capable of identifying and engaging customers and maintaining a greater engagement and connection with prospects across the customer purchase journey.

Also new in 21st century approaches is the ability of companies to influence customers indirectly through influencers, partners and other third parties. Collaborating with third parties to identify and engage customers is required rather than recommended.

Figure 3.3 From funnels to cycles

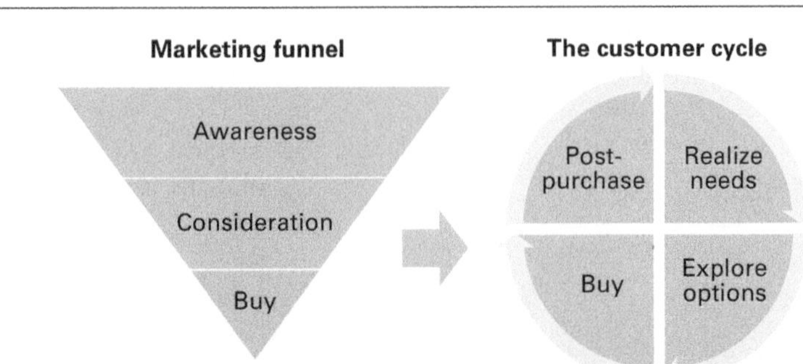

B2B marketing strategies

Marketing strategy is fundamentally about gaining and sustaining competitive edge; it should facilitate and support the business's growth. It needs to includes short- and long-term activities. Most of the current successful B2B marketing strategies can be developed along the areas covered in this book (see Figure 3.4):

1. *Customer-centric strategies* that focus on areas of the customer lifecycle, or focus on a niche target segment such as C-suite, or crafting a strategy based on true solutions for customer needs. Influencer marketing is now evolving in B2B as an effective way to gain mind-share and reach new audiences. Other possibilities are to refocus business and marketing investments across the customer cycle: vertical sector orientation means tailoring marketing content, messaging and budget to specific vertical markets.
2. *Transform through digital and content.* Other ways are to define a new digital marketing mix or create compelling content. Some successful strategies have included capitalizing on social and leveraging platforms to support customer relationship management and amplification of brand-building programmes. More frequent are B2B brands that invest to reposition themselves or to change perceptions of customers. Where the perception of the business differs from the reality or the desired view of the brand, a business will decide to invest in communication and branding that changes the customers' perceptions.
3. *Collaborate with channel partners.* Some B2B brands find success in redefining relationships with existing channel partners or creating new channel partners. An example would be to work with an independent software vendor that has experience of working in a vertical segment and its customers.
4. *Improving marketing execution.* The fourth area relates to improving areas of marketing execution, either by improving the quality of lead generation and nurturing, becoming more targeted with budgets and resources in account-based marketing (ABM), through greater sales and marketing alignment to be more effective as a business in achieving goals, or through improving events marketing.
5. *Collaboration with partners.* Across all the above; marketing partnerships can serve to further strengthen the strategy as well as improve the probability of achieving strategic goals. An example would be collaborating with an industrial association and its marketing resources to reach an industrial business segment.

Figure 3.4 B2B marketing strategies

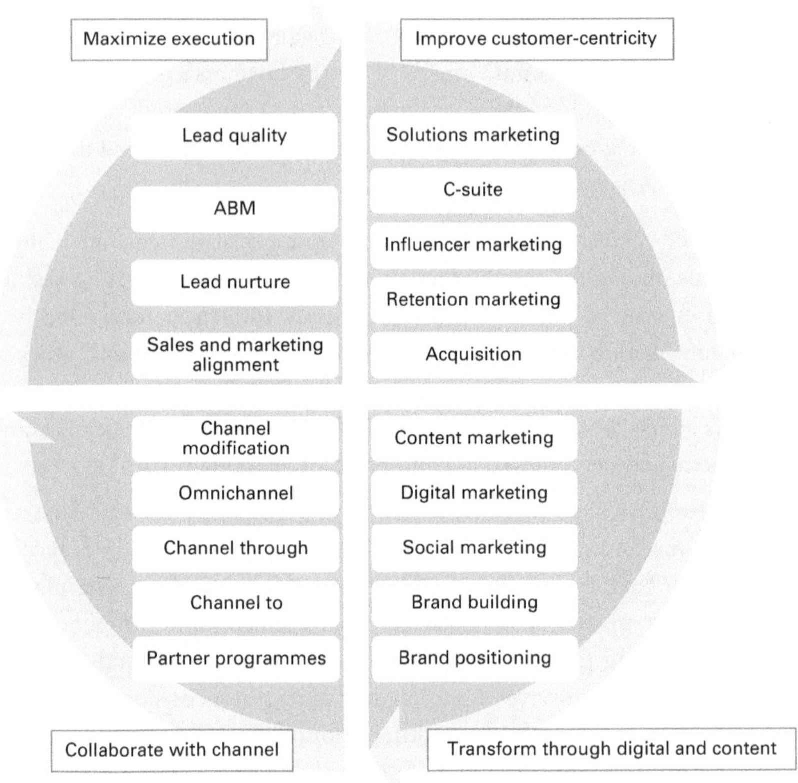

EXAMPLE CSR and business marketing strategy

It has become more and more important for companies to show social responsibility, and having a Corporate Social Responsibility policy in place has been a growing trend. CSR is a way for businesses to connect on an emotional level, to help serve the communities and to demonstrate responsibility to the environment. As a knock-on effect this approach helps businesses distinguish themselves from other companies. B2B businesses may support CSR initiatives through environmental issues and employee programmes. For some, CSR has been an investment issue: public organizations may view purchasing from companies with a CSR initiative as a plus as they can indirectly support those companies in their CSR initiatives.

Grainger is a B2B distributor of products used to maintain, repair or operate facilities. Many businesses and institutions across the world rely on Grainger for pumps, motors, hand tools, janitorial supplies, fasteners and much more. Grainger has put particular emphasis on CSR across four core areas of people, operating responsibility, sustaining environment and serving communities.

PART TWO
Improve B2B customer-centric marketing

Business customers and buying behaviours 04

This chapter will give you an understanding of:

- the importance of business buying behaviours
- the new business buying process
- buyer triggers and how to identify them
- identifying business buyer behaviours
- influences on purchase decisions

The importance of business buying behaviours

Critical to your success as a B2B marketer in creating marketing strategies, plans and activities is understanding how businesses make purchase decisions, how they move from one stage to the next and what influences them within and between the stages.

The buying stages

Six main stages, shown in Figure 4.1, can be identified as part of the business buying process:

1 *Need recognition.* The business recognizes a potential need; the recognition can come from an individual or a group of people within the business and may be the output from a study or other outside stimuli such as vendors or partners. Typically, the need is solved by purchasing a product, a service, or a portfolio of products.

2 *Need quantification and research*. Once a need is identified the next step is to gain commitment to fulfilling the need; in larger businesses this can be a department convincing stakeholders to release capital to pay for a product or service.

3 *Vendor review*. During this stage, the people involved in the buying process seek out information and search for vendors who could supply potential solutions to their needs. Most buyers start with an online search, which can then be followed up with attendance at seminars, trade shows or further searches online. Smaller businesses as well as bigger ones may use contacts as sources of information.

The potential suppliers are then evaluated and suppliers compared. Typically, buyers will weigh vendor alternatives based on a set of purchasing criteria. Different organizations will weigh parts of a proposal differently, depending on their goals and the products they purchase. For example, price may be an important factor for some whereas others may place an emphasis on service and service level agreements. Larger business customers have a more structured process to tender for vendors through RFPs (request for proposals).

4 *Purchase*. Based on findings during the evaluation phase a customer selects a vendor or vendors(s) and proceeds to ordering. The ordering of the products or services can be structured within a longer-term agreement or may be a simple transaction.

Figure 4.1 The B2B buyer process

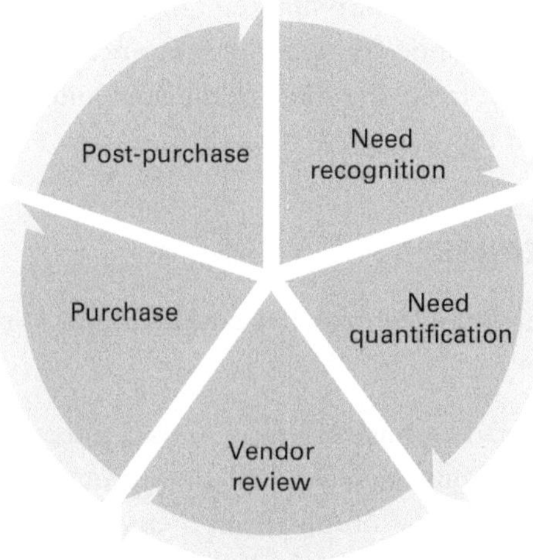

5 *Post-purchase*. Following the initial purchase the customer could repurchase from the vendors when necessary, move to a new vendor, revert to a previous vendor or increase purchasing activity.

Identifying business buying behaviours

Identifying customer buying behaviour can help in business planning across logistics and finance. It can also remove the element of surprise; for example if a business establishes that two-thirds of its customers conduct all their repeat purchases in one quarter, it can plan its resources accordingly. The education sector tends to make most of its purchases of computing equipment in the second quarter, ie between April and June. Other benefits come from improved marketing and improved selling as sales and marketing can engage customers better, in the right way at the right time.

TIP How to identify buying behaviours

Identifying business buying behaviour includes answering key questions such as how customers buy, when and where they buy, how they inform themselves about purchases and who they engage. Identifying buying behaviour is also about understanding business perspectives and outlooks.

Organizations can identify buying behaviours through different approaches; they could set up customer advisory councils or conduct a survey. Other approaches include learning from sales account managers who have in-depth understanding of their customer accounts; or leveraging third-party associations that can engage customers on the organization's behalf.

What to do with the knowledge

Businesses should use their findings to look at commonality in behaviours between business types. This can be based on a similar industry sector or similar business size. Capturing information based on sector or size can help businesses structure their organization; marketing can look at channels to engage, communications routes to use, ways to engage, and using more relevant language.

Business buying influencers

Internal

Purchase process and complexity of purchase

Purchasing can be affected by the complexity of the product or solution; where it is a single product or one bought in smaller amounts the purchase process may be a simple one. For example, a quick review of specifications is all that is required prior to purchasing online; this process resembles that of consumer buying. Where the product or solution is more complex, such as IT infrastructure for a larger business, the purchase process can be longer due to the number of stakeholders involved; there are also typically more steps involved and more time required to move between the buying stages.

The size of the order or number of products ordered

Where the number of products ordered is large the time to purchase typically takes longer, as more products need to be evaluated.

Capital outlay

Where the capital outlay is sizeable, the customer will need more time to review and select a product or service as there are potentially more stakeholders involved in understanding the justification of the spend. In larger organizations it may also require more time, decisions and stakeholders to 'free' up capital.

Company objectives

A company's goal to grow the business at different speeds at different stages may affect how and when it buys.

Purchasing policies

Purchase policies can influence the buying process, and the size of the procurement department plays a role.

Fiscal timelines

A company's fiscal structures and calendar, such as its financial year, can impact when products are purchased. For example, Dell's fiscal year runs from February to January whereas Microsoft's is from July to June.

Organizational structures and interpersonal factors

How people engage as a result of stakeholder personalities, organizational structures or rigid processes could influence the buying process negatively or positively. For example, where the steps in purchasing are cumbersome this may protect against invalid purchases but also dissuade from pursuing opportunities to purchase something that eventually helps the business.

Size of business

Smaller companies will have fewer processes, steps, policies and stakeholders, which could mean that decisions can be made faster. The flip side is that due diligence in reviewing and evaluating may be skipped, leading to less than optimal purchases.

External

Competitive influences may be changes in competitive activity that impact short- or long-term purchase decisions. New entrants to the market that employ disruptive pricing or terms and conditions can affect purchasing quantities or timing of decisions.

Legal factors affecting purchase decisions may be related to the financial and stock markets and black-out periods.

Technological factors may be new technology that renders existing technologies obsolete; customers may decide to shift to the newer technology.

Governmental aspects include businesses delaying or accelerating purchases ahead of governmental election results.

Buyer types

In organizations, buying is usually undertaken by two or more individuals and so it is often referred to as 'group buying'. Sometimes the buying process will involve technical issues or financial decisions whereby finance work with procurement on the best purchase for the business. As organizations grow and evolve so do the number of stakeholders and roles within the organization that influence the buying process. In general, the main types of buyers or roles are:

- *Users*. These are people who will directly use the product or service; in business, this can be a group of individuals who would benefit from the purchase.
- *Influencers*. These are individuals or groups who steer or impact the purchase decision; they may be experts in an area, they may even come from outside the organization where specialist knowledge not found within the company is required.
- *Buyers*. In smaller companies buyers and users may be the same; in larger companies, they can be separate, even from different departments. They typically have formal authority to select vendors but may not have the power to make the final decision.
- *Deciders*. These can be the same as buyers in some organizations or for some purchases. Deciders have the ultimate power to make decisions on purchases; they can be CEOs or heads of department.
- *Gatekeepers*. These formally control information and access to other groups in the buying process.

Types of buying situation

Business buying can take different forms depending on a number of factors, which can include the internal and external influences mentioned above. The main forms of buying situations are repeat purchase, modified re-purchase and new purchase.

Repeat and modified re-purchase

Repeat purchases of the same product or set of products may, if straightforward, occur without any engagement. *Modified re-purchase* is where the buyer amends the previous purchase; the modifications can be:

- *To include new products or services*. An example could be a business buying notebooks and modifying the purchase to include additional or different notebooks due to new processes or technologies.
- *To account for new prices or used to renegotiate new prices*. This could be a business renting office space from a provider and, based on changes in the office rental market, may mean the business wants to renegotiate a better (lower) price.
- *New packaging or other customization*. The buyer may want different packaging or delivery, or the product customized slightly differently.

New purchase

New purchase can come in the form of spot purchase – products are bought as a one-off. This type of purchase may occur online if the product in question is easily understood and the purchase process is straightforward. Alternatively, new purchases can be a range or portfolio of products; the buyer may expect phone contact or a face-to-face meeting to better understand the product or portfolio of products under consideration.

EXAMPLE Domain website service vendors and purchasers

A new purchase could be the customer making the first purchase with the website provider. Repeat purchase could be a repeat service purchase on a monthly or annual basis. A modified re-purchase could be buying extended services such as access to richer content and images or expert online support services that the website domain provider offers.

Changes to business buying behaviour

Business buying behaviour has altered greatly in the past decade. Business buyers used to rely on inputs from vendors for the majority of information for the purchasing process. Because of the wide availability of information online, customers are now able to research on their own and evaluate potential solutions without needing to engage vendors directly for a large part of the buying process.

Nowadays, business customers will typically engage vendors much later in the buying process and the process has shifted from vendor-led to customer-led. This aspect of customer activity means that customers could either be better informed or more misinformed, where they form unrealistic opinions of a possible vendor. Potential vendors may lose out on opportunities to pitch and explain their business offerings.

Selling and the customer process

With customers changing how they engage sales, vendors also need to adapt. Customers decide to make their first engagement with potential vendors further along the buying process, so sales departments need to leverage marketing's support, to influence customers through content and information, supporting them in their purchase process.

The process can shorten as sales staff take on the role of facilitator by providing information via their communication channels. Some businesses have seen real benefit in accelerating buying processes through employee advocacy, as their networks help customers access information more readily, directly or indirectly.

Buyer triggers

A buyer trigger is an event that causes a customer to recognize a clear need. It usually moves a buyer from a state of curiosity or consideration to a more urgent state of need.

EXAMPLE Microsoft XP end-of-life support

In April 2014 Microsoft withdrew its support for the Windows XP operating system; this was announced some time in advance to allow customers and businesses to take the change on board. This in turn led to different buying behaviours: some businesses made short-term decisions to purchase new computer products with the more up-to-date operating system; other bigger organizations invested large sums of money in purchasing and extending support. For example, the Dutch government signed a 'multi-million euro' deal with Microsoft for continued support for its Windows XP systems.

Other examples of business triggers are:

- a product fails and is out of warranty;
- a warranty period is about to expire;
- a company intends to move to the next stage of growth and buy new office space;
- a new technology and related products are launched.

Identifying and exploiting buyer triggers

Organizations can be effective in sales and marketing by identifying and exploiting customer triggers. Identification can come from monitoring and listening activities that help to not only identify triggers but anticipate them. Some possible routes to buyer trigger identification are:

- Taking part in a social forum where customers participate.
- Undertaking needs assessment research with existing/new customers.
- Monitoring market trends through the web or research firms.
- Monitoring technology trends.
- Engaging industry associations that represent the target customer segment.

Organizations can capitalize on the triggers by some of the following:

- Creating customer persona(s) for the trigger event identified.
- Looking at potential reactions the trigger event may initiate.
- Including messaging and content that tap into trigger event reactions.
- Ensuring messaging includes a solution your business can offer for the trigger event.

ACTIVITIES

Look at your own business and industry and try to identify trigger events.

As a customer yourself can you notice any trigger events that have caused you to buy something?

Think about purchase influences for customers you're marketing to and identify at least three internal and external influences.

Further reading

Forbes Insights (2009) The rise of the digital C-suite: how executives locate and filter business information, *Forbes Insights*, June

Acquisition marketing 05

This chapter will give you an understanding of:

- the REAP model
- differences between retention and acquisition customers
- types of acquisition marketing
- the acquisition marketing process
- re-acquisition marketing
- re-acquisition marketing tactics
- acquisition marketing strategies
- measuring acquisition marketing

Customer acquisition and customer lifecycle

Customer acquisition refers to the activity of identifying and engaging potential customers for the purpose of persuading them to purchase a company's products and/or services. Potential customers are sometimes called 'prospects'.

Customer lifecycle

A customer lifecycle outlines the progression of steps a customer makes from point of awareness of an organization's products to the point of becoming a repeat customer of an organization. The main phases are reach, acquisition, onboarding, retention, upsell and cross-sell, and loyalty. The main phases, shown in Figure 5.1, can be described as:

- *Reach.* Where an organization targets a customer and tries to get the attention of the businesses they want to reach.
- *Acquisition.* Where an organization attracts and engages the business for purchasing its products and/or services.
- *Onboarding.* This involves the prospect becoming familiar with the organization's products and/or services, understanding and making use of the offerings.
- *Repeat – retention.* During this phase the organization sells its products to the customer. The customer is a repeat customer for similar products and/or services.
- *Expansion – upsell and cross-sell.* During this phase the organization looks to expand its offering to the customer through upselling and/or cross-selling.
- *Loyalty.* Loyal customers can be defined by the number of purchases made over a period of time.

Figure 5.1 Customer lifecycle

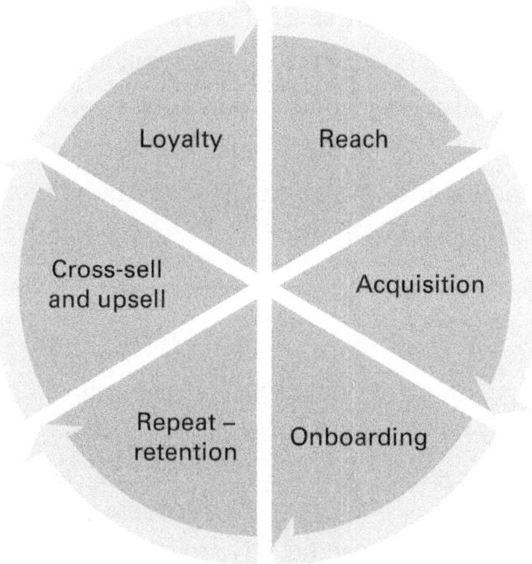

The REAP model

One model to categorize customers is the REAP model; customers according to this model can be defined by level and scope of purchase by retention, expansion, acquisition and preferred customers, where:

- *Retention* accounts are existing customers who may be purchasing more than one of the vendor's products and may be repeat purchasing. They show a degree of loyalty.
- *Expansion* accounts are existing customers identified for purposes of developing business further either by increasing the volume of products/services they purchase or for expanding the portfolio they purchase from a vendor.
- *Acquisition* accounts are customers not purchasing today; they may also be customers recently acquired but needing to be managed via acquisition sales account managers for account relationship reasons.
- *Preferred* accounts are retention accounts that buy in large quantities and show a degree of loyalty over time; without these accounts the business would be struggling to survive. These accounts are also advocates of the company's brand and generally require extra handling and care beyond the key account management activities.

Retention vs acquisition

Acquisition customers differ in several ways from retention customers. As they are not yet customers of the organization they are not yet account managed and, generally, no previous data exists about the customer and there is no pre-existing relationship. Thus the responsibility falls generally on marketing to understand and share insights about such customers. More differences are summarized in Table 5.1.

Table 5.1 Differences between retention and acquisition

Retention	Acquisition
Existing relationship	Not account managed
Data about the customer exists and is accessible	No relationship pre-exists
Future project needs are documented	No current or up-to-date data exists
Behavioural data	No buying behaviour information exists
Easier to engage C-suite	It is typically challenging to engage higher management
Their details are logged in a central database or CRM system	
Account management is possible	

Acquisition marketing and types of acquisition customer

Acquisition marketing is any marketing activity with the specific goal of acquiring new customers. In this case new customers are customers who have never purchased from the organization or who are no longer actively doing so. Acquisition customers can be sub-divided as follows:

- *Prospects.* A prospect is a potential customer or sales lead that has been qualified as fitting a set of criteria.
- *Greenfield customers are completely new customers for the business.* These customers have not previously bought from the company.
- *Re-acquisition customers.* These are customers who used to buy from the business but no longer do so and have been identified as customers to re-acquire.
- *Lapsed customers.* Customers who recently lapsed and no longer purchase beyond an expected period of time. Lapsed customers could be categorized as lapsing if they are purchasing once within three or six months but have not purchased for six months.
- *Inactive customers.* Inactive customers are accounts that have not purchased for an extensive period, eg not purchased for more than 12 months.

The acquisition marketing process

The acquisition process, shown in Figure 5.2, can be split into six main stages:

1. *Analysis.* A company needs to understand the background to customers purchasing competitor products, and what competitors have in terms of value propositions. Other factors to consider are whether customers are aware of the organization's products and offers and their perception of them.
2. *Preparation.* In this phase the organization prepares itself before reaching out to the customer; preparation activities include aligning with sales on the acquisition process and approach; defining the customers and their pain points (ie their main needs or challenges); adapting the business value proposition and agreeing on the hook or how to entice the customer.

3 *Education.* During this phase customers are typically approached indirectly with information to help them in their research phase; this corresponds to the buyer journey where customers quantify needs and research alternative solutions for their needs.

4 *Customer engagement initiated.* During this phase the customer is contacted by the business or a business representative.

5 *Follow-up.* During the follow-up stage sales become more actively engaged with the customer and help in answering any final questions the customer may have.

6 *Acquisition.* The final stage of the process is where the customer decides to purchase and completes a transaction.

Figure 5.2 Acquisition process

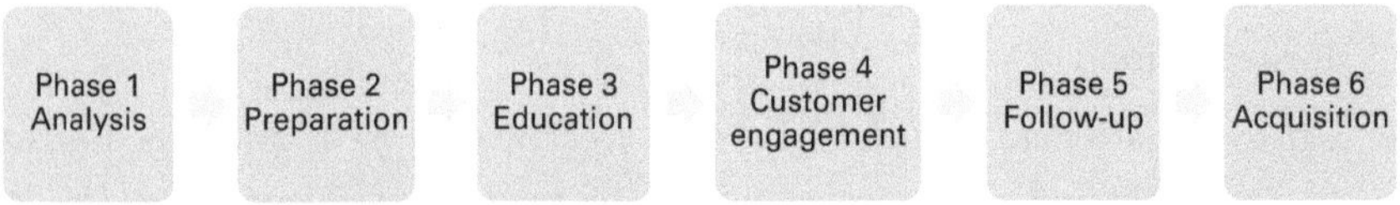

Phase 1 Analysis → Phase 2 Preparation → Phase 3 Education → Phase 4 Customer engagement → Phase 5 Follow-up → Phase 6 Acquisition

Analysis – insights and data

One gap a company has in acquisition marketing compared to marketing to existing customers is a lack of data and insights about new customers. This type of information is critical if a company intends to effectively target and engage customers in the right way at the right time via the right channels.

TIP Key questions and areas businesses need to investigate

- Competition. Why is the customer buying competitor products? What are their weaknesses and strengths? What is their business model? What are their tactics and strategies at a business and marketing level?
- Resistance. Why is there resistance to purchasing our business products and/or services?
- Customer engagement. Who is the customer? Who are the influencers?
- Customer buying behaviours. What do they buy? Why do they purchase today? When do they purchase? How do they purchase?
- Customer behaviours. What are their pain points? What are their top needs?

The ultimate objective of the analysis is to identify a unique angle or opportunity and allow the business to uniquely position itself in engaging the customer.

Preparation

As part of the preparation stage the role of B2B marketing is to support the business with the right go-to-market (GTM) models, define and align on the sales approach and prepare marketing materials.

Right GTM model

The right GTM model approach is dictated by the prospect and the most suitable engagement and channel model for the vendor. For example, in targeting small businesses a company can choose different direct channel approaches to engaging and acquiring, eg via call-centres, online investment or an outbound salesforce. Alternatively, it could look at indirect channel routes, eg online mail order or retailers and their physical or online stores. The selection of the channel can be based on financial capital, in-house competencies, in-house resources, operating locations, and efficiencies in reaching and engaging customers.

Sales

Compared to marketing to existing customers, the efforts in acquisition marketing are typically greater and the cost is usually higher for the business, so ensuring sales alignment and the correct structure is key. Below are some of the main considerations in preparing with sales:

Align to the correct sales group for the acquisition campaign; if the marketing activity is about bringing customers in front of specialists and thought leaders in the organization then be careful not to only include sales generalists who may not be able to answer specialist questions from key customers.

Align on customer type and need. According to the business portfolio gaps and business goals, the business should align on the right customer target, their profile and pain points. Inputs into this phase can come from existing customers who mirror the target customer profile.

Align on process for engaging customer. Marketing and sales need to define when and how to engage within the marketing/sales process. For example, will marketing leverage sales to make outbound inquiries or phone calls? Will sales lead by using hooks or door openers?

Marketing preparation

Marketing in this phase should define messaging, content and materials about the business proposition. The agreed types of hooks needed, eg incentives, compelling articles, services or other types, can be prepared.

Education

The education phase is typically managed by an organization's marketing department. This phase is the major pivotal change point compared to 10 years ago, when organizations had the luxury of being contacted by customers. Marketing needs to position and place information at customer touch points or across media that customers use. The challenge for marketers is identifying which media or information sources are being used by which customers and when.

Engaging the prospects

During this stage marketing typically takes the lead on the first steps by engaging through third parties, through forms, an online website, offline associations, events or by engaging through marketing directly. Depending on the customers and their decision journey the number of touch points before sales engage can vary: some industries highlight an average of 12 touch points before sales are engaged; others talk about three or five. The mix of marketing touch points leading to the final sale can also vary depending on customer type and marketing type.

Follow-up

During this final stage the prospect is not yet a customer but sales need to follow up based on engagement or contact activities. It is generally pre-agreed when and what stage the handover to sales occurs. Acquisition marketers and acquisition sales need to agree in advance and correctly assess the likelihood and timing of conversion to a sale. For example, if a customer purchasing a complex solution is in the early stages of the decision process it is probable they will require more information, more engagement and time compared to existing customers who buy simpler products.

Acquisition

The customer is acquired by the organization as a customer. A customer may remain an 'acquisition' customer for some time in the eyes of the organization until the customer's new business is developed into something more established.

Re-acquisition marketing process

The process for re-acquiring customers can follow a similar process to that of acquisition, although there are differences. During the analysis stage, a company should understand why customers ceased purchasing products or ceased business. These insights can shed important light on how to proceed in the next stages or even whether to proceed. Businesses can find this out through approaches such as ad hoc surveys directly or indirectly with lapsed customers, surveys via customer service, or from reports such as Net Promoter Score reports.

During the preparation phase, channel selection and agreeing on a different sales engagement (eg via more senior sales) may be prepared. Content may be incorporated that addresses solutions to the specific customer challenge, which may have been the reason behind the customer ceasing business.

The engagement phase can include engaging via a third-party partner, channel or even marketing agencies. More than is the case with acquisition customers, the follow-up in a timely and relevant fashion while addressing any input or response from the customer is critical.

EXAMPLE Net Promoter Score

General Electric, Honeywell, Dell, HP and many more companies use Net Promoter Score to identify customer satisfaction. As part of the report there are three categories of customers: promoters, detractors and passives:

Promoters are loyal, enthusiastic fans. They are more likely than other customers to increase or maintain their purchase activity over time.

Detractors are unhappy customers. They are more likely to decrease or cease purchase over time.

Passives are customers who repurchase but are only passively satisfied.

The Net Promoter Score can help organizations in their acquisition marketing or sales by investigating the detractors and understanding why customers lapse or don't purchase; they can help an organization identify areas to fix before acquiring customers.

Why customers lapse

Customers lapse for various reasons; here are just some of them:

- *Poor 'service' from the business.* The business failed to meet the customer's expectations in terms of 'how' it delivered the product or service; this may be the way it handled a complaint.
- *Neglect.* In the initial stages of acquisition the customer was engaged regularly but over time this engagement changed or stopped, essentially making the customer feel neglected.
- *Poor quality of product/service offering.* The quality of the product or service did not meet expectations or was of inferior quality.
- *Competitor acquisition programmes.* A competitor offering a similar product or service increased its price aggression or engagement with the customer, which will lead to customers switching supplier.
- *Change of price position from the vendor.* Some companies over time decide to increase margins on their products or service through reducing costs or repositioning their products; this can affect the purchasing behaviour of customers in that they either buy less or stop altogether.
- *Irrelevant communication.* If the communication form isn't appropriate to the customer needs or not aligned to customer wishes, it may put off customers and their business. Some companies have been criticized for excessive e-mailing to their customers and eventually annoying them.

TIP How to segment for re-acquisition

To better ensure the achievement of marketing efforts, markets need to be more targeted to re-acquire customers. Figure 5.3 is an example of how to segment lapsed customers based on four criteria: 1) how recent their latest purchase was, 2) type of purchase, 3) size of business, and 4) propensity for purchasing high-margin products.

Using these criteria, classify customers against a scale, A, B and C, where segment A is most recent purchase, most frequent purchase, largest purchase and highest propensity for purchasing high margin products. Segment A is the most desirable segment, Segment C the least. The customers that tick all the boxes with an 'A' will be the priority segment.

Figure 5.3 How to segment for customer acquisition

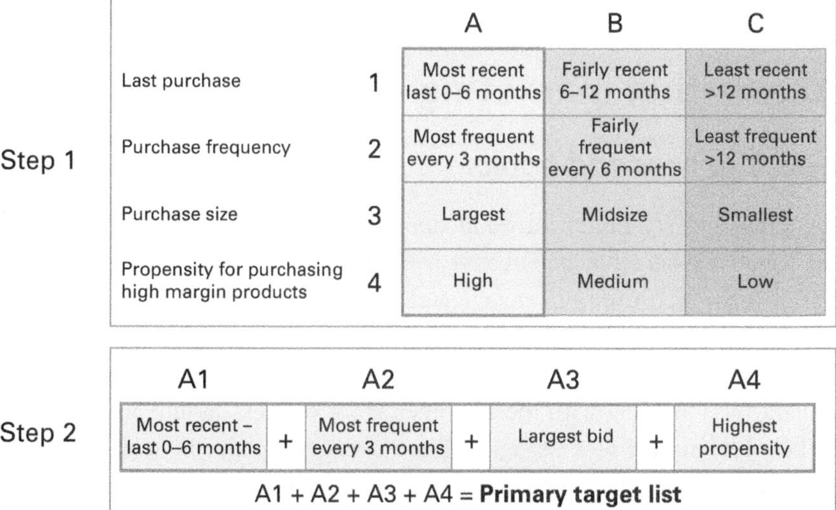

TIP Tactics in re-acquisition marketing

There are a number of different approaches to re-acquiring customers:

- *Lapse red flags.* The business can define red flags or alert systems to understand changes in customer touch rate or engagement rate. Sales or marketing operations can sometimes help with reporting to identify accounts to target in advance.
- *Reason to re-engage.* Trigger activities or events can be included in messaging, highlighting why the business is re-engaging. Such tactics can be effective if they show that the vendor is aware the customer no longer buys and shows the importance of the customer to the vendor.

- *Change communication channel.* Where traditional e-mail hasn't worked; the vendor can employ different approaches such as social InMail, direct mail or other.
- *Use fresh new content.* Use new creatives to engage lapsed customers; use new ways to engage if budgets permit, for example video slabs.
- *Listen and respond.* Organizations can conduct random surveys that highlight key customer needs and therefore provide opportunities to organizations in their marketing and messaging.

Acquisition marketing strategies and tactics

Door openers and hooks

A science has been built up around 'door openers' and 'hooks'. Door openers are usually designed to be effective in capturing attention and in giving the business an opportunity to engage with the customer. Types of door openers include low-cost introductory letters, vouchers and coupons as well as more sophisticated approaches that involve a sales person delivering something of value at a meeting with the customer. Door openers should appeal to the stakeholder targeted for engaging. Door openers can also be service related; for example, some IT hardware companies offer low-cost or free services to demonstrate their capabilities.

Acquisition marketing strategies

There are different schools of thought on how to acquire customers. Less efficient is the 'persistence' approach where a company or its salespeople continuously knock at the door or pester potential clients. Others that embrace marketing techniques are more effective by being more strategic, sophisticated in planning and targeting. Some examples of the more effective acquisition strategies are:

Segment the market; segment the customers

It is important to create a detailed segmentation that can actually be used. For example, a business may have the objective to target all small businesses in the UK, but with over 4 million small businesses, marketing to all of them and subsequently engaging them is not realistic or cost-effective. Segmentation of this large audience could be by vertical type, by region, or by further segmenting by employee numbers. Ideally segmentation should follow a set of criteria, eg all small businesses with more than five employees in each region to be offered consulting services.

Create compelling stories and clear call-to-actions for follow-up

Companies of all sizes have stories to tell; they have something to say that will capture the attention of potential customers. Few businesses think about creating and sharing their proposition or message in an interesting way that then leads to something tangible. As an example, they could offer an article or a thought leadership piece, linking it to an invitation to a webinar or to call and discuss the unique challenge in person.

Advocacy

Creating advocacy programmes is also important for acquisition. Customer advocates are probably the strongest influence on potential customers as customers listen to other customers; this is why Amazon ratings and similar review-type sites are so popular. Advocacy can come in different forms. For example, Glassdoor is an online site giving employees and non-employees opportunities to talk about companies and rate them. Negative comments will dissuade other people from seeking employment, or engaging with the company; positive comments and high ratings can help the organization attract talent and business.

New GTM approach; new resellers

Sometimes the challenge is that a customer wants to buy an end-to-end solution comprised of multiple products, services and applications, whereas the organization usually offers a single solution. Here it's important to understand whether a business should adapt its go-to-market approach if it wants to sell fully fledged end-to-end solutions.

Measuring acquisition

The most obvious way of measuring acquisition marketing activities is by tracking the number of new customers and the revenue attributed to new customer business. Typically, in any given period, while businesses acquire new customers some customers will lapse or stop their purchases, so an important measure of the true impact is 'net new' customers and 'net new' revenue calculated as:

> Net new customers = new customers – lapsed customers in any given period
>
> Net new revenue = new revenue attributed to new customers – revenue attributed to lost or lapsed customers in the same given period

It's important to have a long-term approach to measurement as acquiring completely new customers usually takes longer than expected. Typical quarterly approaches to reviewing for ROI (return on investment) will not work.

In general, the more complex the product or solutions the longer the sales cycle, so for ROI to be determined one needs to take a longer-term view. The reason behind this is not just the large size of business involved but the greater number of decision makers in the purchase of more complex products or solutions.

Cost and benefit of acquisition

Cost

The cost of customer acquisition (CAC) means the price you pay to acquire a new customer. From a marketing perspective this is calculated by tracking marketing activities and campaigns and associated business wins. In its simplest form, it can be worked out by:

> Dividing the total costs associated with acquisition by total new customers, within a specific time period

For example, if a campaign is built on a new proposition and targeting 100 customers, marketing could include e-mail, door opener, event or webinar invite. The costs would be as follows:

> Door opener (× 200): £1,000 (for 200 door openers)
>
> Webinar: £5,000 (infrastructure)
>
> Event: £15,000 (for venue, logistics, etc)
>
> E-mail: £1,000 (for content, creation)
>
> Total: £22,000

Benefit

The benefit is the number of sales resulting from a marketing campaign. For example, where a campaign resulted in acquiring 20 new customers in each period, each delivering £4,000 in revenue and £1,500 in profit, the total benefit in revenue and margin would be £80,000 and £30,000. Using the cost calculation above, the net profit (sales minus costs) would be £8,000; £30,000 minus £22,000.

ACTIVITIES

Look at the key questions to customers box and check whether you're able to answer them. Where there are gaps carry out further research.

Where you see resistance or blocks to customer engagement and acquisition, conduct a mini survey to understand what the resisting forces are and why they exist.

Look at the three core areas of sales alignment and check with senior management on whether this is the situation today.

Further reading

Richardson, N, James, J and Kelley, N (2015) *Customer-centric Marketing: Supporting sustainability in the digital age*, Kogan Page, London

Retention and loyalty marketing 06

This chapter will give you an understanding of:

- customer retention marketing
- customer loyalty
- communication and improving and maintaining loyalty
- top marketing strategies to increase customer loyalty
- customer satisfaction and marketing
- leveraging customer advocacy for marketing
- customer lifecycle communication
- mapping marketing and customer lifecycle stage
- how to increase customer share-of-wallet

The REAP model and retention/loyalty marketing

As we learnt in Chapter 5, there are different stages in the customer lifecycle. Existing customers can be split further into the following categories: retention customers, expansion customers and preferred customers.

Before acquisition

From the current portfolio of customers an organization needs to identify which customers are core to its revenue, which are important as part of its future growth and which accounts to focus to collaborate or promote more. Sometimes this part of the business is ignored: organizations continue to pursue new customers, leaving behind and slightly neglecting their existing accounts.

After acquiring customers

Marketing's role doesn't finish with the acquisition stage. The role of marketing is about supporting the organization in developing business further with customers, in improving relationships, and in identifying which customers are more likely to grow and buy products and/or services either in increased volumes or branch out further by purchasing a wider range of products. This can be tracked based on customers' buying power.

Customers' buying power is their ability or extent to which they 'could' purchase a vendor's products. This is one way to segment accounts. For example, if we define expansion accounts as those with between 10 and 40 per cent buying power this means that they are only spending up to 40 per cent of the potential they could be spending on a vendor's products; there is a further 60 per cent opportunity within the account for the vendor to sell its products. This percentage is sometimes referred to as share-of-wallet (SoW).

One way a business can segment its customers by buying power or SoW is as follows:

- preferred accounts – those that spend over 70 per cent SoW;
- acquisition accounts – spend below 10 per cent SoW;
- retention – spend over 40 per cent but less than 70 per cent;
- expansion accounts – spend between 10 and 40 per cent.

Preferred accounts are those customers that carry a strategic importance for the business; they will typically receive greater attention from their supplier. The role of the supplier is to nurture and maintain close relationships through offering additional benefits compared to the expansion and retention accounts. Expansion customers typically are at the business development stage for the vendor; they may be relatively new customers.

Why focus on customer retention marketing?

According to Bain and Company (Stillwagon, 1990), a 5 per cent increase in customer retention can generate increases of 25 to 95 per cent in profits. Ignoring existing customers can lead to higher customer churn and loss in revenue and profit; and we see indications from Gartner Group that neglect can mean consequences as they tell us that 80 per cent of a company's future revenue will come from just 20 per cent of existing customers (Marsh, 2015).

Some of the main initiatives on developing existing customers are how to increase loyalty, increasing business with the customer and share-of-wallet and building strategic relationships.

Customer loyalty

Customer loyalty is defined as the likelihood of existing or previous customers to continue buying from a specific organization. Great attention is given to marketing and customer service to retain current customers by increasing customer loyalty. Some organizations have structures within the business to support customer loyalty; others go as far as to create loyalty programmes to reward customers for repeat business.

Why invest in customer loyalty?

As we learnt from the previous chapter the cost of marketing in re-acquiring or acquiring customers is significantly more than the cost of marketing to existing customers, so it pays to market to existing customers.

There are some exceptions to the rule. It is sometimes beneficial for businesses to focus away from certain customers that have become unprofitable and disproportionally use up the organization's resources in managing them or serving them.

Customer loyalty process

The main steps organizations take to ensure they maintain or increase customer loyalty are shown in Figure 6.1 and as follows:

1. *Customer research*. During this phase an organization researches customers and their view of the business so as to understand what would make them stay with the supplier or, more importantly, what would make them switch to another supplier. Sometimes the least obvious responses can come back, eg price in B2B is not always the most important factor. Other aspects to identify are how the customer would like the customer-supplier relationship to change or improve.
2. *Summarize and prioritize*. During this phase the supplier summarizes back to the customer what it will do to improve or maintain the relationship in the short- and mid-term, outlining priorities.
3. *Short-term fixes*. During this phase short-term fixes are carried out; this phase is important as it is about delivering according to the supplier's promises.
4. *Implementation*. Longer-term fixes are implemented and communicated to customers; examples of this could be new services or products, improved value propositions, assigning a sales person with more specialized experience or a dedicated service manager.

Figure 6.1 Customer loyalty process

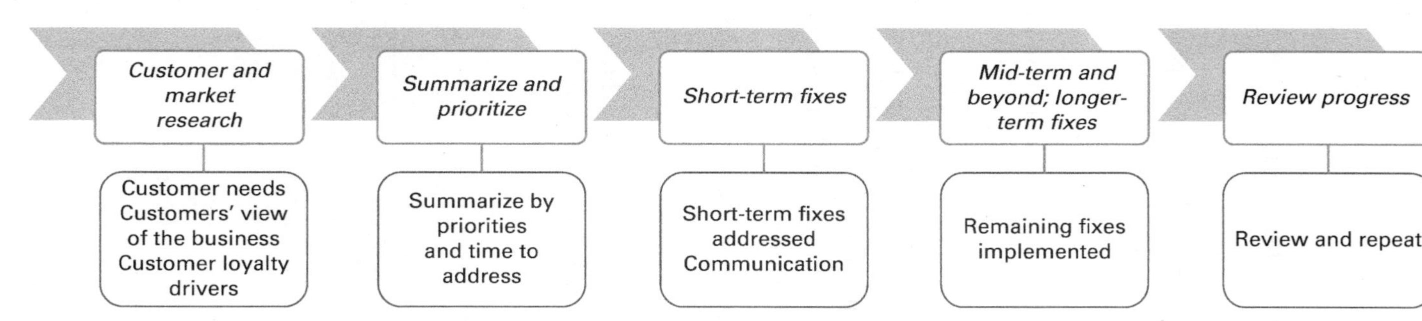

5 *Review.* This is about reviewing more formally the progress with the customer, and ensuring all facets noted within phase one have been captured and addressed successfully.

Customer loyalty spectrum

Customer loyalty is the result of consistent positive experiences, positive emotional experiences and perceived positive value of an experience. Customer loyalty can be viewed as a spectrum from a minimum or a low degree of loyalty to the customer being not only an advocate but a champion for the company.

Five different types of customer loyalty can be identified (see Figure 6.2):

1 *Spot customer.* A customer with low degree of loyalty. Looks at provider as a short-term and tactical means to support its business; may decide to purchase again but not to be relied upon.

2 *Repeat customers* are customers who come back to purchase more from the supplier; the loyalty is confined to re-ordering or purchasing a second time from the organization.

3 *Customer advocate* is a customer who advocates your products or services; if contacted by another customer or potential customer it would rate your organization positively overall; can be relied on.

4 *Customer champion* is a customer who champions the organization's products and rates them very positively; if impacted by a negative experience it may quickly shift to a lower degree of loyalty.

Figure 6.2 Customer loyalty

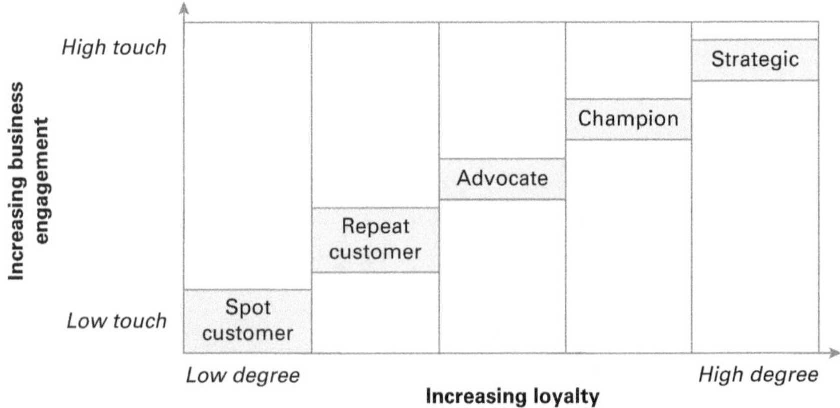

5 *Strategic champion* is a customer that demonstrates a strong customer loyalty, champions your products and is heavily ingrained with the supplier; this could be due to collaborative ties, even family ties. Champions are typically not put off by one-off negative experiences.

The communication factor

How businesses retain or lose business customers can be influenced by how they communicate with them. The main success factors in retaining and building relationships with customers are:

- *Communicate consistently and regularly.* It is often the case in the acquisition phase that businesses over-communicate, but once the customer is acquired there can be a drop-off in communication. It's important that the frequency of communication is consistent and, with digital technologies and applications, it is easier than ever before to achieve this.
- *Appropriate communication.* Appropriate communication is also important. Where customers are experts in their field and knowledgeable about their business needs, the communication needs to account for this. Organizations' marketing departments need to arm their sales people with relevant information to support these more technical or specialized conversations.
- *Listen and respond.* Improving stickiness and loyalty with customers is down to better listening and responding. Digital marketing and new applications support organizations both in listening to customers' conversations and in responding with content that meets their needs.

How to increase customer loyalty

The ways organizations can increase customer loyalty include the following:

Create customer-tailored content

Create content that is tailored or specific to the customer, the customer's business or industry. Creating and including content relevant to the target group can be effective in improving engagement rates and response rates.

Redefine customer value across the company

Increasingly customers place more emphasis on value compared to price. In the technology sector, commoditization means technologies can be offered to more people at lower prices, forcing organizations to provide more value through combined offerings and services and products.

Reward customer loyalty

Many organizations offer rewards to channel partners through programmes providing incentives to sell more of their products. With more incentive points, channel salespeople win more prizes.

Reward large volume purchases

Most businesses offer discounts based on sales volume over a period. For example, large framework agreements in the public sector set pricing over a period of two or three years as well as discounts over that period.

Reward repeat purchase

Discounts are based on quantities over time; this can be through framework agreements that can run for extended periods of one or two years or even longer.

Update with valuable information and news

Customer satisfaction can be maintained or improved through timely updating of information. Some organizations inform customers about trends or activities that could impact them both positively and negatively. In updating customers it's important to understand how customers wish to be informed, and ideally offer solutions to capitalize on opportunities as well as dealing with potential challenges.

Personalized treatment

Personalized treatment can be through dealing directly with a customer contact or set of contacts. Marketing may decide to turn the spotlight on customers by telling their story through its communication channels, which in turn helps promote customers and their business. Another way to offer a more personal touch is to invite the customer to speak at an event the supplier has set up.

Facilitate peer-to-peer networking

One way for businesses to support their customers is through helping them network with other customers, either from the same industry or facing similar challenges due to their position. Facilitating customer-to-customer networking through online information, social forums or webinars and events is a powerful way of offering value to customers without a business overtly pushing its products or services.

Leveraging customer advocacy for marketing

Building a referral programme can come in different forms. These can range from simply developing and communicating customer stories and case studies to more sophisticated approaches involving organizations in branding campaigns and leveraging customer advocates to promote the business across multiple media: online video, adverts, social, event promotion, etc.

Customer satisfaction and marketing

Although often an initiative led by the wider business, customer satisfaction and the process of surveying it touches on aspects for which marketing is accountable. Typical surveys include questions about product or service satisfaction, business operations such as logistics, customer services levels, the quality of sales engagement, pricing, and the company overall. Such surveys can come in the form of Net Promoter Scores, a reporting system used by many organizations. Marketing can influence these aspects directly and indirectly across three core areas:

1. *Marketing mix elements.* Product quality may not meet customers' requirements or may not satisfy their need as expected. Pricing may too high for the product they're purchasing. Communication, whether excessive or not aligned or appropriate, can impact on customer satisfaction.
2. *Sales.* With sales, the customer relationship or satisfaction can be impacted by a change of sales account manager or reducing the frequency of the manager's contact with a customer. Time of engagement can also have an impact: sales engagement can be improved through marketing identifying customer needs, and providing sales with information and content that address those needs, in a timely fashion. Marketing can help by providing material through third parties so customers still stay informed but aren't bombarded by e-mails or too-frequent sales calls that may be regarded as a nuisance over time.
3. *Corporate and wider business.* Other factors impacting customer satisfaction are company values and reputation; in modern day business, an organization's business affairs are transparent and very public so where

organizations don't conduct themselves well per customer values this can also impact customer satisfaction. Marketing can help improve perception of the company through PR and branding activities.

Customer lifecycle communication

Customer expansion and retention marketing is about following customers' journeys and their business growth. Customer communication can also revolve around the lifecycle of engagement where there may be dips and peaks in customer/vendor relationships for different reasons. The dips can

Table 6.1 Marketing and the customer lifecycle

Stage post-acquisition	Customer behaviour example	Marketing tactics
Retention	Repeat purchasing	Update via newsletter Invitation to retention account events Support sales in regular communication Marketing supporting sales phone calls with company news Share latest on market trends, information
Dips in vendor/customer relationship	Customer fails to repeat purchase in a given period	Reminder e-mails Invite to webinar, events Offer incentives to purchase Invite to customer advisory council Use detail from NPS report to engage customers
Expansion	Customer increases purchase level through increased amounts or range of vendor's products	Marketing expand content, engagement Support increased sales engagement through broader set of marketing activities Offers-based marketing to upsell Highlight benefits of other products in portfolio
Promotion-preferred	Customer becomes champion or strategic partner	Collaborative marketing Inclusion at vendor-led events Include in brand marketing Hospitality marketing 1x1 marketing at senior level Include in executive visits

be due to customer business troughs and therefore lack of need or ability to purchase, or vendor-specific due to rotation of sales people as well as customer satisfaction factors mentioned before.

Customer lifecycle dips can be mitigated through marketing initiatives as marketing can craft news and messaging as well as provide unique opportunities to improve customer engagement.

Mapping marketing and customer lifecycle stage (post-acquisition)

In managing customer lifecycle post-acquisition marketers can prepare for the different stages such as retention, customer satisfaction dips, expansion and premium-based marketing. Table 6.1 outlines some marketing activities for the different lifecycle stages.

Customer loyalty measurement

Customer loyalty can be measured across the core areas of engagement, purchasing behaviours and advocacy (see Figure 6.3 for more detail).

Engagement metrics differ between business type and their marketing channel usage; for example, a digital channel savvy small businesses could be measured on time spent online and returning visits. Other metrics for customers who are account managed may be their frequency of use of a customer portal or their usage of customer solution tools; or downloading of information.

Purchasing behaviours reflecting loyalty can cover the number of repeat purchases in each period, renewal rate if the product is software based, share-of-wallet and churn rate. Low churn rate for a given customer group or segment would indicate a good degree of loyalty.

Advocacy could be based on likelihood to recommend or leave; these are typically qualitative and measured through surveys such as Net Promoter Score.

The degree of usage of a loyalty programme and membership numbers are a measure of loyalty, although as an absolute measurement this may be misleading as customers may be members but be completely disengaged. It's important to understand how engaged the customer is with the loyalty programme.

Figure 6.3 Measuring customer loyalty

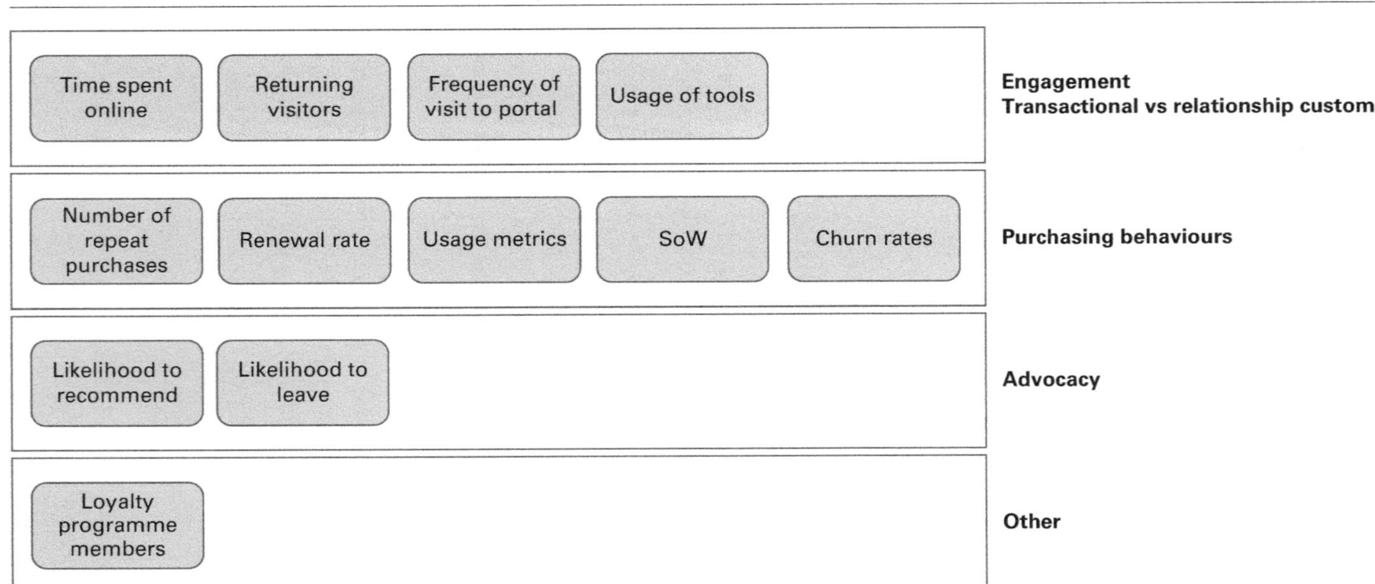

ACTIVITIES

Identify marketing activities today that are oriented towards customer retention; do you see any gaps?

Look at how you measure customer retention or loyalty marketing. What do those metrics tell you? Are there any different metrics that can be used?

References and further reading

Ahmad, R and Buttle, F (2001) Customer retention: a potentially potent marketing management strategy, *Journal of Strategic Marketing*, **9**, pp 29–45

Ahmad, R and Buttle, F (2002) Customer retention management: a reflection on theory and practice, *Marketing Intelligence and Planning*, **20** (3), pp 149–61

Marsh, B (2015) 4 musts for serious customer success in 2015, Salesforce Blog, 16 January, available at: https://www.salesforce.com/blog/2015/01/4-musts-serious-customer-success-2015-gp.html (accessed 10 February 2017)

Payne, C M and Ballantyne, D (1991) *Relationship Marketing*, Butterworth-Heinemann, Oxford

Stillwagon, A (1990) Did you know: a 5% increase in retention increases profits by up to 95%, available at: https://smallbiztrends.com/2014/09/increase-in-customer-retention-increases-profits.html (accessed 10 February 2017)

C-suite marketing

07

This chapter will give you an understanding of:

- C-suite – who they are
- importance of C-suite
- C-suite marketing challenges
- C-suite and personas
- C-suite marketing success factors
- C-suite contact strategies
- measuring C-suite marketing

C-suite and C-suite marketing

'C-suite' is a term commonly used to refer to the senior executive level of companies and includes all executives described as CEOs, CIOs, CMOs or other 'Chief' or 'C-level' positions. 'C-suite' for the purposes of this chapter also includes those who may not have a C-based acronym to their title but who operate at the senior executive level within an organization. In a similar fashion 'C-suite marketing' refers to all aspects of marketing oriented towards C-level or senior executive decision makers in a business.

C-suite roles

The main C-suite roles are as follows:

- *CEO*: concerned with the success of the company and is involved in creating its vision. CEOs hold their management team accountable; they think about revenues, margin and performance of the business on a regular basis. In engaging a CEO, marketing needs to communicate at a business level rather than on a technical or product level.

- *CFO*: manages and reports on the financials of the business. CFOs report financials and highlight any red flags; they're interested in marketing from a point of view of what it can deliver and the return on the overall marketing resources – budgets, people, etc.
- *CIO*: handles all IT requirements for the company. CIOs handle the internal IT support and ensure the business and employees are supported through equipment and infrastructure.
- *CSO*: sometimes known as the general manager, head of sales. CSOs lead and direct the salespeople in the organization; they are responsible for sales targets and all aspects of sales.
- *COO*: concerned about the operations of the business from a logistics and supply perspective.
- *CMO*: is concerned about the brand, marketing communications and supporting the business growth through delivering new business opportunities through leads, clicks or calls, or supporting sales through sales enablement. CMOs are also typically responsible for market research, market insights and providing greater customer insights through data.

C-suite trends

Within the executive level of companies there have been some recent shifts and changes. CMOs are gaining more influence due to the advent of digital technologies and applications in marketing that can help businesses become more efficient and effective. From a recent study conducted by the CMO Council (2013), according to both marketers (85 per cent) and IT executives (85 per cent) who participated in this study, the relationship between the two is critical to the execution of customer-centric programmes. In the future it is expected new positions such as chief data officers will be in place to support CEOs and COOs in managing streamlined companies by using the mass of data available to them and to draw insights.

EXAMPLE The emerging CDO role

CDOs or Chief Digital Officers were unheard of 10 years ago. They act as the main driver behind digital transformation, leading companies into the next stage of their development. They are also looked to for coordinating digital initiatives across the enterprise, not just marketing. Various sectors have seen CDOs appear, such as higher education, healthcare and manufacturing. They work closely with the CMO and are concerned with the digital ecosystem and company touch points as well as heavily invested in data use and applications.

The importance of C-suite

Why C-suite?

C-suite marketing is for organizations that want to think of longer-term, strategic and essentially more profitable business relationships with customers, through building more senior executive relationships and marketing to them. Where the sale is thought of as a transaction and to non-senior executives, the chances are that the supplier is missing out on potential opportunities. Typically, engaging the senior executive level of companies means suppliers can enter into more strategic conversations, propose different value propositions and solidify business relationships, which opens up wider business opportunities.

Broader view of needs

Senior level executives or C-suite will have a broader view of the company direction and will be interested in unlocking potential through capital, resource or other means. They could also be looking for partners in the forms of suppliers who can offer a different relationship. It may be that the vendor organization can offer something the company hasn't thought about or that the proposition being offered needs to be considered with a long-term perspective, which at a lower level in the company may not be appreciated. For example, a proposition which in the short term costs a lot more but over a year reduces energy bills or other operating costs may be more positively considered by a financial head who is looking at long-term benefits rather than a more junior person in the purchasing department who is taking a short-term view of the business.

Early in decision cycle

We discovered from earlier chapters that the main challenge today for B2B marketers is to influence or engage customers or decision makers earlier in the buyer journey so they are more informed and influenced to purchase an organization's products or services. One way to resolve this challenge comes from deepening engagement with the C-suite of a customer who then can influence purchase decisions within the organization earlier on in the purchase decision process.

C-suite marketing challenges

C-suite are probably particularly challenging to engage; they're generally extremely busy people, with packed calendars. They tune out of traditional marketing messages more than non-C-suite, skip TV ads and don't click on digital advertising. In the office they receive masses of e-mails and brochures and, more than others, need to be very discerning in what they read and respond to.

C-suite typically have a set of gatekeepers that protect them, such as PAs, heads of department reporting into them, assistants who filter e-mails, phone calls, etc. C-suite executives will also typically have very specific interests and motivations depending on their area of responsibility and topical business challenges, so unless potential vendors are on top of the latest trends and challenges and unless they tailor those to the sector or language used by such C-suite executives they may find very little or no response to marketing.

Once a C-suite executive is engaged and interested in a vendor's value proposition and what it can deliver, the time between the first engagement and concluding a deal is likely to be much longer than engaging purchasing departments directly. However, the potential benefits are much greater in terms of broader business arrangements and more profitable business. It does mean that success from marketing or business activities aimed at the C-suite can be difficult to demonstrate due to the length of the purchase process. Other challenges are that in some organizations the C-suite is large, consisting of many stakeholders, so detailed targeting and sub-segmentation are required.

With the above taken into considerations it's clear that approaches such as database or e-mail marketing will probably not work to engage a C-suite executive.

C-suite persona and persona creation

Before marketing to a C-suite it's important to gather insights about the different personas within the executive suite of companies being targeted. In building personas, it's important to define exactly which C-suite to target, as in larger organizations C-suite can be large teams.

The main process for creating C-suite personas is as follows:

1. *C-suite buyer/potential buyer research.* The first step is to conduct research of the C-suite or executives. Ideally this is conducted by C-suite type to be able to structure and group feedback later. The research could be groups of CEOs, of CMOs, of CIOs or of CFOs depending on the objectives of the marketing department. Typically interviews and insights can cover such as things as latest challenges, future objectives, what information sources are used to keep up to date, and how they want to be engaged by companies such as yours.
2. *Capture insights.* In this stage common behaviours are captured across different groupings. Assuming it's CIOs who are the intended target, groupings could be by size of company where, for example, CIOs in smaller companies may be concerned about building IT infrastructure in line with business growth.
3. *Build personas.* Next is building personas per type, age, interests, role, size of company, main concerns, main challenges and main requirements from potential suppliers.
4. *Content mapping.* Finally, content and messaging are created in line with the gathered insights and mapped per industry or C-suite type; ideally the content is per C-suite buyer behaviour and decision path.

Key success factors in C-suite marketing

Unlike marketing to heads of departments, marketing to a senior executive group of people means adjusting elements of the marketing mix and strategy such as communication vehicle, content, niche target group, contact strategy, go-to-models involving vendor sales or other groups. For example, a newly appointed account manager with few years' experience is probably not the best person to engage a C-level executive in the prospect company. In general, marketing to C-suite will differ from the usual sales and marketing channels, and typically requires extra knowledge, resource and budget. Few companies conduct C-suite marketing successfully.

TIP Core areas of success factors in carrying out C-suite marketing

Consistency in segmentation
Contrary to perceptions, tribalism exists between and within the C-suite; it's important when engaging C-suite in forums, etc, to be sensitive to this. A CEO of a small business will have different challenges from a CEO of a midsize or large company.

Taxonomy
C-suite tend to respond to different content compared to others in an organization; their concerns are generally more strategic so if marketing is to be successful it's worth creating tailored content.

Business vs product benefits
Executives tend to care about how to solve business problems; they are less interested in engaging potential vendors about technologies and products. Therefore, when thinking about products or services businesses should position solutions in terms of the bottom line and what can help grow the business. Peer stories of how executives of other companies managed can lend credibility to business propositions. Marketing should employ multi-step or business benefit thinking in communicating with senior executives, ie rather than the immediate benefits of the product, highlight the indirect benefits to the business derived from rolling out the offerings (see Figure 7.1).

Niche segmentation – C-level
Where the focus of a C-suite marketing programme is to engage only specific representatives, separating out these roles and contact details from the rest of the C-suite is critical.

Figure 7.1 C-suite messaging

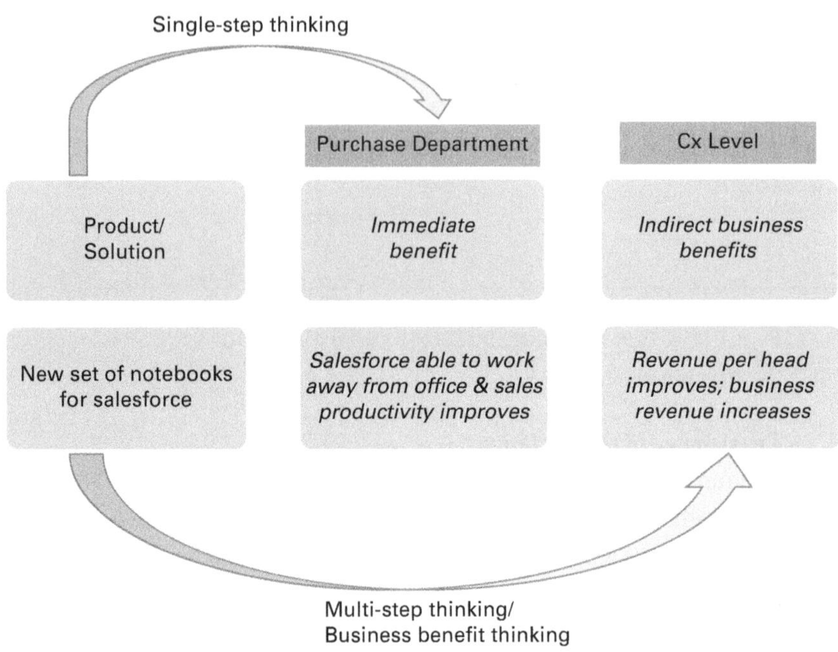

C-suite contact strategies and tactics

One of the main challenges organizations have with C-suite marketing is contacting and engaging C-suite people. Even vendors that have been doing business with a customer may find there is a complete lack of engagement with any senior executive at the customer site.

Why the challenge in contacting?

As mentioned earlier, C-suite members will have gatekeepers in the form of department personnel or personal assistants who manage post and e-mail on their behalf. As you can see from Figure 7.2 the gatekeeper is not just one person and if the marketing department needs to target more than one C-level member the challenge multiplies.

Other stumbling blocks can be behavioural. Where an organization has started to engage a customer through a sales person, that person may be reluctant to refer a vendor to someone more senior in their organization. This could be for a number of behavioural rationales, such as protecting territory.

Figure 7.2 C-suite and their gatekeepers

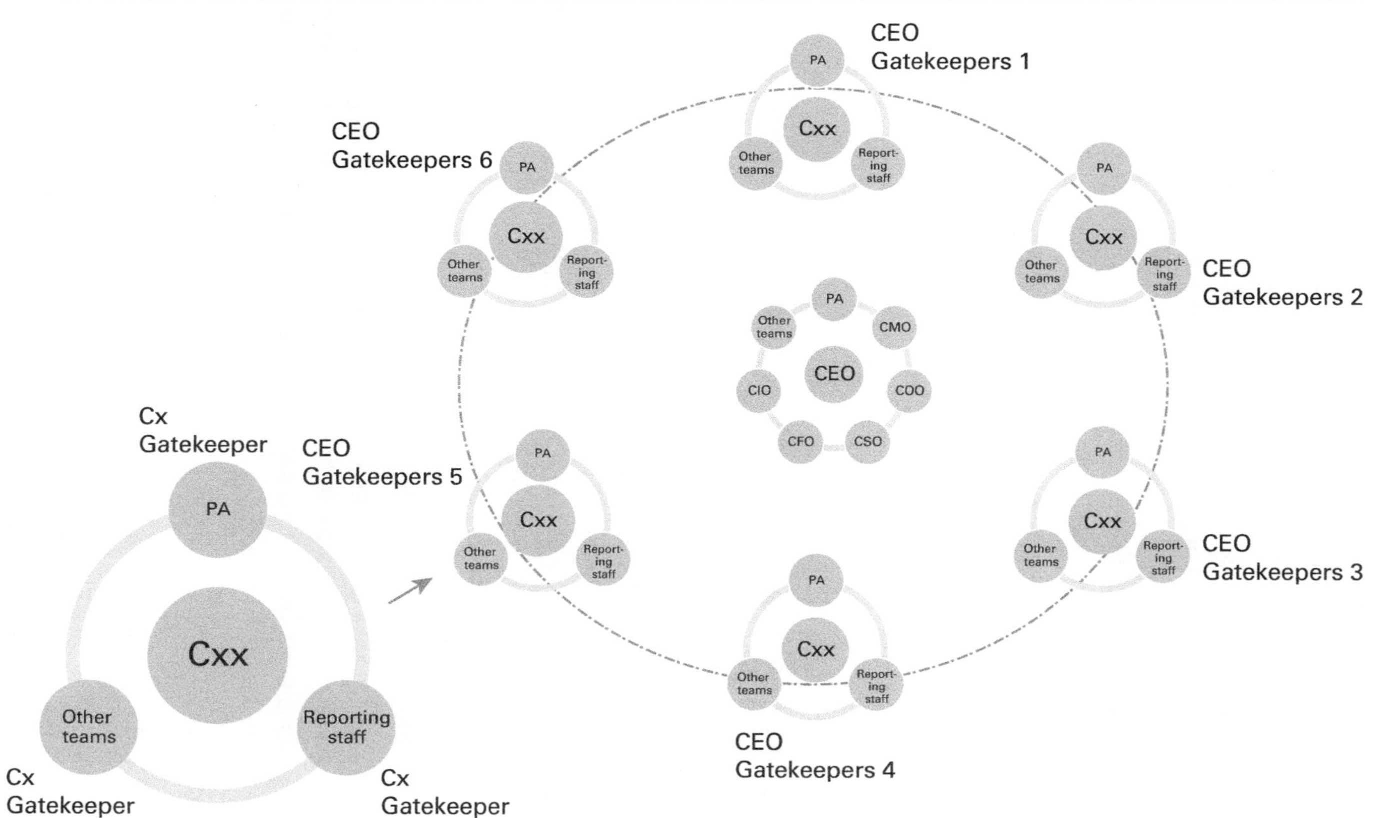

The contact strategy and tactics will differ depending on whether they are new or existing customers; here are some of the possibilities of engaging C-suite. With new customers:

Third-party research

Use third-party research companies to improve contact data; marketing can help to identify organizations that have contact data profiles.

Via industry associations

Executives are often part of multiple associations depending on function, background or business interests. For example, a CFO may be part of a financial organization or an accounting organization as well as leadership organizations. Reaching CFOs may be more effective through financial bodies or associations that have a long-standing relationship with the company's executives.

New content, reports or research

One way to engage executives may be through data or research that is particularly relevant to their interests.

New services

Provide information on a new service or product and how this benefits the top- and bottom-line of customers. For example, a new service may improve efficiencies such that financial or headcount resources are freed up, or it may help the customer achieve the same thing faster and so support them in gaining competitive edge in their field.

C-suite forums and memberships

Vendors can ask their executive level to engage and participate via forums on social platforms; sometimes this type of activity is supported and managed by PR to ensure the message is right and the right social platforms are leveraged.

With existing customers:

Vendor executive engagement

Marketing can enlist the company CEO or other C-suite representative to engage an existing or potential customer at a more senior level. Through having the C-suite of the vendor engaged, the communication would be directed to the right level in the customer.

Create a C-level event

Creating a specific event exclusive to C-suite will encourage customers to ensure the right level of people attend.

Build PA peer-to-peer relationships

A vendor could request their executive PA to build a relationship with the client's own PA by offering opportunities for lunch or other forms of engagement opportunities. In turn this relationship-building serves as a way to remove the barrier of the main gatekeeper to the C-suite contact person.

Two-pronged communication

E-mails directly to executives will either go to PAs or into a spam folder, so having a two-pronged communication approach involving e-mail plus some other form of communication will ensure a higher probability of the message reaching the intended target person.

C-suite loyalty

How do companies gain C-suite loyalty? How do they sustain such loyalty with executives, and what is the role of marketing? Essentially C-suite loyalty is a two-way process where both supplier executives and customer executives see a benefit in the executive relationship. There are a number of ways such executive level loyalty can be sustained; some are:

- *Offer information that only executives are privy to.* This can be through simply creating content only meant for executives, their pain points, or through more sophisticated approaches by providing access to specific online sites only for C-suite executives.
- *Three-way networking.* Facilitate a relationship between the customer's executives and between executives at the vendor and customer site. Marketing's role here is to develop executive engagement opportunities for executives to come together.
- *Provide insights.* A vendor could share interesting insights or tips with the customers' C-suite to keep them abreast of the latest news and market trends.

Measuring C-suite marketing

One challenge marketers face is measuring the impact of C-suite programmes. Some stumbling blocks for marketing are the inability to articulate the benefit of C-suite programmes, which can often can lead to such programmes being dismantled or kept for vanity purposes. Poor information-capture mechanisms or untimely capture can mean that the data is not captured or the wrong type of data is captured.

Short-term measuring can impact C-suite marketing success. A C-suite marketing activity is typically strategic in form and a final purchase is tactical, so the time to move from C-suite engagement to purchase can be lengthy. Where a vendor fails to incorporate a long-term measurement approach the wrong assumptions about ROI can be made.

TIP How to measure

Define metrics
Define the right metrics and articulate how they tie to the business and marketing goals; eg if a C-suite programme is defined by the number of C-level executives engaged, where the number has been reached this is one KPI achieved. Another possible metric is the number of touch points a target C-suite makes over different marketing vehicles, eg digital banners, e-mail, social, advertising or events.

Interpret metrics
A company can do this itself or engage an external company to do so. Marketing can look at CRM and data analysis by doing control group vs random sampling to understand the impact of C-suite programmes.

Blend the metrics
Ideally marketing needs to use metrics that include the beginning, middle and end of the customer journey for the intended C-suite marketing activity. By highlighting metrics in this way marketing can show how metrics evolve over time; for example, early C-suite marketing metrics could be awareness and engagement reach, and later on metrics could be opportunities and pipeline based.

Time the metrics

Marketing should define times according to measurements, eg the early phase metrics may be reviewed in the first three to six months and include engagement and participation level metrics, while metrics towards the end of the activity (eg after 12 months) may include revenue.

ACTIVITIES

Look at your top 30 accounts and ask your account manager what level of relationship the company has with their C-suite. Is it just with the CEO or with others?

Where you have an existing C-suite relationship, look to build a forum or an event to discuss with them the latest trends regarding C-suite, sharing any observations from your company and its executive leadership.

Reference and further reading

Accenture (2014a) Cutting across the CMO-CIO divide, Accenture Interactive, available at: https://www.accenture.com/au-en/~/media/Accenture/Conversion-Assets/DotCom/Documents/Global/PDF/Dualpub_16/Accenture-Interactive-Cutting-Across-the-CMO-CIO-Divide-Pdf.pdf (accessed 10 February 2017)

Accenture (2014b) CMOs: time for digital transformation – or risk being left on the side lines, Accenture Interactive, available at: https://www.accenture.com/th-en/~/media/Accenture/Conversion-Assets/DotCom/Documents/Global/PDF/Industries_14/Accenture-CMO-Insights-Web.pdf (accessed 10 February 2017)

CMO Council (2013) Big data's biggest role: aligning the CMO and CIO, CMO Council, available at: http://www.sas.com/resources/asset/big-data-biggest-role-106349.pdf (accessed 10 February 2017)

From product to solutions marketing

08

This chapter will give you an understanding of:

- product and portfolio marketing
- product marketing: hardware, software and services
- building effective value propositions
- how to create a solution
- challenges in marketing a solution
- enabling the solutions marketing integration
- solutions marketing strategies

Product and portfolio marketing

Product marketing is the science behind marketing products, where products take the centre stage. Product marketers are sometimes called 'brand managers' as they manage the product as a brand.

Twenty years ago hardware product marketers were common; increasingly one finds more software and service marketers as businesses look to differentiate themselves and their offering, reflecting also the economy moving more to solutions, software and services marketing.

Portfolio marketing

Few marketers today market just one product; most will market multiple products across hardware, software, services or a combination so the correct description is marketing of 'offerings' or 'portfolio' marketing. Portfolio marketing is about managing multiple products, each as discrete products or product categories.

Portfolio management

Marketing departments typically have the responsibility of managing product and service offerings and to manage the product mix to achieve business revenue and margin targets. Often there are products that serve to achieve unit/revenue targets while other products or services serve to achieve margin targets; it is rare that a business looks at the same product to achieve and maximize both margin and unit volumes.

Portfolio marketing for many marketers brings the challenge of managing a marketing mix per product, and with multiple products or product types it means that marketers or marketing departments need to be able to manage different marketing mixes across each product type or category. Marketers and businesses tend to create portfolios according to customer type, size and segment or tailored to a different mix of customer need, eg where the vendor's portfolio is broad.

Product marketing: hardware, software and services

Product marketing can differ depending on whether the product is hardware, software or a service. Some of the similarities and differences are:

- Product hardware marketing refers to something tangible, whereas services and software tends to be less tangible.
- Sometimes product vendors will use services to differentiate or to help with selling products, eg free services to capture the customers' attention.
- Tangible products are more susceptible to lifecycle impacts than services, which tend to be more easily adapted.
- Both hardware and software can come in packaged forms; for example, Microsoft offers customers delivery via the internet or offline channels such as retailers or the post.
- Hardware (and sometimes software) products need storing so the logistics in delivery and warehousing become more time-consuming.

- Services are based on people delivering them. They are dependent on their skillsets and the quality of their output; they are less controllable than hardware or software products. One could view the person delivering the service as part of the product.
- The quality of services is based more on subjective opinion of the customer; hence frameworks such as checklists or quality controllers are important.
- Measurement of service is subjective so evaluation approaches are needed such as questionnaires and surveys.

The shift away from 'products'

The core product and the extended product and solutions

In product marketing there is typically one or multiple core products which can be hardware, software or service based. Beyond the core product there are additional aspects such as warranty, packaging, brand and customer care known as the 'augmented product'. In solutions marketing the core product can be multiple products tied together.

Within B2B the augmented product is of great importance. For example, for software and hardware core products, service is a major way that businesses can differentiate themselves and demonstrate value add. Even for software, vendors such as Microsoft and Apple make the product tangible by using cards for buying iTunes or boxes for office applications. Services augmentation is through customer care, brand or other aspects. A business needs to leverage augmented aspects of the solution in order to connect with customers, engage them and appeal to them.

Why evolve to become more solutions focused?

Solutions marketing is all about being customer-centric; businesses have seen real benefits from moving to a customer-centric business model. By identifying customer needs, organizations can create better solutions; often customers have a need but are not aware of how to articulate the solutions or features they require.

Take the example of dictation software. The customer needs to reduce the burden of typing at a keyboard throughout the day but may be unable to state that he or she needs a software application that can perform this task.

Product focused vs customer-centric

So what is the difference between product focused and customer-centric product marketing? Product focused marketing typically has a more specific value proposition or a value proposition that doesn't align with customer needs; the products developed are off-the-shelf rather than oriented towards customers. Customer-centric product marketing is demonstrated through needs-focused messaging and products, configuring and tailoring offerings to the customer, and the design of products is bottoms-up or built on expertise from customer input, whether directly or indirectly.

From product to solutions

In B2B one hears more frequently the term 'solutions marketing'. The background to this focus will depend on sector and segment: in the IT sector, personal computers, laptops and notebooks that were once regarded as luxury items or business purchases are now affordable for all. Businesses are under greater pressure to demonstrate the value they offer and how they can support business customers with solving current challenges.

Building effective value propositions

One of the main ways to effectively market to customers is in creating and messaging value propositions. Value propositions explain the value and experience a customer will receive from a product, service or solution. It states specific benefits and highlights why it is a superior offering compared to alternatives.

Creating the value proposition

Creation of the value proposition is the foundation to effectively engaging customers in solutions marketing. The main process, outlined in Figure 8.1, is as follows:

1 *Identify customer needs, desires, challenges.* What are customer pain-points today? What keeps them awake and what problems do they have that are not getting solved? Identification of needs can come through talking to customers, engaging them in exploratory discussions or through listening forums via social, etc.

Figure 8.1 Value proposition creation

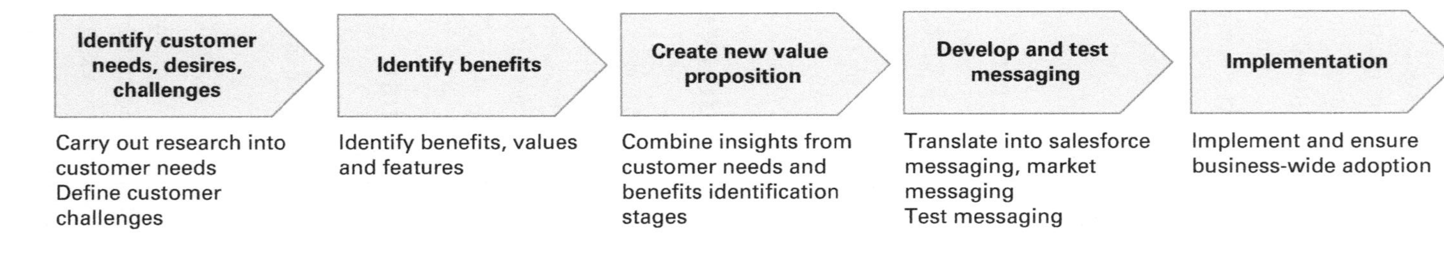

2 *Identify benefits.* Benefits from the product or offering are defined and adapted to customer needs, desires and challenges. Product value is then mapped according to features, benefits and experiences for the customer. In this phase competition is reviewed.

3 *Create value proposition.* Insights are gathered and the value proposition created.

4 *Create and test messaging.* The value proposition is translated into sales-force and market messaging, and tested.

5 *Implementation.* The final stage is implementing the value proposition internally by ensuring enterprise-wide adoption, and integrated into external marketing materials and messaging.

TIP Key questions to answer

In creating a value proposition, organizations need to answer the following key questions regarding product and service offering:

What value does it deliver for the customer?

What needs does it fulfil?

What problems does it solve?

Why should a customer purchase it over the competition?

Towards solutions marketing

The difference between solutions marketing and portfolio marketing is that the marketing of a portfolio tends not to be messaged or designed around a solution; it tends to be presented in the form of ranges of business offers.

Portfolio marketing or marketing of offerings can sometimes be marketed as a solution or in piecemeal fashion as some customers may not require or want to purchase a complete 'solution'. They may have already purchased some of the solution, for example a customer who is creating a home office may already have a computer and only need a screen and a printer.

Types of solution

Solutions can come in different forms to fill different needs and gaps; the main ones are:

- *Technology*: where the customer needs to draw on the benefits of different technologies to fulfil a need.
- *Business*: where the customer has internal or other organization needs, eg office space, and looks to a vendor to fulfil them.
- *Specialized*: where the solution may need adapting to the customer's specific needs, or involve purchasing a specialized service or software. For example, an organization may provide specialized consultants to help with a customer's challenge; in the IT sector this may be designing a data-centre specific to the customer's back-office space requirements.
- *Verticalized*: like the specialized solution but required for a vertical customer; this could be for the construction industry where the customer requires more robust and rugged outdoor computing equipment.

TIP Mechanisms for creating solutions

Marketers are increasingly challenged with constructing a solution; this can be done from the main options below:

- *Adaptation.* The organization creates a solution from its offering or through adapting its portfolio to be able to offer a solution. For example, IT vendors such as HP and Dell have acquired many companies in the past decade to be able to offer not only the hardware for a solution but also the software and service aspects.
- *Alliances.* Some organizations will create an alliance with another company; these typically are organizations that complement each other's portfolio and are generally not competitors.
- *Channel partners.* Organizations decide to sell their products through a channel partner with the objective of offering a full range of products or a solution to a customer. This can be a loose arrangement or a specific arrangement when using value-added resellers.
- *Specialized channel resellers.* Independent software vendors or specialized channel resellers that offer solutions for a specific sector can also be used by vendors to offer end-to-end solutions.

Challenges in marketing a solution

One of the main challenges facing marketers is in marketing a solution, even where all the components of the solution are owned by one vendor. Marketing a solution is about integrating marketing, whether within one company or between companies. Integration means integrating marketing processes, marketing information and people.

Five areas can be identified that support solutions marketing:

1. *Customer-oriented value proposition development.* This can be achieved through better PR, improved customer segmentation and account-based marketing.
2. *Customer intimacy.* Customer intimacy is about maximizing exposure to customers through customer events, where companies listen to existing and potential customers. Customer engagement is facilitated via social forums or through loyalty programmes.
3. *Internal integration processes and approaches.* Supporting the external marketing, internally there needs to be cooperation between departments and product units in formulating solutions. This can be done using processes that orient the business towards customer segments rather than inward approaches focusing on the product.
4. *Strategic alignment.* This is about aligning the organization strategically towards relevant market segments for the current and future business and building capabilities to support the business in offering solutions.
5. *Sales integration.* Sales integration within and across the organization can help with future implementation; where the solutions require handover between departments any niggles can be resolved in advance. Sales integration can ensure a level of buy-in is already in place when it's time to roll out.

TIP How to integrate for solutions marketing

1. *Integration starting point.* The integration starting point is to create a forum for different companies or departments to engage, share and agree on the objective, scope and process. This can be through regular calls and meetings.

2 *Prioritize customer segment.* The different companies or departments need to agree on the customer or priority customer segment(s), eg where there are multiple segments in play. This step is critical to ensure the next steps in integration take place smoothly.

3 *Define customer challenges, needs.* Next the combined departments/organizations need to define the core needs and challenges that customers face.

4 *Ensure the solution is complete according to detailed customer challenges.* From the previous step it may become clear that an aspect of a solution is missing, eg for an office documentation solution up-to-date software that helps archive documents may be missing even if all the hardware is present.

5 *Integrate messaging.* With solutions marketing the biggest challenge marketers face is in integrating components of marketing into one cohesive message. It is important to highlight the overall benefit as well as individual benefits of each of the elements of the solution.

6 *Test the message.* Before proceeding with marketing materials and content it's prudent to test the message and solution with customers to understand if the solution and its message resonate; this should then be incorporated and tweaks or changes made if necessary.

7 *Create combined marketing materials and content.* Once the message is defined, marketing should create marketing materials or content, such as a digital brochure, a video or advert.

8 *Create combined marketing activities.* These can be combined webinars, events or other marketing vehicles.

Enabling the solutions integration

For solutions integration of messaging and marketing to occur a few things need to be established. The first is executive sponsorship. A business needs to visibly support this through formal communication and executive sponsorship; this will allow for any process or other stumbling blocks to be overcome and ensure buy-in across business units. The second requirement is overall marketing leadership; it should be agreed that one of the partners needs to lead the overall process. Where both regard themselves as leading this can result in duplication and potential friction in the process.

Figure 8.2 Integrated solutions marketing

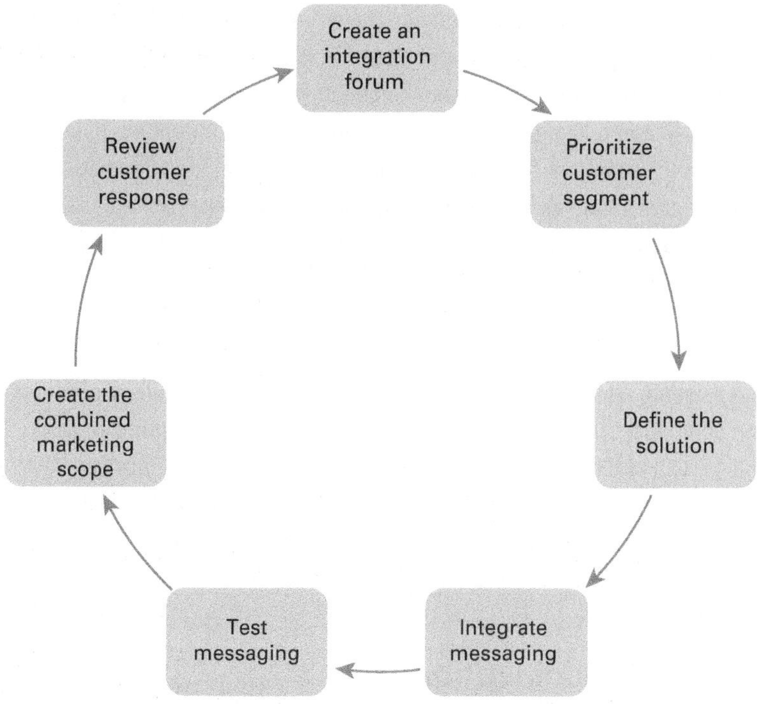

EXAMPLE Dell solutions marketing programme

In 2013 Dell UK Public Marketing decided to embark on a new approach to marketing its public information technology solutions. The impetus for this initiative was sales feedback which highlighted the need for a more end-to-end view of the Dell information technology offerings as well as the need to make customers aware of the full extent of Dell's portfolio.

The solutions marketing programme involved a multi-step process that kicked-off creation of the outline to support this new solutions marketing approach, buy-in from the public sector followed by alignment sessions with the senior sales executives to map out content requirements. Following this first draft of requirements, whiteboard sessions were set up to document information technology needs and blueprint end-to-end solutions. The external marketing agency then compiled the solutions content in the form of a guide which would be reviewed by sales people from external and executive sales. In the background, marketing communications (marcom) would ensure compliance with brand guidelines. The final stage involved the document being reviewed again by the general manager for sign-up prior to the solutions guide being launched.

The success of this programme hinged on various aspects; sales integration and full support were key in ensuring the content and final brochure were relevant for the customer. The external marketing agency played a facilitator role for sales and marketing as well as an integrator role between different departments. The general manager played an executive sponsor role, which ensured all departments were bought into the process.

The initial feedback from sales and customers was strongly positive as sales were able to enter into new conversations with customers, new and existing, and sell a broader range of information technology products and solutions. Customers were vocal about how easy the guide was to understand and how clear they found the information and diagrams. Now the solutions guide is a successfully established format for all public verticals and some verticals in the non-public space within Dell.

Dealing with competition

The strength of a vendor's solutions will be directly linked to its resilience in resisting competition; the strength can be the comprehensiveness, the level of customization, the level of integration with customer's business or quality of its components. Where a solution is missing some of these it will be more exposed and vulnerable to competitive displacement.

Marketing has the ability to articulate clearly the benefits of a solution that customers find important. Although a solution may be the sum of different products, vendors still need to ensure that organizations are managing product transitions and lifecycles to keep them as up to date as possible. Competition may offer more up-to-date aspects of the solution, which can persuade customers to move away from their existing supplier.

Updating solutions

Probably contrary to perception, solutions have a shelf-life; even those more complex and tailored to customers' needs will reach maturity or end-of-life. The complexity and sum of the parts of a solution tend to mask some of the needs for updating or replacing. Situations where solutions need updating or changing include:

- *Where customers' needs change.* If this is a dramatic change of business needs, business purpose or growth, a vendor needs to ensure it capitalizes in time.
- *Products within the solution reach end-of-life.* For example, application software as part of a home office solution is replaced by updated office software and is no longer supported.
- *Products within a high-end technology solution* need to be updated with new technologies.
- *Competition challenges by offering new benefits.* For example, a telecommunication provider offering new tariffs for multiple phone contracts will influence alternative vendors in updating and improving their solution or offering.

B2B influencer marketing 09

This chapter will give you an understanding of:

- types of influencer marketing
- what an influencer is
- influencer marketing process
- preparing the influencer strategy and programme
- finding influencers
- identifying the right influencers
- engaging influencers
- measuring influencer marketing

What is influencer marketing?

Influencer marketing is a form of marketing where the focus is placed on specific individuals (or groups of individuals) as a means of influencing the target customer. It identifies individuals who have influence over potential buyers and orients marketing activities around such influencers with the goal of leveraging their influence.

The idea of using influencers to market a product or service is not new. Most consumer commercials include influencers (professional athletes, movie stars, etc) though most B2B marketing budgets are not sufficient to cover the costs of such influencers and fortunately these influencers may not be the most suitable to influence business customers. In B2B there are influencers with a smaller reach but influence over a very specific set of target customers.

Types of influencer marketing

Influencer marketing can come in different forms: testimonial advertising, key events where speakers and influencers are advertised, bloggers who have a reach.

EXAMPLE Dell

In 2010 and 2011 Dell employed a brand campaign 'Take Your Own Path' which included some of their main customers at that time. The campaign meant the owner of the company became the main advocate and influencer for highlighting the benefits of buying solutions from Dell. As part of the campaign multiple advertising vehicles were employed as well as multiple content formats across adverts, banners, videos, PR and TV interviews. This campaign was designed to build credibility for Dell as a B2B solutions provider.

Why use influencer marketing?

The application of influencer marketing in B2B is increasing. This is due to three factors:

1. Social platforms have matured and become more sophisticated.
2. Customers in general are using social more and in more versatile ways in the business world where Twitter, LinkedIn and YouTube have grown in usage and sophistication.
3. Content is growing at an overwhelming rate and influencers provide a different angle with which to engage customers.

At the heart of influencer marketing is the fact that people trust people, especially people who have credentials of some sort. This part of B2B marketing is sometimes called B2P as it's about the human component of B2B marketing.

Influencer marketing is great where one is trying to reach an audience or sway an audience in a direction. Influencer marketing can overcome the following issues:

- *Audience reach.* The current perception of the brand or marketing hinders its ability to reach a given audience.
- *Credibility.* The influencer's advocacy can help the company improve its credibility.
- *Resonance.* Current marketing messages and activities aren't resonating with the target customer; they're not compelling enough. Influencer marketing helps support and substantiate messages with a customer.

Recent research shows:

- 72 per cent of B2B buyers use social media to research a purchase (Demand Gen, 2014).
- More business buyers (53 per cent) are relying on peer recommendations when they make a purchase. This number has increased from 19 per cent in 2012 (Demand Gen, 2014).
- B2B customers want to know what subject matter experts think. In fact, vendor subject matter experts were rated the most trustworthy or credible source of information, beating peers, analysts and digital influencers (ITSMA, 2015).

Influencer types

An influencer is a person who is well-connected and regarded as influential and in the know; someone who is looked to for advice, direction, knowledge and opinions. Business buyers can be influenced by these types of people:

- peers who are regarded as leading in their field;
- analysts for a subject area or market – through white papers or papers they are deemed experts;
- magazine writers or journalists;
- specialists in each field who are regarded as experts by customers;
- bloggers: typically specialists or experts in their subject who communicate opinions and views via blogs.

The influencer marketing process

Influencer marketing can be split into five steps, shown in Figure 9.1:

1 *Prepare.* The customer or audience intended to be reached is defined. Activities to carry out in this phase are creation of stakeholder maps, identification of how stakeholders are influenced, purchasing influencers within the buying journey.
2 *Identify key influencers.* The next step is to discover or identify the right influencers. During this phase digital applications can be used to identify the best placed influencer(s).
3 *Select influencers.* In this stage influencers are selected based on criteria such as followers, reach, strength of recommendation, level and so on.
4 *Engage and activate.* During this phase influencers are engaged directly or indirectly.
5 *Measure results.* Results from the influencer campaign or activity are measured.

Step 1. Preparation

Before launching into the influencer search, engagement, etc, one needs to prepare the ground. It's important to define the customer target and then map the influencer ecosystem for the customer target set.

Influencer marketing goals

Influencer marketing goals are defined formally or in brainstorming forums. Defined goals can be about reaching a customer set, or increasing credibility or opening new business.

Customer target set

The customer target set can be a customer segment, sub-segment or another grouping. Typically, influencers are engaged to reach a specific niche target segment; where there are multiple segments it's likely that more than one influencer is required. This specificity will help with the impact and effectiveness of the influencer marketing campaign later in the process.

Figure 9.1 Influencer marketing process

Influencer stage	Prepare and plan	Identify influencers	Select influencers	Engage influencers	Measure influencers
Activities	Define influencer marketing goals Define customer targets Build influencer map	Leverage social Leverage third party knowledge Market activities Engage subject matter experts	Research Marketing budget review	Forum participation Engage indirectly Incentivize	KPI selection KPI review
Tools/Methods	Brainstorming forums Stakeholder maps Audits	Social monitoring Social listening Influencer identifier	Influencer grid Influencer selection overview	Engagement outline	Marketing automation CRM Influencer tracking software

Building the influencer stakeholder map

The influencer stakeholder map is created using two approaches that may substitute or complement each other. The first is auditing the existing customer base using in-house resources. Customers can be engaged through sales or directly to understand their influencers during their purchasing journey. Customers may not refer to such people as 'influencers' but as key contacts, information sources or experts. This method is ad hoc and low in cost, which means most businesses can carry this out; it assumes a good relationship between vendor and supplier. The second method is using a research company where organizations can use existing and/or external customers; the benefits of this approach are that in-house resources are not burdened with additional tasks and external expertise can be leveraged.

Steps 2 and 3. Identify and select influencers

In B2B the process of finding influencers can be different to that of the consumer space, where influencers have great exposure and are often very public. If the business is actively engaged in business conversations, themes and members of associations there's a likelihood that there are already several influencers in its network, whether digitally, socially or offline. Some ways of identifying influencers are:

- *Social listening tools.* Using social listening applications with influencer search plug-ins and key words or terms one can find several influencers.
- *Twitter activity.* Influencers can be found by viewing Twitter activity and associated number of connections and number of followers. It's likely that influential speakers or speaker associations are already being engaged.
- *Industry associations.* Industry associations will typically be connected to key experts in the industry and know of influencers. Within the industry association itself, some of the senior executives may be influencers.
- *Events and speakers.* Event management organizers will probably know of relevant keynote speakers who are influencers.
- *Peers.* One can ask peers, in the company or in other companies, who may know of influencers or be in touch with them.
- *Subject matter experts.* In-house subject matter experts who are bloggers may be influencers themselves or be in a social network that includes influencers.

Figure 9.2 Influencer identifier

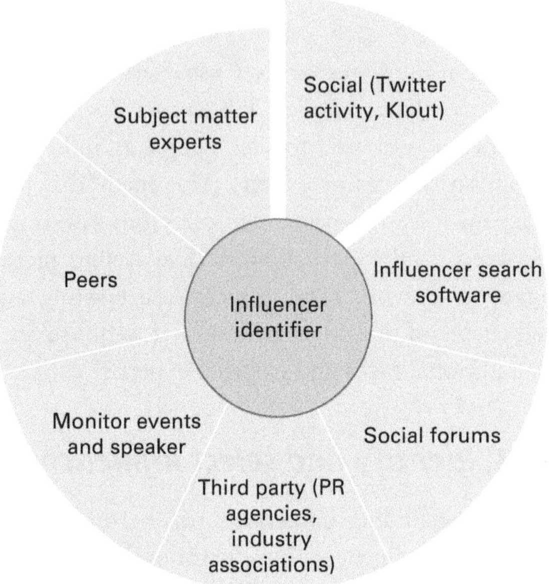

TIP Finding influencers in the B2B enterprise marketing space

It is possible that the influencer being searched for is not yet using digital or social in the same way as in the consumer space. If the B2B customer being targeted is a niche one, the influencer and their way of engaging customers may be selective. So how does one find such influencers? For example, how would you find an influencer talking about technology usage in healthcare? Here are some thoughts:

- Ask contacts working in the healthcare or IT industry.
- Look at trade fair events and key speakers.
- Look at trade or industry associations and senior people who are responsible for public relations.
- Ask a PR agency.
- Look at editors of healthcare IT journals.
- Ask customers who they think of as credible spokespeople.

Where research finds multiple influencers, marketers will need to select the optimum influencer type and the best one per category. Even if the marketing budget supports the use of multiple influencers at the same time, this may lead to different messages, which could be confusing for the customer.

One can narrow down the choice of influencers as follows (see Table 9.1): 1) measure using digital metrics such as Klout score, reach or posts. Reach can include aspects such as Twitter reach, and activity levels in terms of number of blogs, posts and how many people like, share or comment on such posts. 2) Offline, which may require qualitative research, eg a survey with customers asking them to highlight their sources of information or influencers. Overall the digital and non-digital weighting can be across influencer type and based on type and level of influencer strength.

Table 9.1 Identifying the right influencers

Stage 1: Influencer type selection

Criteria	Journalist	Analyst	Peer	Industry	Subject matter expert
Reach					
Posts					
Activity – Klout					
Followers					
Customer mention					
Qualitative					

Stage 2: Influencer weighting

By type	Journalist 1	Journalist 2	Journalist 3
Reach			
Posts			
Activity – Klout			
Followers			
Customer mention			
Qualitative			

Step 4. Engage and activate

Once the influencers have been identified and the choice narrowed down to the right influencer(s) the next stage is to engage them. Ways of doing so include:

- Be their fan and follow them online.
- Participate in their forums.
- Engage through customer referral and recommendation, on- and offline.
- Engage through PR agencies or industrial association referral.

Engagement model

Engaging influencers is about building relationships. Every influencer will probably require a different engagement approach so it's important to think about how to engage.

Incentivizing them

Engaging influencers, like most business relationships, is a two-way approach. It involves a balance between offering advantages for the influencer partnership and receiving benefits; the partnerships tend to be long term so creating the right engagement environment is important.

Advantages offered to influencers may be providing access to market information or specialized information about the business's products and solutions. Like partnerships the influencer relationship can be a loose one or a heavily integrated one where the influencer is treated as an extended member of the company; however the risk of over-integration of influencers is that they are no longer perceived as impartial by the customers they're trying to influence. Other advantages may be participating in company or customer events, offering them platforms to speak to customers and access to information. Benefits from the influencer are reach, credibility, resonance and ultimately in converting prospects to customers or in increasing customer stickiness.

Step 5. Measure results

Before an influencer marketing campaign is implemented KPIs (key performance indicators) linked to objectives need to be determined. Measurement of influencer marketing will vary and depend on goals stipulated within the preparation phase. Types of measurement can be vehicle level, campaign level and according to the customer journey.

The influencer KPIs should align with the influencer goals. For example, if the objective of the influencer campaign is customer reach then possible metrics could be audience reach by social platform; or circulation of an article or advert if the activity is an insert within a magazine. Where the objective is to improve awareness for a particular product or service, the KPI can be a perception survey linked to the influencer activity. If the objective is in generating leads, the measurement can be about leads or opportunities linked to the influencer campaign.

Influencer marketing for the long term

Once influencer campaigns have been completed the typical behaviour for businesses is to move to the next thing; unless this is a deliberate choice, a business should try to avoid this as influencer relationships take time to build and to leverage and maximize. Stopping an activity before ROI stage means wasting budgets. Influencers hold the key to customers, so switching on and off a campaign may mean customers follow the same behaviour. An influencer campaign may take time to move the customers along the buyer journey; where the business objective is in improving consideration or lead generation, the vendor needs to ensure enough time is taken for the campaign to take effect.

EXAMPLE IBM and influencer marketing – Skyword

IBM's main challenge was to build presence and awareness of its digital applications; for this it turned to influencer marketing. IBM set up an influencer blogging programme known as the 'Skyword programme' focused on midsize business marketing. It brought together different influencers from IT analysts and independent bloggers with the focused theme for the activity being competitive advantage and how midsize business can achieve it through information technology.

As part of the campaign influencers created content which in turn educated the target market. The objective was to create a knock-on effect of reaching and engaging intelligent individuals within midsize businesses to be able to impact change within that company. It challenged these individuals to use information differently, to empower their teams to make better decisions that would ultimately drive business growth.

The campaign's success was built on identifying influencers correctly aligned to business goals. Where the business goals were aligned to product and service portfolios, IBM chose particular influencers as they had credibility and were authentic; the independent nature of followers and networks was a key component of the campaign.

ACTIVITIES

Based on your industry, start to identify potential influencers through digital applications such as Klout and Twitter.

Use partners, associations, PR or anything else to build influencer identification through non-digital means.

Compare the results from the digital and non-digital approaches in terms of influencer names. What are your observations?

References

Demand Gen (2014) B2B buyer behaviour survey, available at: https://www.demandgenreport.com/industry-resources/research/2508-the-2014-b2b-buyer-behaviour-survey (accessed 10 February 2017)

ITSMA (2015) *How Buyers Consume Information Study*, abbreviated summary, ITSMA, London

PART THREE

Transform through content and digital marketing

Digital and content marketing 10

This chapter will give you an understanding of:

- digital marketing evolution
- B2B digital marketing channels
- how media has changed
- digital and sales
- digital and marketing

The digital marketing evolution

Even in the past five years B2B marketing has undergone some dramatic shifts. Recent years have seen the rise of content marketing, an increase in content formats, the use of digital in marketing, the increase in marketing technologies and the changing behaviours of customers in how they use digital and online information.

Within B2B marketing there are two distinct forms of digital marketing: transactional and relationship (or enterprise as it is sometimes called); see Table 10.1. Transactional digital marketing is digital marketing centred on business purchases of product; this is very like consumer marketing and is typically the form used to market to small business customers. The customer buying process and behaviours across the journey are easier to measure as almost all of it occurs online. Relationship digital marketing is built on a business requiring sales relationships to market and sell; this requires integration between offline and online or at least an appreciation that some aspects of the decision journey are not all digital.

B2B customers are becoming more selective, more demanding and vocal about how they want to be engaged by potential suppliers. E-mail marketing in some areas has become overused or applied inappropriately, leading

Table 10.1 Transactional digital vs relationship digital

	Transactional digital marketing	Relationship digital marketing
Products	Point products	Multiple products
Customer	One decision maker	Multiple decision makers
Targeting	Large sets of consumers based on segment/persona	Fewer groupings of customers based on segment/account/persona
Price	Important	Less important
Time to purchase	Short	Long
Main digital marketing objective	Website traffic and conversion	Lead generation
Communication channel mix: online vs offline	High mix (to full use) of digital channels	Balanced mix of digital vs offline channels used

to customers perceiving it as a nuisance and subsequently requesting e-mails from vendors to be stopped. Because of digital marketing and technologies, business customers expect more from an organization; they expect to be engaged in a timelier fashion per their needs.

Changing B2B digital marketing channels

Digital channels are the channels used to reach customers via online; over recent years their breadth and versatility have increased. For companies still making the shift, this will feel like a maze and somewhat impossible to navigate.

Digital marketing channels are sometimes called vehicles; the main ones are SEO (search engine optimization), online PR, social media, e-mail, video, webinars, digital advertising, website marketing and mobile. Their application and mix will depend on the customers, their buying phase, a vendor's goals and marketing budget.

Marketers' growing digital focus is being driven by technology and an increase in user demand via mobile and social. As a consequence, marketers need to adapt their marketing content and communication channel mix to include more digital channels.

Driving forces

So why the change in digital marketing and in digital marketing applications? We know from previous chapters that customers' behaviours have had an impact. The three main driving forces that have influenced the usage of digital marketing and digital applications are: accessibility, availability and versatility of information.

Accessibility

In the past 10 years mobile devices have changed. As recently as 2003 smartphones were regarded as a luxury item used by senior level executives, determined by pricing. Today virtually everyone can own a smartphone. Smartphones have become more powerful for using, consuming and sharing information. Ultra-mobile devices, tablets and such have become more prevalent. According to *Forbes*, the top 25 per cent of SMEs (small and medium-sized enterprises) are seeing big gains from mobile. In some parts of the world, over 90 per cent of SMEs use their smartphone to help manage their business.

Because of this shift businesses provide more information and content that can be accessed through mobile device. Terms such as 'mobile optimized' or 'mobile responsive' have become common. B2B marketers in turn are allocating more of their budgets to mobile marketing to ensure they reach potential buyers.

Some recent trends show total mobile advertising spend was expected to reach $40 billion in 2016 (Stengard, 2016); it is surpassing desktop spend. In-app mobile advertising spend will account for almost 75 per cent of total mobile ad spend.

Customers can obtain information in real time; they are able to be engaged almost any time of the day. However, being able to access a customer all the time doesn't mean vendors should do it.

Cross-device marketing

A new feature of mobile advertising is that of cross-device marketing; this provides advertisers with information on the user's use of devices and their interplay by looking at mobile exchange, desktop activity and geo-specific locations. Cross-device is a hot topic in B2C marketing and now a growing trend in B2B. While B2C is about targeting an individual across multiple devices, in B2B it's about both the individual and the company targeting across multiple devices. If multiple employees from the same company have visited an organization's website with some regularity, this can mean either that they are more likely to convert to buyers or that they are somewhere along the buyer journey.

Understanding multiple device usage and behaviours gives marketers insight into building unique user profiles. In B2B it is important for creating content that is mobile friendly and helps understand when, how and where to engage prospects.

Availability

Another major driving force is the availability of information; information and content is growing at a rate faster than users can consume it. Today the challenge is not about getting information but understanding which pieces of information to access, read and keep.

Management of information is becoming more the trend. In the business world the challenge is how to digest it, store it and then use it. 'Big data' as a term has become popular as some businesses require specialized applications on powerful servers with massive storage to crunch data and draw insights from it to help them improve their operations and marketing.

Online one can find how data is being created in real time. For example, in 60 seconds over 100 LinkedIn accounts are created, over 70 domains are registered, 700,000 search queries are carried out and 168 million e-mails are sent.

Versatility

The final driving force is versatility of information. Although the types of content have mostly been available for a long time, the range of content formats used by B2B marketers has grown in the past five years; for example, B2B marketers are employing 12–14 formats of content on average (CMI, 2016).

This is probably due to customers spending more time online and business customers looking for more information and possibly to access customers. Users expect information to be easy and quick to read, which has led to easily digested pieces of content being created. As a knock-on effect, infographics have become popular, SlideShare has become more widespread and the technology has become more accessible for B2B marketers, from both an ease of use and cost perspective.

Figure 10.1 Content marketing tactic usage

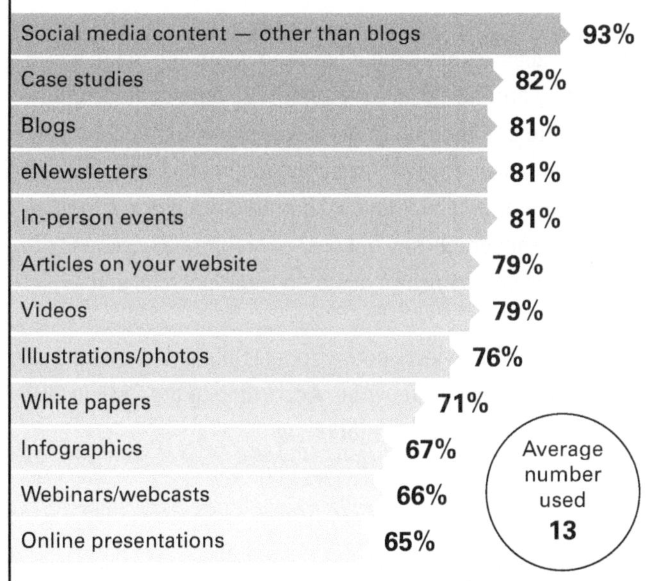

SOURCE CMI (2016) B2B content marketing: 2016 benchmarks, budgets and trends – North America, Content Marketing Institute, http://contentmarketinginstitute.com/wp-content/uploads/2015/09/2016_B2B_Report_Final.pdf

The changing face of B2B

Associated to the evolving and changing digital landscape, B2B marketers have experienced a change in media and media consumption. Video has become more widely used; more and more B2B customers turn to video to learn about products they're interested in, and the increase in YouTube views, year on year, is in double digits.

Social media has matured and evolved to become more than just a conversational platform. LinkedIn, which was regarded by businesses as a great networking or HR recruitment platform, has now evolved to become a marketing and sales platform. Twitter is used by businesses to connect and engage potential customers. According to recent research (Bullas, 2012), articles with images get almost double the views of articles without.

EXAMPLE YouTube

YouTube, founded in 2005, is today the most used video site in the world. In 2016 it was used by around 1.3 billion people, 72 hours of video was uploaded every minute and four hours of video were watched monthly.

YouTube originated as a site for amateur videos but has become a site to effectively distribute original content. B2B marketers use YouTube at different stages in the buyer journey not only to promote awareness of products and solutions but to nurture customer relationships and even to help in closing sales.

More than half of YouTube views come from mobile devices and 9 per cent of US small businesses use YouTube. According to the CMI, in 2016 76 per cent of B2B marketers use video marketing.

Marketing automation

Businesses that use marketing automation to nurture prospects experience as much as a 451 per cent increase in qualified leads (Moore, 2016). Marketing automation, which was perceived initially as an e-mail management tool, now can manage and track all marketing channels, measure them and in doing so help marketing better understand customers' behaviours online and offline.

Marketing automation has evolved to support easier and quicker integration of offline tactics. For example, at events badges can be more easily scanned and sent to CRM systems, allowing leads to be captured faster and more easily nurtured and tracked.

Digital and sales

In the past the emphasis was on salespeople discovering customers' problems or challenges and then presenting them with the right solution; this allowed salespeople to steer customers towards vendors' own solutions or offerings. The salespeople could provide the solution and articulate how their particular solution was better.

Digital has inverted the relationship between sales and customer, giving customers more power to manage their purchase decision journey, to educate themselves and to decide when and how to engage a potential vendor. By inverting the relationship, digital has also meant that engagement with a vendor can and does take place much later in the journey.

This shift means sales need to appreciate the new digital channels and for some to adopt and use them. For example, some sales specialists have become bloggers in their field, and others have adopted social media platforms such as Twitter and LinkedIn to engage a wider audience. Others work more closely with marketing to help with the creation of content that they can use later to send to a potential prospect. Advocacy programmes have become more important where sales as well as other employees embrace and use social content.

Sales are becoming marketers and the most successful salespeople are the ones embracing different forms of digital, adopting social platforms to engage customers in different ways and understanding how to use different forms of content to manage customer relationships across all purchase phases.

Changing models and approaches

Digital marketing has also impacted the linearity of customer buying phases. Customers used to move from one step in the process to the next, using a piece of content or marketing tactics as they moved through their journey; today customers can, in an instant, digest a piece of content, share on social; then be messaged through their mobile device via e-mail or SMS. At each stage customers can digest different content and use different marketing vehicles. This means that the traditional way of tracking and measuring media and ROI by each channel in isolation is no longer possible or if it is done it does not reflect reality. New measurement and tracking models are being developed to account for this lack of linearity, such as attribution models across the journey in a blended or allocated fashion.

Funnels are also becoming more complex. Customers don't always move clearly from awareness, through consideration to purchase. The reality is probably more stages for a business customer, extending from early in the buyer journey to the end. Instead of using marketing funnels in their pure form, marketers need to complement the funnel approach with buyer cycle stages, breaking it up into early, mid and late in the cycle.

References and further reading

Bullas, J (2012) 6 powerful reason why you should include images in your marketing – infographic, availabe at: http://www.jeffbullas.com/2012/05/28/6-powerful-reasons-why-you-should-include-images-in-your-marketing-infographic/ (accessed 10 February 2017)

CMI (2016) B2B content marketing: 2016 benchmarks, budgets and trends – North America, Content Marketing Institute, available at: http://contentmarketinginstitute.com/wp-content/uploads/2015/09/2016_B2B_Report_Final.pdf (accessed 10 February 2017)

Columbus, L (2015) Mobile technologies becoming a growth engine for small and medium businesses, *Forbes*, availabe at: https://www.forbes.com/sites/louiscolumbus/2015/02/08/mobile-technologies-becoming-a-growth-engine-for-small-and-medium-businesses/#45be4f574edb (accessed 10 February 2017)

Moore, K (2016) 25 marketing automation stats for 2016, SessionCam, available at: https://sessioncam.com/25-marketing-automation-stats-for-2016/ (accessed 10 February 2017)

Stengard, J (2016) 15 must know marketing automation stats, emarketeer, available at: http://www.emarketeer.com/blog/mustknow-marketing-automation-stats/ (accessed 10 February 2017)

Digital marketing strategy and planning

11

This chapter will give you an understanding of:

- digital strategy objectives
- digital marketing framework
- digital planning/strategy enablers
- digital challenges and opportunities
- digital marketing value chain
- paid, earned and owned digital
- digital marketing measurement
- digital marketing technologies

In this chapter, we'll look at digital marketing objectives, a framework for digital marketing planning, and how to embrace new digital technologies that enable digital marketing success.

Digital marketing strategy objectives

As digital marketing has become part of every stage of a buyer journey and digital technologies flourish, the objectives behind a digital marketing strategy can vary greatly as can the implementation and use of digital marketing techniques. Some examples of digital strategy objectives include increasing leads and customer engagement, reaching new customer segments, raising brand awareness, reducing marketing and customer service costs. For each objective the application of digital marketing can be very different.

Strategy and planning framework

To develop digital marketing plans and strategies we need a framework to work against; Figure 11.1 outlines how this is broken into six stages:

1. Goal definition.
2. Strategic analysis, forecasting (market assessment).
3. Strategic options development/marketing mix development.
4. Evaluating strategic options.
5. Implementing and activating, optimizing the marketing of the digital content and channels.
6. Analysing and reviewing.

Enablers

Supporting the strategy and planning framework are several enablers for carrying out and implementing a digital marketing strategy:

Capabilities are marketers' know-how; they are important in designing the right digital marketing strategy and in implementing it effectively.

Technology selection. Technologies and applications may be needed to collect and crunch data related to the strategy as well as track customers across the journey. If the focus of the company is to further embrace social media then social monitoring and listening applications may need to be invested in.

Content optimization. Content may need to be optimized according to gaps in the buyer journey, or in creating new formats not yet available. For example, where a customer is expecting SlideShare content to help later in the evaluation phase, the organization should make sure to have this available in time.

Buyer journey mapping. Although it seems like an obvious task, it may not be so for some companies. In this case it's not just about mapping out stages in the buyer journey but what customers do with which information, leveraging which channels, whether digital and non-digital.

Vehicle mix testing. Where there is little existing information it's prudent for marketers to test digital mix assumptions on a target group either directly or via an agency.

Figure 11.1 Digital marketing strategy framework

1 Digital goal definition	2 Digital strategic analysis/ forecasting	3 Digital strategic options development	4 Evaluate strategic options	5 Implement	6 Analyse and review
1. Digital goals or goals to achieve through digital	1. Digital performance 2. Digital audit 3. Digital trends 4. Digital channel trends 5. Factors influencing	1. Customers via digital 2. Digital mix (comms, content) 3. How to get there: influencers, use of SEO, application of social 4. Where to focus 5. Digital partners 6. Digital applications and technologies	1. Digital resources 2. Digital capabilities 3. Digital skills 4. Digital ROI, KPI	1. Digital activation 2. Digital amplification 3. Content curation	1. Digital measures 2. Digital tracking 3. Digital analysis 4. Digital optimizing

Step 1. Goal definition

So how can digital marketing support different marketing strategies? To understand more about this, below are some examples of B2B marketing strategies and how digital marketing and applications can be aligned.

Targeting and reaching customers

Traditionally, if a marketing department wanted to reach masses of business customers it would need to think about hefty marketing budgets to cover direct mail, e-mail, public relations, advertising and maybe TV advertising. Businesses today can suddenly reach thousands of customers at very low or even no cost.

Digital marketing plays an important role in targeting and reaching customers through the organic multiplier effect digital channels have: through shared, liked and referred content businesses today can quickly target and reach customers and gain exposure not possible in the same way with offline marketing. Marketers putting together a digital marketing strategy designed to reach customers have to think about how to do so effectively, ie how to reach the right customers at the right time in the right way.

Engage

Marketing automation technologies allow businesses to engage huge volumes of customers through nurtured communications and targeted communications. Social platforms and online communities mean that businesses now can engage potential customers much easier through questions, dedicated forums or other aspects of social media platforms.

Ad-serving technologies make it possible for advertising to be placed on website pages whose content is deemed relevant. Native advertising means customers get to see additional content similar to what they are already viewing in a similar format; this means organizations can share content without interrupting the customer. Other forms of engagement are through online chat functions; vendors employ chat possibilities for customers to ask short questions in real time rather than being burdened with the time and cost of making phone calls.

Online webcasts or webinars allow businesses to present directly or in partnerships with others key messages or information. Customers, regardless of location, can attend lectures, seminars or virtual events.

Customer nurture

Prior to the increase in digital and digital technologies businesses were limited in ways to nurture customers along their buyer journey; digital has made it possible to nurture customers through their purchase process. A nurture strategy could involve a mix of the following digital marketing applications: software to retarget customers with additional content, e-mail management software or marketing automation software that manages e-mail send and response rates and sends subsequent e-mails and associated social banners to customer profiles and industries. Digital channels and formats for nurturing customers along their buyer journey can be social forums, own social downloads, webcasts to update on latest product information and new videos.

Customer conversion

Digital can help with converting customers to purchase through webinar platforms geared to answering pre-order questions. As part of events, digital plays a role in helping customers engage better with content or to view content before, during and after the event.

Step 2. Strategic analysis, forecasting

The second stage is about assessing the market and forecasting digital market dynamics. During this step, marketers need to identify what is changing, why it's changing and how the market is changing.

Step 3. Strategic options development

During this phase different marketing mix options are developed according to goals. Options for reaching, engaging, nurturing and converting customers are explored. New elements of the marketing mix such as social are also defined within this phase, including which social channels to use and how.

Step 4. Evaluate strategic options

Options are evaluated against budget, resources available, internal skills and capabilities as well as reviewing ROI projections.

Step 5. Implement and activate

Digital plans are implemented according to schedules. Activities are readied where needed to support implementation and technologies leveraged so that marketing can optimize the use of digital content and channels.

Step 6. Analyse

During this stage the activities and plan related to goals, objectives and KPIs are reviewed and analysed.

Digital challenges and opportunities

With digital marketing technology there are several challenges facing marketers; on the flip side, digital technologies have brought with them some solutions and answers to alleviate these challenges. It's important marketers embrace and capitalize on these digital opportunities.

Digital challenges

The main challenges digital marketing and technologies have brought have been in content diversification, the evolving social media marketing space and the move away from traditional marketing funnels. Regarding the increased diversification of content formats, marketers need to create not only more content but content in a richer variety of forms. Some of these content formats would, only 10 years ago, be challenging or even impossible due to limited resources, bandwidths and capabilities.

The social landscape is evolving as business customers are using social more and in different ways due to the increased sophistication of social media platforms. LinkedIn, for example, now offers new and different capabilities beyond helping people network; it supports advertising, lead generation and different content formats. Social has become part of business customers' DNA and their business processes. Marketing funnels have been erased and in their place is a maze of interconnected channels reflecting the organic way in which customers use channels and consume information.

Digital opportunities

Digital marketing and digital technologies have brought about new opportunities from which B2B marketers can benefit:

Lower cost of digital marketing

Those who used TV or offline media in the past will find digital more cost-effective in reaching the same customer segments.

Speed of connecting

With digital, the pace of marketing to customers and connecting with them has become much faster; at a touch of a button businesses can engage and share information with prospects. Digital and social platforms facilitate ease of engaging and reaching customers and even in building relationships with them.

More detailed analysis

Digital applications enable businesses and marketers to analyse behaviours at a micro-level; where customers use digital throughout their buying process marketers can track them and their behaviours more easily.

Richer content

Richer and more varied content has become easier and possible even for less experienced marketers.

Content distribution

New technologies mean marketers can distribute content easier in a targeted manner and through retargeting can tap into buyer journeys and areas of interest by retargeting customers with additional pieces of content.

Media buying

Digital applications have made it possible for marketers to purchase media more easily, either directly or through agencies.

Competitive levelling

Digital also supports smaller businesses in marketing in the way larger businesses do; they can compete regardless of their size. Traditionally a smaller retailer would struggle to match the finesse of the approach of its larger competitors.

Native advertising

With digital it is possible to use native advertising to catch content and use it to build trust and engagement with potential customers. Native advertising doesn't disrupt the user experience and offers helpful information in a format similar to the other content on the site, so users engage with it more than they would with, say, a banner ad. According to the CMI, in 2015 34 per cent of B2B marketers used native advertising to promote content; although not a large number this trend is expected to increase in the coming years (CMI, 2015).

Digital marketing value chain

The digital marketing value chain should be used as an auditing tool to review the value add of all the digital marketing-related elements according to business and customer objectives. By working through the value chain back-end to customer-facing front-end, businesses are able to understand how each digital marketing element impacts the next stage in the value chain and thus understand if there is a value-added or redundant (non-value-added) component. A typical digital marketing value chain is split into four core areas:

1. *Background infrastructure* can be split into owned online resource, in-house content resource and general cost of infrastructure. At this stage the challenge for marketers is to understand the potential need and value-add prior to incurring costs in using or purchasing such applications and technologies.
2. *Digital preparation – awareness based.* Such digital applications can be through using apps to buy media and serve ads. In the cost of creating content (as opposed to cost of resource) this can be the cost of paid search rather than organic search.
3. *Digital preparation – lead generation based* can include social paid targeting activities, content syndication associated with lead generation, webinars or other digital channels directly attributed to generating leads.
4. *Digital performance tracking and review* – such technologies can be CRM with marketing plug-ins, marketing automation to analyse marketing activities more broadly, or specific monitoring programs to monitor SEO quality, or social listening to monitor conversations on social.

Figure 11.2 The digital marketing value chain

Back-end infrastructure	Digital preparation	Digital activation	Digital performance tracking	
Owned website(s)	Co-creation	Programmatic	Social monitoring	
Owned social platforms	SEO content	Content licensing	Search tracking	
Owned content (existing)	SEO	Retargeting applications	Marketing automation	Customer
Owned resource, know-how	Content formats	Paid social, search, advertising		
		Content syndication		

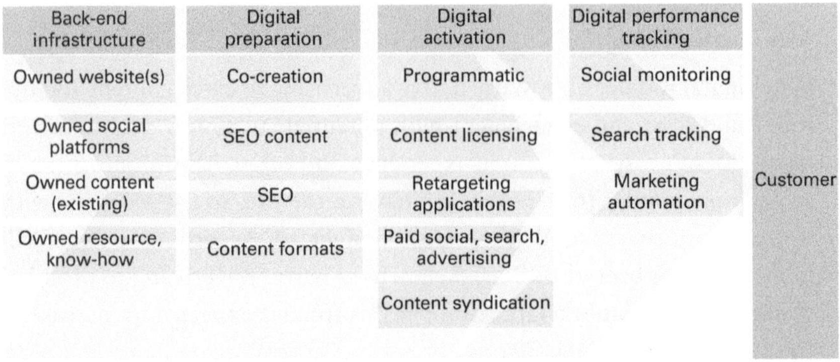

Why conduct a value chain audit?

The costs of digital marketing can mount up alarmingly unless controlled. Technology has grown at a phenomenal rate and marketers could spend all its budget on new technologies and none on 'marketing'. Additionally, business leaders will need to understand how marketing can justify new investment and what such investments can deliver for the business; sometimes an audit can surface new opportunities for improving the business.

Paid, earned and owned

Another way to develop strategy is to look at the mix of owned, paid and earned media channels:

Owned media is any online property that a vendor owns or controls that is unique to the brand. Examples are own websites, own blog sites and own social pages. The social media blogs are extensions of the own website.

Paid media is media the business pays for, and can include everything from social, through to online video to promote to customers, reach them, and increase traffic coming to owned media. Businesses do this to help achieve objectives not possible with pure owned media. Even with social you can pay for advertising (pay per click ads and display ads) that boosts content and gains exposure. Paid search also helps improve rankings, and one can pay influencers to promote content.

Earned media is media is neither owned nor paid; it can be described as online word-of-mouth. Examples are mentions, shares, reposts, reviews, recommendations or content picked up by third parties. One of the most effective driving forces of earned media is usually a combined result of strong organic rankings on the search engines, and content distributed by the brand. You can also have earned influencers who you haven't paid for but support the brand's messaging. One big driver behind earned success is content: compelling, timely, informative content such as blogs, infographics, videos, etc, can help improve the impact of earned media.

Digital marketing measurement

Before building tables of metrics it's important to answer a number of questions. Digital marketing and technologies produce more metrics than other areas simply because they have the ability to track more easily and support more granular views than traditional offline marketing. Marketers need to be extremely focused on what they measure and how, and in overall management of digital measurement to ensure success:

1. *Set measurable goals.* During this step goals that can be measured are defined, along with how they are to be measured.
2. *Define business-associated KPIs.* The KPIs should be linked to business performance in some way; even KPIs early in the buying cycle should be linked to engagement or reach. For example, the number of repeat visitors to a website or number of pieces of content being viewed can be linked to customer conversion statistics.
3. *Track and report.* During this phase the activity is tracked and reported back to key stakeholders.
4. *Review.* The activity is reviewed in terms of performance against set KPIs, how the activity is supporting business goals.
5. *Optimize.* Optimization may be needed when results are below plan. Where performance is above plan, optimization may still be possible by looking at implementation or how to take it to the next level, for instance where the activity was a pilot before the full implementation.

Digital marketing measurement can be split into some core categories:

- general performance – traffic, leads, reach;
- digital channel based – website, blog, social networks, search engines;
- customer lifecycle – acquisition of new customers; existing customers;
- campaign-based performance – lead generation, click-through, conversions.

Some other considerations and questions are:

- How will we use the metric? This question should help marketers think about which KPIs are going to be used rather than collecting sheets and sheets of metrics.
- How frequently will we need to use it? Some metrics may not need collecting or reviewing so frequently; limiting the number of metrics to review on a regular basis to a manageable number helps save time.
- Who is the audience of the metric? This question will help marketers think about how metrics are understood and whether they need interpreting or explaining before presenting. Rarely is it the case that marketers can understand and articulate all metrics they receive; this line of questioning will help marketers challenge the metric before sharing it further.

Attribution models

One of the areas B2B marketers need to grasp is how and where to attribute marketing spend across the buyer journey; these engagements are referred to as touches. For some sectors these can stretch beyond 10 or 15 touches before a customer engages a vendor salesperson. Figure 11.3 shows the main attribution models:

First touch – this model means value is given to the first marketing touch in a sequence of touches. An example could be a business buyer receiving a message via a mobile phone and many steps later purchasing online from his or her desktop computer.

Last touch – this models means value is given the last touch in a sequence of customer touches. The example above means the weighting is given to the online website purchase.

Non-weighted – value is attributed equally across all touch points regardless of their relevance or importance.

Time based – value is attributed increasingly to touch points closest to conversion. This is often used because it is where it is easiest to measure and assign value; the risk is that investments earlier on in the buying cycle that are more awareness based are neglected and undervalued.

Measurement based – value is attributed to the touch points most easily measured; this can be where digital activities are measured even if offline

Figure 11.3 Attribution models

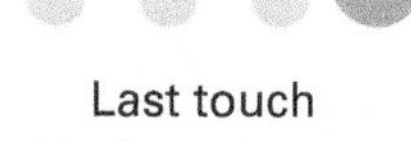

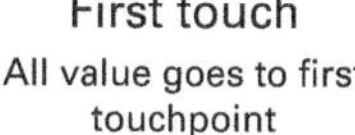

activities contribute greatly to the purchase. This is the case in sectors where integration between offline and online marketing hasn't been put in place; the risk is that offline marketing is undervalued.

Position based – value is attributed to touch points at the start and end; the middle touch points are usually not attributed.

Digital tools and technologies

As mentioned before, marketing technology is vast with literally thousands of applications to choose from. To simplify things, one can place these in four core areas: back-office infrastructure, customer-facing, monitoring/review and intermediary marketing. Examples are:

- *Marketing back-office infrastructure*: includes CRM, marketing automation, content management and e-commerce engines.
- *Customer-facing*: includes webinars, search, e-mail marketing, blog, display.
- *Monitoring/review*: includes social analytics, SEO optimizing.
- *Intermediary marketing*: includes data management platforms (DMPs).

Technology selection

Various criteria will determine which technology to select, such as:

- business size: number of employees within the company;
- business goal: short, mid or long term, the goals to be achieved within one, two or more years;
- objectives and priorities: aligned to short- to mid-term goals;
- technology needs case: per above, highlighting benefit of the technology/ies;
- budget and budget ceiling: the budget available and the limit to spending;
- in-house vs external: where in-house is required this may depend on in-house competencies.

ACTIVITIES

Look at your current marketing approach and identify which media are owned, paid and earned.

Consider your main target audience today. What do you know about their time spent online? Where do they go? What do they use online for?

Reference

CMI (2015) B2B content marketing: 2015 benchmarks, budgets and trends – North America, Content Marketing Institute, availabe at: http://contentmarketinginstitute.com/wp-content/uploads/2014/10/2015_B2B_Research.pdf (accessed 10 February 2017)

B2B digital marketing channels 12

This chapter will give you an understanding of:

- key digital marketing channels
- importance of website within B2B digital marketing
- how to use search and SEO
- B2B e-mail
- B2B mobile marketing
- online PR
- digital advertising
- webinar marketing
- video marketing

What is a digital channel?

A digital channel can be thought of as a transport route, where the traffic is the content the digital channel delivers. Different content formats can be thought of as different types of transport vehicles. The 'digital' part of the term is because it's via the internet or online. Non-digital is any form of communication channel not online or on the internet, eg hard copy magazines, newspapers and brochures, physical events, printed advertising and word-of-mouth.

In the digital world, some of these channels will merge and cross-over as they are used together (see Figure 12.1). Marketers need to view digital channels as an interconnected universe, in the same way as customers using digital do, not only using a mobile or a website for purchases. The main digital channels are:

SEO: SEO is search engine optimization and search engine marketing; it's about being ranked high in search results when buyers search for topics related to your products.

Online PR: online PR marketing is linked to reputational marketing; it's about telling stories through effective PR activities.

Social media: social media sites are born out of community participation, user-generated content, ratings and interactions.

E-mail: this continues to be integral in B2B marketing strategies and a great way to engage and nurture some business customers.

Digital advertising: this is sometimes referred to as 'online advertising'.

Mobile: mobile marketing involves communicating with the customer via a cellular (or mobile) device, to send a simple marketing message, to introduce them to a new audience participation-based campaign or to invite them to visit a mobile website.

Webinar: a webinar is a presentation, lecture, workshop or seminar that is transmitted over the web using video conferencing software.

Video: video channels are used to provide digital video, eg YouTube.

Website: website marketing is using a company's own website to support the communication and marketing of the business, value proposition and other information.

Figure 12.1 Hub and spoke

The business website: the top priority

A company's website is its window to customers; it can help drive perceptions either negatively or positively depending on how customers access the website, navigate it and how they perceive its content. The website should be the place customers come to from elsewhere in the digital world so having traffic directed to a business's website is key. It should be thought of as the central hub for a business and for its channels, digital and otherwise.

TIP Traffic direction and business buying process

In Chapter 3 we learnt about business buying stages and behaviours. For a vendor it's important to direct customers to its website in a timely manner. Too early may mean customers feel pushed into the sales process if the page they are directed to talks about pricing, commercial terms and products. Too late may mean that businesses lose out on opportunities where customers have already purchased something elsewhere.

Business customer type and website development

Most businesses need to engage different stakeholders within their customer target set. Typical distinctions are between more specialized or technical targets and those more interested in business impact, such as business decision makers or senior executives. Therefore, it's important that businesses create separate pages for each type of stakeholder.

Measuring effectiveness

Effectiveness of websites can be measured by repeat visitors, time on site and/or bounce rate. A high bounce rate would indicate that the customers are leaving the website quickly and are not compelled to stay. A short amount of time on site indicates they are not staying long enough to read and digest the content. Another way to measure is by using heat maps, which show how much time is spent on different areas of the website pages.

SEO and search

SEO and search marketing remain one of the top priorities for any B2B marketers. According to some recent surveys (eg Snyder and Hilal, 2015), 71 per cent of B2B researchers start their research with a generic search and it is the number one vehicle for customers.

In B2B 'searching' can be the customer researching more about the product/service solution they're interested in. Vendors trying to engage prospects can facilitate search through better optimization of their web and setting up links and key words that will direct people to their website. This is search engine optimization, where the optimization refers to a business's own website and related websites. The other main area is paid search; it refers to businesses spending money on key words. In line with the amount of spend against key words, the website is ranked based on search queries.

Optimizing SEO

There are several digital applications businesses use to understand how or whether their website is SEO optimized; typical criteria are performance of the website, navigability, security and mobile-applicability. Optimization can be conducted in-house if the competence and resource are available. Essentially SEO is about being found without paying for keywords, through an intuitive website, by building links from content on other digital sites to the company's own website.

Optimizing paid search

One way B2B marketers can leverage paid search is by optimizing and selecting key words related specifically to a vendor's business and its USP (unique selling proposition). The advice is to stay clear of peak seasons as bidding on key words may prove expensive: the more businesses bidding the higher the price of key words. Sometimes it may be more beneficial to bid on the key word directly after the peak season.

B2B e-mail

B2B marketers use e-mail more than ever: 83 per cent of marketers use e-newsletters as a content marketing tactic according to CMI's 2016 report. Within B2B there are different types of e-mail marketing ranging from a very basic e-mail through transactional e-mails to rich content e-mails.

Transactional e-mails are basic e-mails without any rich content; they are designed to influence a call-to-action or transaction. Direct e-mails are based on traditional marketing and don't always take account of a customer's journey or needs; they are there to communicate a promotional message. Personalized e-mails have some form of personalization whether through simply using the recipient's name or individualizing the content throughout. Fully personalized e-mails can be very effective and are sometimes used to improve open and response rates. Rich content e-mails include an image, video link or other; the inclusion of richer content can help with improving open rates and engagement with the customer. Retargeted e-mails are used to retarget a customer who may have clicked or opened another form of content.

TIP Using e-mail in enterprise marketing

In enterprise or relationship marketing, e-mails are still widely used but in different forms; aside the above different forms of e-mails, the way e-mails are managed can differ where the relationship is being built or where sales want to lead the way information is communicated. The e-mail can be a lead into a phone call or be used to communicate something during a phone call or a way to follow up a phone call. This type of e-mail mechanic is sometimes called assisted e-mailing, as the e-mail is not sent on its own but assisted by another activity.

In some companies automated e-mail sends are restricted, as blanket e-mails are regarded as ineffective or even damaging to customer engagement. E-mails are therefore provided to sales to use according to their judgement.

TIP Nuisance e-mails – how to avoid them

If customers want to receive information or be engaged by a vendor at the right time in the buying process, e-mails can be welcome. They are only perceived as a nuisance if they're not timely or if they are over-used. Where companies send too many e-mail to customers they can feel bombarded and ask the vendor to stop through suppression requests.

One way around the risk of over e-mailing is to create preference systems allowing customers to opt-in to e-mail only for selected topics. A common example of preference systems can be found in magazine or event companies that offer topic selection options for information or e-mail themes that customers are interested in.

Figure 12.2 E-mail and the B2B buyer journey

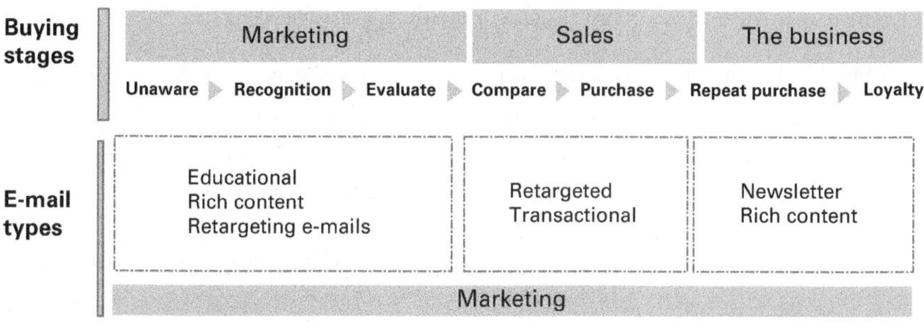

© Simon Hall, 2017

Social media

Social media channels cover a wide range of different types of social channels including social listening, social platforms – eg Facebook, LinkedIn, Twitter, social e-mail and social commerce. You'll find more about how this digital channel can be used by B2B marketers in Chapter 15.

Mobile marketing

Mobile marketing offers multiple benefits to B2B organizations, as well as being one of the main influencers of digital marketing. According to a survey by Google, 57 per cent of customers say they won't recommend a business with a poorly designed mobile site and 40 per cent have turned to a competitor's site after a poor experience. Another survey from emarketer (Sukhraj, 2016) highlighted that among the group of SMEs (small and medium-sized enterprises) that had or planned to create a website, just 33 per cent had a mobile-optimized site in September 2015.

Mobile provides customers with anytime, anywhere access; vendors looking to target customers can access customers in many more ways than with desktop-based activity. Other benefits of mobile marketing include the ability to personalize or target customers, the greater response rate and effectiveness of mobile channels, immediacy and distribution.

B2B mobile marketing tactics

The main mobile marketing tactics include the following:

- *SMS* is simple and involves sending a text message. SMS can be effective in delivering very simple messages and in response rates as it boasts extremely high open rates; on average around 98 per cent open rate. Average response rates for SMS are also high.
- *QR codes*. Quick Response codes are like a barcode that can be read using smartphones; they can be used to provide access to additional content, eg as part of a campaign.
- *Mobile display ads*. Through different options such as click-to-call and click-to-video, mobile display is great for engaging prospects with the brand. Mobile adverts can be used in conjunction with geo-targeting to advertise to customers within a given area.
- *Mobile optimized and responsive websites*. Considering the amount of time prospects or customers are away from their desk using smartphones, having a mobile site allows users more possibilities to see a brand's content; responsive content means adapting the content according to the device whether a mobile, a desktop or tablet.
- *Mobile applications* include software downloaded and installed on mobile devices. B2B event companies use mobile applications to better engage with audiences before, during and after events to share information and capture feedback and comments.

Online PR

Online PR is very similar to traditional PR in the sense that it's about influencing people rather than buying placement for brand content. The influence could result in a story in a magazine, newspaper or blog. It could also result in other online pick-up, including social media.

As people are influenced through more digital stimuli and usage, PR has made a shift in the past decade over to digital; we'll explore this digital channel more in Chapter 15.

Digital advertising

Similar in many ways to advertising in print media, with online advertising one pays for the space online, with the additional benefits that organizations can determine where the advert is placed and who sees it. With digital advertising one can target customers by behaviour, which can be a good way to reach professionals. This is done through advertising networks, which basically track the behaviour of users who visit their site network, then catalogue a user's behaviour based on site content. Types of digital advertising in B2B covers mobile advertising, social media advertising and e-mail advertising.

Retargeting

One of the main benefits of digital advertising over offline advertising is the ability to retarget customers. Retargeting in digital covers audience retargeting, key word retargeting and CRM retargeting.

Ad serving

Ad serving is sometimes known as 'advertising display' and is about displaying text or rich media content online on a company or third-party website that has auctioned off digital real estate. Adverts are typically displayed as banners or pop-ups. Ad serving applications can offer the option to automatically optimize ads, thus reducing workload such as A/B testing. Many B2B ad serving and retargeting products, eg Demandbase and Everstring, are supporting more account-based ad targeting which is part of the Account Based Marketing movement (more on this in Chapter 21).

TIP Using Google AdWords

Google AdWords is an online advertising service enabling advertisers to displays ads in a timely manner to specific audiences. AdWords' success for B2B marketing depends on three main factors: 1) carefully selecting relevant key words; 2) speaking to customers' pain points; and 3) making sure ads are written for B2B buyers and have key word qualifiers that can help filter out B2C traffic.

Webinars and webcasts

A webinar's main feature is its interactive elements. Webinars come in the form of lectures and tutorials, presentations or mini events online. Webinars are useful in some of the following circumstances:

- When budgets don't allow for physical events.
- When the target customers are in different locations or across different sectors.
- Where multiple topics at different time periods need to be planned.
- Where customers' preference is for a short engagement approach.
- Smaller businesses may consider webinars as an alternative way to showcase their value proposition or present on a topic that is current and topical.

Webinars as alternatives to events

Webinars can be considered as event alternatives as they allow different speakers to present from different locations. Where businesses have operations spread across different locations or even countries, a webinar allows them to include the highest quality internal speakers to be put in front of customers.

Types of webinar

Webinars can be one of three types. They can one-way educational, where the focus is to update and educate the audience and where the communication is only to the audience; two-way interactive where audience response is facilitated; or awareness focused where the objective is to create awareness of a product or service. Webinars are also great tools for improving retention by keeping customers up to date on the latest products or solutions.

TIP Webinar optimization

The main areas where webinars can be optimized are:

- *Speaker quality*: involving the best speakers means webinars can be executed to the highest level possible.

- *Interactive where appropriate*: facilitating opportunities for interactions will allow participants to engage; this can be managed or unmanaged depending on the business preference.
- *Sales engagement/inclusion*: with sales involved in the process, opportunities arising from the webinar sales can be followed up in a more timely fashion.

Figure 12.3 Webinar marketing goals

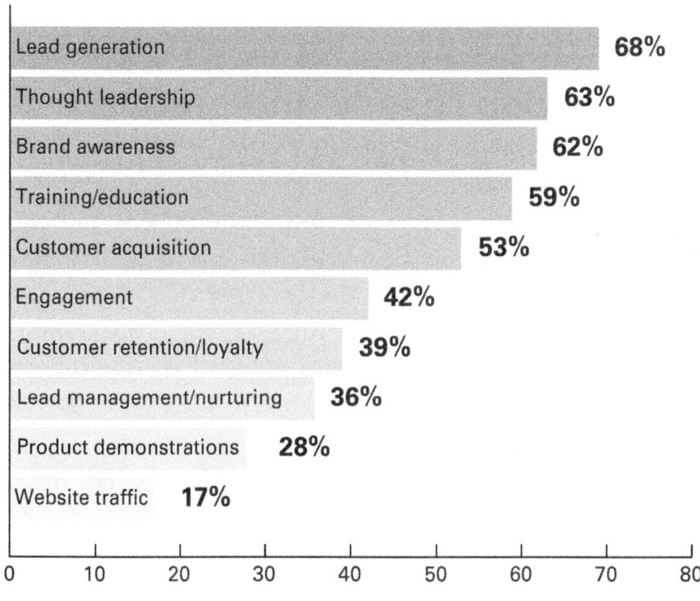

SOURCE Rose, R (2015) Webinars: they're not just leads anymore, CMI, www.slideshare.net/CMI/webinars-theyre-not-just-for-leads-anymore

Digital video

Digital video is becoming more and more effective in B2B marketing and YouTube is increasing in popularity and is used by most businesses today. Typically, video channels are used for demonstrating or launching new products and technologies, in providing expertise, sharing events or demonstrating leadership in a subject area.

YouTube is one example of a video channel supporting SEO of its videos, which in turn helps boost rankings. Video can come in different forms: as pure advertising, as something to solve business challenges, or to demonstrate thought leadership.

Video and the customer journey

Video can be used across the customer journey and is becoming increasingly effective not only in the awareness stage but during the consideration and final purchasing stages. This is through case study videos and videos demonstrating a solution or product.

Communication channel integration

In B2B marketing, digital has become more important and marketers need to be aware of the customer's information needs and consumption behaviours. Offering up a pure digital approach may mean that either some customers or stakeholders are left out, or customers are not included at certain buying stages, such as where they require more direct engagement via phone, or face-to-face in the consideration or purchase phase.

With that in mind, B2B marketers need to understand when, where and how to integrate digital and non-digital channels. There are different approaches to integration:

- *By stage of purchase*: one way is to look at early buying cycle mix, where the early part may be more digitally led and the late part may be mostly offline where customers may require some face-to-face interaction.
- *By customer type*: small businesses may be chosen for a pure digital approach while larger enterprises will require a mixed approach.
- *By customer decision maker*: even where targeting an organization may require a mix of digital and offline channels, certain decision makers could be regarded as being engaged purely through digital; for example, a CMO or chief digital officer in a company may be singled out as using mainly digital channels.

References and further reading

CMI (2016) B2B content marketing: 2016 benchmarks, budgets and trend – North America, Content Marketing Institute, available at: http://contentmarketinginstitute.com/wp-content/uploads/2015/09/2016_B2B_Report_Final.pdf (accessed 10 February 2017)

Sukhraj, R (2016) 31 mobile marketing statistics to help you plan for 2017, emarketer, available at: https://www.impactbnd.com/blog/mobile-marketing-statistics-for-2016 (accessed 10 February 2017)

Snyder, K and Hilal, P (2015) The changing face of B2B marketing, available at: https://www.thinkwithgoogle.com/articles/the-changing-face-b2b-marketing.html (accessed 10 February 2017)

Content marketing 13

This chapter will give you an understanding of:

- what content marketing is
- benefits of B2B content marketing
- types of B2B content
- the content marketing process
- content marketing planning
- key tools to support content marketing
- content curation and how to take advantage of it

Content and content marketing

Content marketing can be defined as the process of creating and distributing relevant, timely, compelling content with the purpose of attracting, engaging and acquiring target customers. Content marketing in the past five years has become a hot topic; in Chapter 10 we reviewed the three main driving forces of digital, which has given marketers greater access to more information and content and the ability to create more types of content. Where customers are exposed to more information and content, the need to make that information more compelling, relevant, digestible, readable and timely becomes paramount, hence the increasing importance of content marketing.

The benefits of B2B content marketing

Content marketing allows B2B marketers and businesses to reap different rewards; it builds a community of loyal customers; good quality free information can seal connections between a community of customers loyal to the vendor's brand. Regular sharing of content will incentivize customers to stay connected to the brand. Content marketing also helps instil trust; with good quality content the brand can become more of an authority and trusted supplier or provider in the eyes of the customer; this trust will influence purchase decisions.

Compelling content will improve SEO; good quality content tends to get cited and shared, which will mean a greater likelihood of people going to a brand's website. Content helps drive inbound traffic: with great content, businesses can benefit from more inbound traffic and more interest without having to go out and seek customers. Easy to read and understand content can help customers make better decisions; it can mean customers educate or self-educate better, which in turn allows them to make better decisions for their business.

According to other recent research from Forrester and Sirius Decisions (2013), about two-thirds of B2B buying decisions are being investigated, evaluated and compared before the brand is contacted. Most B2B purchasers say that content has a moderate or major impact on vendor selection.

Types of content

Content can come in many different forms: videos, banners, mobile content, SMS messages, white papers, tutorials, advertorials, adverts, testimonials, SlideShare, demos, infographics, blogs, webinars and forum content. It encompasses digital and non-digital forms, although many marketing articles refer to digital as this is the area that is evolving faster and becoming more innovative.

B2B content marketing differs in several ways from B2C marketing; ultimately the user or recipient of the content is very different. There are similarities but there are also differences such as thought leadership, used more in B2B marketing; thought leadership content is content demonstrating leadership on a specific topic. The digital channels used can also vary between B2B and B2C; in B2B there are social media digital channels that are more effective in reaching B2B audiences and webinars are used a lot more. In B2C more traditional advertising such as TV or online TV is used; this is rarely the case with B2B. The message being delivered can also vary: in B2B this can be more rational, fact based and appealing to business concerns.

What is great content?

Great content is:

- *Compelling*. It resonates with the audience and compels them to view more closely.
- *Timely*. It reaches customers at the right time for their needs; retargeting or redirected links make this possible.
- *Digestible/readable* for the target customers and their buying stage.
- *Relevant*. Information is relevant to the customer, their business, industry, etc.
- *Original*. It is something different, new, fresh rather than a repetition of what's already out there.
- *Emotive*. It inspires an emotion such as an urgent need or a desire.

EXAMPLE American Express Open Forum

Amex's Open Forum was launched in 2007 and has been regarded as the gold standard content marketing programme. The site was originally designed for small business: a major feature is facilitating small businesses discussing between themselves and sharing advice, asking questions and rating the advice given. The site features content by key business theme, eg raising finance, and multiple types of content, from articles through to videos. The forum is also a source of leads for new card members.

Content creation

So how does one create content? Below is a six-step outline for content creation, shown in Figure 13.1:

1 *Customer needs assessment*. Customer needs and associated digital channels and content are identified. The needs of different organizational stakeholders are reviewed. Buyer triggers are identified, account profiles and personas are created. Core themes are then agreed upon based on the research.

2 *Planning*. In line with the budget content requirements are documented, timelines are drawn, processes are mapped out and editorial calendars built. The editorial calendar is the main tool to document content, timing of content, availability of distribution and different messages. There may be decisions to change content or reduce the amount of content based on the output of planning or to adjust the budget if it doesn't allow for both creation and implementation.

3 *Content creation*. The main content is then created; this could be a large piece of research, or a piece involving a case study. The main content includes all messages and is the basis for the content creation that surrounds a marketing or brand campaign.

4 *The content portfolio is then created*. Different content formats are developed based on the main content. This part of the process is sometimes called 'content fragmentation'.

5 *Content activation*. Content is distributed or activated. During this step content is made ready and accessible and distributed according to content calendars. Part of this step is content amplification where techniques are employed to maximize the audience reach for the content.

6 *Measure and optimize*. Content is measured in terms of effectiveness and against a set of criteria and metrics such as downloads, clicks, click-throughs, time spent or other if the content is offline.

Figure 13.1 Content creation process

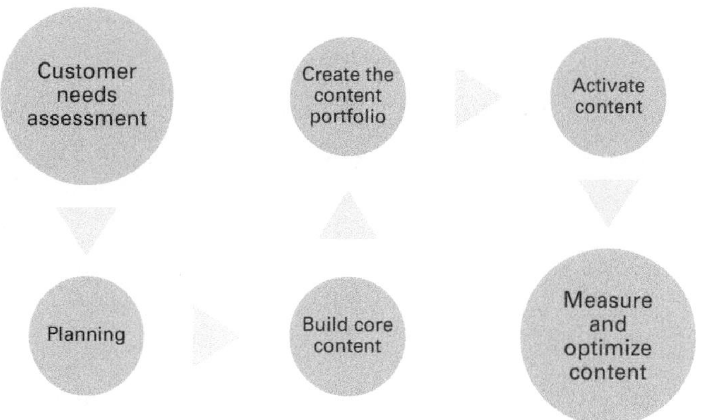

1. Customer needs assessment

The first step in creating content is to understand the target customers, their needs, their pain points. One way to capture this information is in the form of a buyer persona. Buyer personas are fundamental to understanding the customer; despite this only 44 per cent of B2B marketers use them, according to ITSMA (Schwartz and Weaver, 2014). They require resources, effort and competency to build.

TIP How to create buyer personas

Are you finding it difficult to define the right content for your target audience? Is the challenge in mapping content to the step in the buyer journey? If yes then the answer lies in buyer personas.

Buyer personas can be created in three main ways: 1) interview with customers directly or via a research company; 2) using marketing automation or CRM database which captures information source insights regarding what buyers use; and 3) website download forms which include insights such as information sources and priorities.

A typical buyer persona includes the following:

- *Needs.* What are the pain points of the customers?
- *Drivers and motivators.* What motivates them workwise?
- *Role and level.* What role do they hold, and what level in the organization?
- *Key media used.* What media do they use?
- *Communication channels used.* How do they like to be communicated to?
- *Organization interdependencies.* Who do they engage within or outside the organization?

TIP Identify buyer triggers

Another step in creating compelling content is identifying buyer triggers. A buyer trigger is an event or occurrence that spurs buyers to make purchases. Buyer triggers come from different influences such as technology, legal, competitive, business growth, governmental or economic.

2. Planning

Within this stage content mapping, content audit and content plans are carried out. Timings for content creation, availability and distribution are defined as well as corresponding budgets.

Content mapping

Content mapping is the mapping out of content formats and requirements according to buyers and their stages in the purchasing process. For example, in the awareness stage content formats could be videos, demonstrations and banners; as buyers move further along the buyer journey they require SlideShare, different types of video, infographics or even white papers.

Typically, content is mapped against two core areas (see Table 13.1): 1) buyer journey: content is created to cover each part of the journey and gaps in types of content or by buyer stage are identified; and 2) by format per buyer journey: the most used and required formats per buyer stage are created. Following the content mapping by buyer stage, the next step is to review content according to buyer type (see Figure 13.2). The buyer type can alter the content needs, formats and the buyer stage to focus on.

Content audit

The content audit follows the content mapping stage. It is the analysis of the market communication material the organization developed for internal and external purposes. The objective is to determine content

Table 13.1 Content map

Buying stage	Awareness	Evaluate	Compare	Buy and post-purchase
Content stage	Educational content	Research support content	Comparison support content	Usage and optimization of content
Content types	SEO Videos Infographics Research reports Industry article	Webinars Case studies Testimonial Content syndication	Webinars Case studies Testimonial Content syndication Comparison tools SlideShare	User forum content Tutorial Forums Blogs

Figure 13.2 Stakeholder content mapping

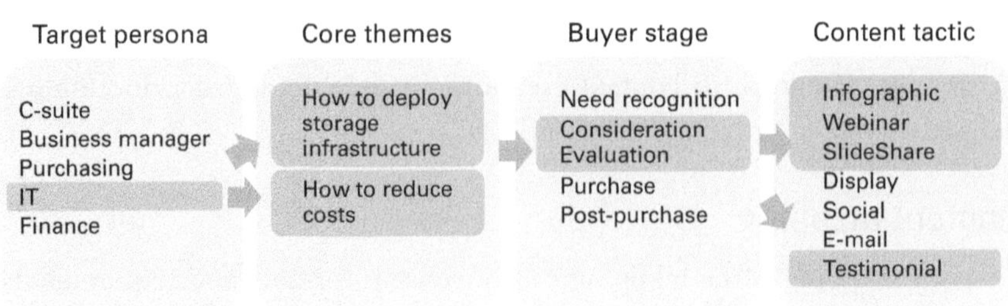

availability compared to content requirements. It's about uncovering opportunities and gaps within the content portfolio: are there enough formats to capture buyers and help them move from a consideration stage to purchase stage?

A content audit can be conducted in its simplest form as an inventory list documenting all that is available in terms of content – white papers, infographics, etc, the date or age of the content, ownership of content and details regarding target customers. The next step is to understand the content's usability, share-ability and tone: can customers easily find it, is it shareable, relevant, does it have a call-to-action?

Other content marketing planning tools

- *Provisional editorial calendar* mapping out themes or requirements by time period – month, week, etc. It is quite possible that all content is already created before the start of the campaign and content is released and activated according to timings. The benefit of this is that the messaging is controlled and fewer messages are in the market; sub-themes can be emphasized by month. Also, the customer can digest and follow rather than receiving everything all at once.
- *Creation vs activation review.* This essentially is reviewing budget allocation between the content creation and content marketing; some marketers can get so excited about creating content that they leave little budget to share the content, promote and distribute it.
- *Budget planning.* Based on scope, themes, and personas, next is determining budget requirements to create different formats. According to a CMI report (2016) the average marketers in 2014 created 14 different formats for every theme compared to nearer seven in 2010.

3. Core content creation

Core content is the main, original core piece (or pieces) of content upon which the content portfolio is built. Examples of core content are:

- a piece of research;
- a story the company wants to tell;
- an event or trigger event in the market that the company has an answer to;
- a new message or theme the company promotes;
- a customer story;
- a market trend around which the business focuses key messages.

What the core content looks like depends on the customer target, the business goals and other influences.

4. Build the content portfolio

Once the core content is created the next stage is to fragment or atomize according to content format requirements, eg taking a research piece and the results and transforming them into infographics, banners, SlideShare or other formats according to the content map.

Business marketers can encounter numerous stumbling blocks in content creation; the main ones are:

- *Knowing how much content to create.* Putting a cap or ceiling on content is difficult, particularly when there is a trend of increasing content and content consumption. Defining the volume comes down to understanding the buyers and their use of content across the buyer stages.
- *Lack of buy-in to the value-add of content.* Having an organization not fully bought-in to the value of content can mean content is not created to the right scale or quality.
- *Knowing when to refresh.* The timing of refreshing may be misunderstood; updating content too late may mean the business loses out on opportunities to engage.
- *Too many formats.* With too many different content formats managing and sharing content can prove challenging; good content can get lost in the maze of poor content.
- *Content creation know-how.* In-house technical knowledge for creating content could be lacking.

TIP Content creation considerations and solutions

In creating content marketers should be aware of the following:

- *Co-creation.* Businesses tend to find greater response rates to content co-creation than purely building content in-house; co-creation can come in multiple forms such as through analysts, case studies with a customer, a collaborative provider, by teaming up with a channel, etc. The content collaborator can substantiate a brand's credibility.
- *Ageing of content.* Content freshness can be very subjective and the B2B marketers behind the creation and managing of campaigns will typically have a different relationship to the content than its the recipients. Vendors are quick to view content as old after just three months as they are exposed to the content so frequently. B2B marketers should think about how much exposure customers have over a period of time and use that as an indicator, rather than internal fiscal quarters or planning cycles.
- *Curate it.* Where resource is limited or timelines are tight companies can look to partners for licensing content.

5. Content activation and distribution

During this phase content is promoted and distributed across different channels according to media plans and editorial calendars. Below are some of the mechanisms for distributing content:

- *Content syndication* through third parties who place company content on their website.
- *Media placement and distribution,* media or advertising slots are booked across online and other sites, directly or via media agencies.
- *Via content licensing,* through content licensing and posting companies who act on behalf of the vendors.

Content can be amplified beyond these distribution mechanisms through self-sharing of the content, eg through social; or by leveraging influencers or encouraging advocates to post and share content relevant to the topic.

> **EXAMPLE** Self-amplification
>
> Business self-amplification has become popular in B2B, partly because marketers' budgets have become more constrained but also because businesses have been conscious of how powerful people networks have become. An employee advocacy approach has helped companies such as Dell, HP and Cisco in promoting their brand and key messages.

Content syndication – how to promote and distribute content

Content syndication is the process by which third-party sites cite or use your content. It drives more engagement with an organization's content, and more traffic to a company's website; it generally increases exposure of the brand. Content syndication normally forms part of a larger marketing campaign or initiative. It can be used when the content syndicator is regarded as a trusted provider, which can help instil credibility in the content, or when the content syndicator provides customer accessibility benefits, eg a network of different customers. It helps build awareness by offering additional exposure.

Content curation

Content curation is content provided by other people, eg influencers. It involves organizing content from a selection of sources and using it to support messaging; it's not about creating 'new' content. Content is curated when the content plan has gaps in terms of amount or type of content and when budgets and resources don't allow for in-house creation; it is also a quick way to secure content.

The process of curation involves four core steps: 1) discovering – sorting the content, 2) compiling the content, 3) placing per themes, and 4) publishing the content. Using curated content means an organization can share other parties' content, as well as including commentary on the content piece. It is important to credit the author of the content by adding an attribution.

> **TIP** Checklist for content curation
>
> 1 Careful selection. Topics are carefully selecting according to initial customer research, understanding of needs, pain points, etc.

2 Content check for trustworthiness. Content is reviewed in terms of sources, stories.
3 Content should support marketing and/or brand efforts.
4 Relevancy. Content is checked for relevance to the target group and for the goal of the activity.

Content amplification

This is about bringing the content to life. It can be thought of as the process of helping content reach wider audiences than through standard media planning and placement. Some ways to amplify the content are through influencer marketing (see Chapter 9) and the following:

- via influencers – by employing influencers to share content;
- encouraging referrals – customers post and share their stories;
- where partners or channel partners share and promote content further;
- native advertising using new technology applications.

6. Content measurement

The effectiveness of content marketing is something marketers need to demonstrate if they're to protect their budgets. Measuring content marketing can be split into four core areas using the TELS framework:

Traffic metrics. Metrics relating to number of visits, unique visitors.

Engagement metrics include bounce rates, repeat visits and time spent. A bounce rate of 80 per cent means that 80 per cent of customer landing on a page and content leave immediately. A measure of how much time an audience spends on content can say a lot about the content quality. Finally, having a high repeat visit level is a positive sign as it shows customers are willing to come back.

Lead generation metrics. These include number of leads, leads converted to sales opportunities and ultimately leads closed as deals.

Sentiment metrics. These include metrics such as comments, likes and shares.

> **TIP** Website heat maps
>
> There are many great applications out there that illustrate how a vendor's audience is engaging with a page and its content. Heat maps show where on the website the customer is clicking and how much of the website is used.

Content marketing examples

Xerox developed the 'Get optimistic' campaign in early 2012; it was about positioning itself better through integrating content marketing with a sales outbound programme. Bi-weekly e-mails were sent to prospects that directed them to a personalized website. The campaign helped Xerox add 20,000 new contacts.

Sage wanted to engage with 'micro-businesses' (those with fewer than 10 employees) so it decided to focus on searches to meet objectives by targeting 100,000 business searches across seven defined user themes. Unique content was developed according to the themes used in an SEO and PPC (pay per click) campaign. Overall this resulted in 85 per cent of the UK micro-business sector being reached and 130 million impressions.

> **ACTIVITIES**
>
> Identify by campaign which pieces of content could be used for different stages of the buyer journey: beginning, middle and close.
>
> Identify your key target personas of a recent campaign and check whether your content is really tailored to them through formal or ad hoc surveys.
>
> What are your KPIs according to the TELS framework? Where do you focus today? How would you adjust the KPI discussion depending on a marketing or sales audience?

References

CMI (2016) B2B content marketing: 2016 benchmarks, budgets and trends – North America, Content Marketing Institute, available at: http://contentmarketinginstitute.com/wp-content/uploads/2015/09/2016_B2B_Report_Final.pdf (accessed 10 February 2017)

Schwartz, J and Weaver, A (2014) The marketing strategist: what's behind the customer mask? ITSMA, available at: http://www.itsma.com/whats-behind-the-customer-mask/ (accessed 10 February 2017)

Sirius Decisions (2013) How to get started on marketing and sales alignment, available at: https://www.salesforce.com/blog/2013/10/align-marketing-sales.html (accessed 10 February 2017)

B2B social media marketing 14

This chapter will give you an understanding of:

- social media business benefits
- social media channels and how to select them
- social and the customer cycle
- how to implement an advocacy programme
- social media marketing strategies

Social media evolution

Social has evolved in the past decade from a conversational forum to a full end-to-end marketing and business tool. Businesses are now embracing social in different ways and those that evangelize and embrace social are set to reap huge benefits across the business and business functions.

Social media is a collection of online platforms and tools that people use to share content, profiles, opinions, insights, experiences, perspectives and media itself, facilitating conversations and interactions online between groups of people. Social media is an ever-growing and evolving collection of online tools and toys, platforms and applications that enable all of us to interact with and share information.

Benefits of social media for business

Social has shifted in the way it impacts and benefits business; about 10 years ago social media platforms were forums oriented towards consumers. Today businesses benefit from influencing customers without engaging them, in messaging and marketing at a low cost (or even no cost). Social has become a new element of the marketing mix that helps position and promote the brand as well as generating leads. For small businesses, it's one of the easiest way to get started: beyond networking it can help them promote their offerings.

Social media can drive traffic to a website; can boost a site's SEO. Great content on social platforms means search engines are more likely to pick up a business's posts. Social can help businesses understand their audience; eg Facebook insights can help them learn about customers.

Social media channels

B2B social media channels have evolved to support business needs and customer needs; they have become more fragmented into the following areas (see the 'new' B2B social media navigator in Figure 14.1):

- *Social networks.* Network platforms designed to allow people to connect with each other; the main social network platforms used by businesses in most countries are LinkedIn, Twitter, Google Plus and Facebook.
- *Social video.* Rich and streaming media sites including YouTube and Vimeo help to engage customers early in their buying journey through richer content.
- *Social display.* Banners, typically provided through social media platforms, are a form of paid advertising.
- *Social knowledge.* These are social networks used also for business reference purposes, like Yahoo! Answers, Quora, Ask and Wikipedia. Businesses use them for reference or to get quick answers on questions and topics.
- *Social business forums.* Business communities that may also be part of social networks or separate as paid or unpaid memberships. Such business forums include members from a similar industry, function or to discuss similar challenges. For example, IT decision makers (who are considering any IT purchase) use Spiceworks to engage other IT decision makers.
- *Social e-mail.* Social networks' own e-mail services, for example LinkedIn 'InMail' can be an effective way for targeting customers and potential customers.
- *Social blogs.* Company blogs, industry specialists' blogs or specialists blogging on platforms or forums.

Figure 14.1 B2B social media navigator

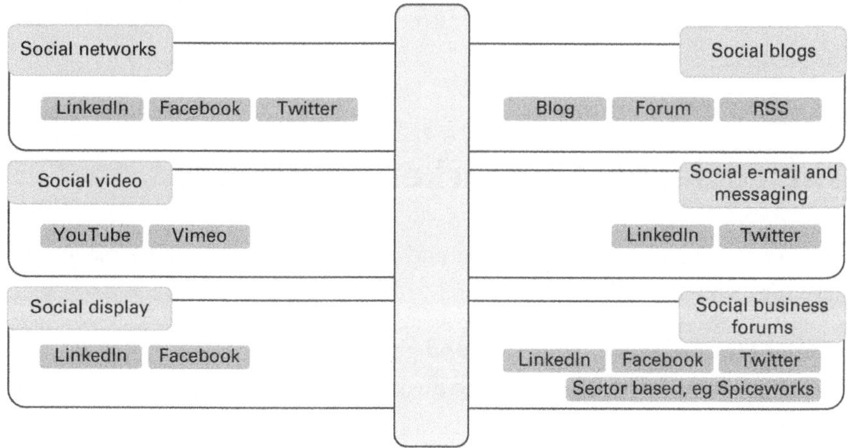

EXAMPLE Spiceworks

Over the past 10 years, Spiceworks has been effective in creating a rich IT decision maker community; it is regarded as the world's largest social business network for IT professionals. In 2011 alone, IT professionals spent almost 3 billion minutes in Spiceworks, making it one of the most active sites in the IT industry.

Social sales and marketing

Social media is a channel used by business customers to self-educate. Here they can learn about new products and vendors, engage peers and potential vendors to ask questions. Now that customers are increasingly using social, both sales and marketing are using social more to educate customers, to target, identify, acquire, engage and retain customers; they can learn more about customers' interests, behaviours, challenges and business needs.

So, who is responsible for social media within an organization? Sales need to become more social savvy to use social channels, to educate, engage, directly nurture prospects and customers. Marketers need to use social to learn about customers, to identify and attract them, to nurture them indirectly through their buying process. Clearly social media and the customers' use of this channel has forced a stronger cross-over between sales and marketing.

The social media marketing process

The six-step process in developing and rolling-out social media marketing activities, shown in Figure 14.2, is:

Step 1: Social media objectives and goal setting
The first step is to align with the business and marketing goals as well as the audience to target.

Step 2: Social media audit
The next step is to conduct a social media audit across four core areas: customer and social media channel usage; vendor employee business usage of social platforms; vendor-owned social platforms; and required social media platforms. The audit should start with the target customers' social media usage: what, how and when. The next level of the audit is to what extent owned platforms are used internally within the company compared to the required extent; eg where social is being used simply to network and add contacts and the business needs to use the platform to target and engage through additional licences.

Step 3: Social media channel selection
According to the social media audit and budget, social media channels are selected and prioritized.

Step 4: Social activation
Once the channels are selected, content should be prepared and readied as part of the overall media and content marketing plan (see Chapter 13) where content timings, paid, owned and earned plans come together to activate social across different channels.

Step 5: Social review
Once implemented, social media activities should be reviewed against pre-agreed KPIs.

Step 6: Social optimization
Based on what has been learnt during the review stage, social media activities are optimized further, whether this is content, implementation, type of social advertising or marketing.

Figure 14.2 Social media marketing process

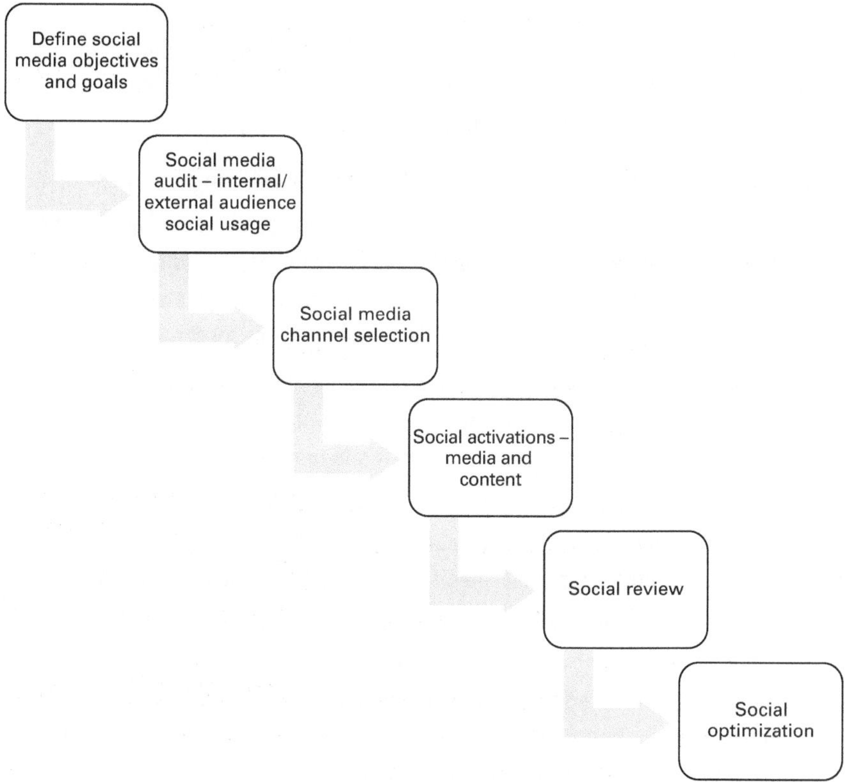

Social media marketing enablers

The success of social media marketing not only hinges on good planning and innovative usage of social media but also on some key foundations or enablers. Success typically relies on sales engagement and support; ie their buy-in. Business buy-in in this context is the respective business stakeholders being fully aware of the social media benefits for the wider business as well as being supportive of social media activities.

Sales adoption, ie sales readily using social media platforms, is key. Some sales specialists may already be bloggers within the business. Where senior business stakeholders have adopted social media, whether for private or business purposes, this can also benefit the business.

Having the business actively using social media is fundamental to any business social media activities. Where a business has little or no social presence, a social media marketing strategy will struggle. Business customers today expect all businesses to have a presence and know how to use business social platforms.

TIP How to gain buy-in

So you need to get your business and sales department participating in your social media initiatives but there isn't the buy-in? Here are some key steps to achieving this across four approaches:

1. *Leverage third-party advocates.* The typical scenario within businesses is that the marketing department takes the lead on social media and in using it for marketing and even broader business purposes. One way to support the marketing voice within a company is introducing outside advocates or experts who can explain the potential of social media for the business.
2. *Competition activities/monitoring.* Sometimes highlighting how competitors are using social and how they benefit from it can be a great way of showing how an organization needs to catch up.
3. *Customer insights and viewpoints.* Leveraging customer views on how they use social, when and to what extent can play to marketers or others trying to get buy-in for social media marketing. One simple way could be to get sales people to ask their key accounts about their use of social media.
4. *Identify internal non-marketing advocates.* Marketing departments are usually expected to be social media advocates so having non-marketers emphasizing and supporting the benefits of social can be a great way to influence other non-marketers.

Social and the customer cycle

As social media platforms have become more sophisticated, so business can leverage social at each stage in the customer lifecycle, from finding them, to engaging, acquiring and retaining them. Following are examples of business goals aligned to the customer lifecycle and how social could be used for each of the stages; see Figure 14.3.

Finding and targeting customers

Social media can be used in various ways for finding and targeting customers: through targeted display advertising on social media platforms or through monitoring third-party social forums. Vendors should check if the targeting mechanism is a help for the prospect or a disruption for the customer,

Figure 14.3 CLC social media

Buyer stage	Need recognition	Evaluation	Purchase	Post-purchase
Social media tactic	Banner on social website	SlideShare adverts	Click-based Inmail	Participate in social forum
	Sponsor content, eg on LinkedIn, Facebook	Infographics on social platform	Gated content, eg infographic on social platform	Share news via social forum
	YouTube awareness videos	Sponsored Inmail, eg Linkedin	CPC Sponsored updates	Post new content
		Build follower base	YouTube Demonstration videos	SlideShare update material
				Q&A social

eg banners that pop up like chat windows when a user is doing something completely unrelated may be off-putting.

Engaging customers

Customers can be engaged via a social forum, whether the company's own or a third party. Another possibility is sharing banners and retargeting customers when they click on a banner. Influencers or referrals can be used to engage and offer some credibility and trust to an unknown organization reaching out to potential customers.

TIP Nurture the engagement – don't rush it

During this phase vendors can easily lose potential customers. With social marketing it is so easy to connect, contact and communicate with customers, sales may not be able to resist the temptation to ask for a phone call or to ask questions about potentially selling something. Businesses need to remember the word 'social'; in B2B this is about building some form of relationship prior to any pitch or sale. Some social sites offer blocking mechanisms to restrict a vendor connecting or engaging unfamiliar contacts, so watch out!

Other possibilities for vendors to engage customers:

- *Invite to a forum based on a relevant topic.* The forum could be a tutorial via SlideShare.
- *Via InMail, personally engage a customer.* Based on defined personas or business types, companies can engage customers through social e-mails or texts.
- *Respond on social questions.* Where customers ask for help with a question or challenge, vendors can demonstrate capability and even thought leadership on a topic.

EXAMPLE Dell

Dell set up a social forum 'idea storm', which is a social crowdsourcing forum to capture input and ideas related to new products and services.

Users post their own ideas and vote and comment on other ideas. One of the key inputs was the need to integrate cameras in notebooks to support online chatting and phone calls, leading to Dell's notebook range being designed with integrated cameras. This was an effective way to engage on a topic that the customer was interested in as well as the vendor.

Social for acquisition

Social can be used for acquiring customers by using social e-mails or messaging (eg LinkedIn, InMail) offering the latest solutions to customers' needs or interest; or downloads from a social website with the opportunity to hear about latest offerings; or gated content in the form of SlideShare, infographics, e-books, or white papers.

Social for customer retention and loyalty

Post-acquisition, social media is a great tool to increase loyalty and stickiness with existing customers. One of the ways is sales updates. These may include news about technologies, about the business, or latest offerings. Rather than using e-mails all the time, this form of updating can be more powerful and less invasive as information can be shared through links or likes, and it reduces traffic to the customers' own e-mail box.

Conversations
Businesses can listen and respond on their own social site to customer mentions, or questions; this may be about sales or other business stakeholders actively engaging customers on key topics through the company's social blogs and posts.

Social mention
Organizations can support customers through mentioning them in their news updates via social or posting about an achievement the customer has had; this can help the customer's profile in the industry through 'free' marketing.

Collaborative social marketing
The vendor and customer participate together on social blogs, where they co-advertise through videos or banners.

Post-event engagement
Companies can include a follow-up message to an event through social in the form of additional content or news.

Customer service
Dealing with complaints in a timely manner can help put a customer at ease and address a problem. Integrating sales operations can also be beneficial where social is used to provide updates on delivery or other aspects.

Implementing a B2B social media advocacy programme

More and more organizations are looking to actively encourage internal employees in using social for business purposes, known as employee advocacy programmes. Here are some of the main steps to implementing a targeted social media advocacy programme, known as the TIPSS model:

Target audience and groupings
The first step is defining the target customer audience, eg specialists within an industry sector or general customers in all businesses.

Internal audience grouping
Based on the target audience, the next stage is to build internal groups, which could be general sales, specialist sales, or different business functions.

Prepare
Internal employees are trained to use social, content is prepared, and mechanisms for internally sharing social content are created.

Share content that is easily shareable
Accessible content is sent on.

Structured review against core KPIs
KPIs could be reach, influence, activity level, etc.

EXAMPLE Dell SMAC programme

Dell, like many larger companies in the IT sector, has set up its own social media programme and policy known as SMAC (social media and communities). Dell was one of the first to create a social policy; the background is to ensure all its employees leverage social media channels responsibly and according to guidelines. This helps employees understand how to use social effectively as well as avoid misuse.

Social listening and monitoring

Social listening and monitoring is another great way to understand social usage by different segments. Social listening or monitoring is about searching the web to see what's being said about your company, your competitors and other topics of interest.

Social listening can be used in different ways to help businesses, for example to find out platforms and websites customers use online, to listen and respond and eventually generate leads, to identify influencers or to improve marketing effectiveness. For example, a business can monitor key words related to business's pain points and by responding on those can generate new leads. A survey by Oracle (2013) found 43 per cent of users interact with brands on social media for a direct response to a problem or question; additionally, 31 per cent interact with brands to gain direct access to customer service representatives or product experts.

Social media channel selection

Selecting the right social media channel depends on the target customer audience. For example, a healthcare professional may have a profile on LinkedIn, be present on Facebook and be in an online community with a separate platform but may not use Twitter. Some of the main criteria in social media channel selection are:

- *Audience usage and propensity to use.* What do they currently use? This information can be found in the persona profile (see Chapter 13).
- *Where is your competition on social?* Through understanding competitors' social activity and channel use, one can avoid falling behind.
- *Buying stage focus.* What stage of the buying journey are you targeting? The answer may determine the type of social media channel.
- *Budget.* What budget do you have for social, or is the idea only to use owned and earned material?

- *Accessibility/reach*. Which social platform allows you to reach and/or engage your target customer?

CASE STUDY Schneider Electric/Invensys Better Together

In September 2014 Schneider Electric launched a communication campaign using social media channels to promote the merger/acquisition of Invensys with the aim of reaching global customers. The objective was to address two major concerns: 1) existing customers were concerned about the company's future investment in products they used and thus were holding back on new projects; 2) new customers did not yet recognize the value of the combined Schneider Electric and Invensys portfolio and demonstrated higher resistance to moving to Schneider Electric/Invensys solutions.

The focus of the campaign was to demonstrate the combined value and benefits and to reassure customers in their business with either or both companies; as part of the campaign an internal competition was launched to encourage employees to use their personal accounts to tweet about the power of being 'Better Together'. For every tweet posted using #BetterTogether the firm committed to donate a corresponding amount to 'Habitat for Humanity'. After five months about €20,000 was raised and donated. Confidence in existing customers was re-established. Aside from the business numbers, internal productivity improved as both companies were working better together and both could see the benefits of a combined business.

ACTIVITIES

Identify which social media channels your current customers are using. Does this match the social media channels included in your marketing activities or campaigns?

How often are your customers using social and for what purpose?

Identify social forums, groups related to your function, industry or business challenge and join one of them.

Reference and further reading

Khan, U (2016) 'Social listening' can help you play a marketing detective and unlocking customer success, available at: https://medium.com/kodenext/social-listening-can-help-you-play-a-marketing-detective-unlocking-customer-success-a2c3f28bd217#.no9e4zfhu (accessed 10 February 2017)

Oracle (2013) eMarketer mobile commerce roundup, available at: http://www.oracle.com/us/products/applications/emarketer-mobile-commerce-roundup-2188367.pdf (accessed 10 February 2017)

B2B brand building 15

This chapter will give you an understanding of:

- brand building and impact on business growth
- key brand elements
- what prevents a business from building a brand
- the brand building process
- how to engage employees to communicate the brand
- how to build a B2B brand tracker
- B2B brand ROI and measurement
- how to ensure brand consistency

Introduction

There are several differences in building a B2B brand compared to a consumer brand. Business brands don't have the same day-to-day exposure as consumer brands; they also tend to use different communication channels. Business brands need to appeal to different needs and requirements and the messages they use aren't as sexy. So how do B2B brands establish presence and how do brands that have B2B and B2C manage the different messages?

Brand and brand building defined

A brand starts with the identity of a company through the way it presents itself: name, description and logo. For a company the consistency of these different elements forms a brand. A brand is much more than just a logo: it is the consistent value systems a company communicates to the outside world.

Such brand consistency needs to cut across all its collateral and communication elements – this is the corporate identity. If there is inconsistency in look and feel, this can undo all the efforts of a company to position itself.

Why invest in brand building?

Several indices point to links between business performance/profitability and brand strength. For example, Brandz creates a report tracking the top 500 US stock exchange companies, and according to its recent report (Brandz, 2015) the top 100 brands grew by 81 per cent in market value while the top 500 grew by 22 per cent. Additionally, research has shown that strong brands secure loyalty, drive choice and command a premium.

Brand building in B2B is less emotive – wrong!

B2C customers may purchase the wrong brand of marmalade but that is easily rectified. What if the IT storage infrastructure for a business doesn't function or worse, loses data; such things if known to a business's customer can hurt a company's performance, earnings or its credibility. This higher level of emotionality in B2B becomes more obvious on closer inspection: B2B purchases can entail personal risks, more so than for B2C. For example, the person responsible for having purchased the datacentre or choosing the supplier will have invested emotions as their credibility and time are impacted.

B2B brand touch points

The B2B brand touch points are the points at which customers could engage with a brand directly or indirectly; the sum of the touch points usually helps the customer form a view of the brand. Figure 15.1 shows the main brand touch points across the customer journey: before, during and after purchase. Some of these elements are typically more specific to B2B, such as product training, channel partner reseller or distributors and the touch points where they represent the brand: unveiling events, user conferences, business cards and collateral that businesses receive.

Within B2B relationship marketing, customers are a lot more exposed to sales or physical opportunities to engage, such as webinars and events, so managing messages and associated branding elements is important if an organization intends to build its brand effectively. Even for small businesses,

Figure 15.1 B2B brand touch points

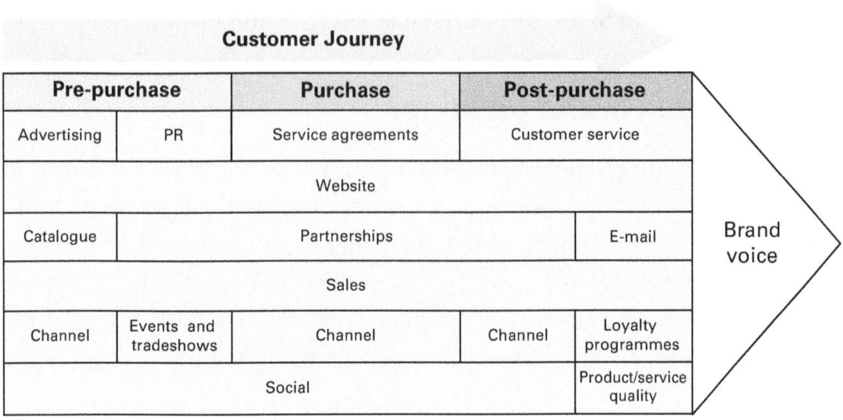

Customer Journey

Pre-purchase		Purchase	Post-purchase	
Advertising	PR	Service agreements	Customer service	
Website				
Catalogue	Partnerships			E-mail
Sales				
Channel	Events and tradeshows	Channel	Channel	Loyalty programmes
Social				Product/service quality

Brand voice

it's important to manage the touch points shown in Figure 15.1. Early in their business life, getting these right and managing this mix could impact the future success and growth of the business.

Brand building obstacles

So, if brand building is proven to be a success factor for a business and its profitability, why don't more businesses invest in it? The reality is that businesses encounter some of these challenges:

Pressure to invest elsewhere
Pressures can come from different areas that influence other investment areas for marketing or even the business; pressures can come from shareholders, from internal stakeholders or even external stakeholders (non-shareholders).

Short-term view of marketing investment
Building a brand is typically a long-term investment and needs to be carried out consistently over time if it is to be impactful. Some companies that measure themselves every six or three months look for quicker results, which is not consistent with brand building or repositioning.

Failure to articulate benefits
If marketing fails to articulate the benefits of brand building or where sales fail to understand them, this can lead to brand building initiatives being negatively impacted.

Competitive pressures
When dealing with competitors that employ aggressive sales tactics such as dramatic price reductions, a vendors' brand activities can be impacted as longer-term investments aren't seen as a priority.

Complexity in sustaining, and rolling out
Building brands and maintaining brand building activities over time usually involve different skillsets, investment in resources and budget. Brand investment needs to be carefully managed to ensure the correct media mix and media placement. There is also a need to review return on advertising spend (ROAS).

B2B brand building goals and programmes

The main goals for investing in brand building initiatives are repositioning of the brand, increasing awareness for the brand, acquiring new business, building loyalty or demonstrating value-add. The main types of B2B brand building initiatives linked to these goals are:

- *Brand positioning*. This relates to the positioning of the company. For example, in the last 20 years a lot of companies in the IT sector have repositioned their brands either into more premium price brands or as solution providers.
- *Sponsorship*. B2B sponsorships usually help brands in reaching different or extended audiences. Examples are sponsoring a piece of research intended for a specific customer, sponsoring an event or a campaign for an industrial association, or larger-scale sponsorships such as major sporting events. Ideally the sponsorship speaks to the audience and highlights to the intended customer the background of the B2B brand sponsoring the activity. Sponsorships can also help brands acquire new business and reinforce loyalty in existing customers.
- *Employee advocacy programmes* for brand building can be powerful in B2B; they can potentially serve all the above goals.
- *Social amplification programmes* are used more and more by B2B brands; they can serve to deliver on all goals. Social amplification through sales as well as partners can help disseminate messages and content much faster.
- *Partnerships*. Partnerships can include member partners that cover a target segment or sub-segment, alliance partners that offer complementary products or services to the B2B brand portfolio, or channel partners who work closely with the B2B brand to develop a market.

EXAMPLE B2B sponsorship – Deloitte and the London 2012 Olympics

Deloitte provides an example of how a professional services organization can leverage a sports sponsorship to highlight its business expertise. Deloitte sponsored the London 2012 Olympics and was the official provider of professional services for the London Organizing Committee of the Olympic Games and Paralympic Games (LOCOG). This role involved responsibility for services to support delivery of the games through more than 750,000 hours of support. Deloitte helped the organizing committee through various complex challenges such as sourcing 1.8 million items of sporting equipment in six weeks. Deloitte's professional services spanned a number of operational areas for LOCOG including catering, procurement, tax and technology; through this wide array of services Deloitte could showcase the breadth of its services and depth of expertise, while demonstrating its contribution to society.

Brand loyalty

Brand loyalty is the level to which a customer stays with a brand; it can be viewed in terms of how tied a customer is to the brand, despite temporary issues or challenges it may have with the brand vendor.

Brand loyalty can be viewed as a two-way relationship: organizations that engage with their customers or potential customers; and customers that demonstrate how they engage with the vendor through purchases, positive feedback or even how they defend a brand where it is receiving unfavourable criticism.

Creating brand loyalty can be based on different brand elements or touch points. Loyalty benefits cover several areas: with increased loyalty, organizations don't need to devote as much marketing to persuading customers to purchase or consider purchases: with greater brand loyalty the marketing costs reduce. Through brand loyalty more customers talk about the brand or advocate it. This can be thought of as 'earned' media. Earned media (or free media) is publicity gained through marketing efforts other than paid media marketing. Through loyal customers, other potential customers are persuaded to try the brand. With greater brand loyalty an organization is more likely to have stable repeat business.

Importance of brand consistency

B2B brand consistency is very important: it's about being consistent across customer touch points, ie where customers engage directly or indirectly with the brand. Ensuring consistency is about having a touch-point management programme spanning customers by buying stage. In establishing such a programme there are a number of characteristics which could be managed to support brand consistency. Creative, look and feel should be consistent. Messages across a campaign should also be consistent, as should over-arching corporate messages. Where business unit silos exist this can lead to messaging silos where eventually the company appears fragmented and confusing for the customer.

Websites and micro-sites should be consistent in look and feel, and means of navigation. Having a policy governing how to use social media, how to post, how to engage customers and what to message, send and share should form part of the B2B brand social media policy (see Chapter 14). Employee communication includes how employees apply e-mail signatures, type of font used, usage and placement of any logos as well as how employees conduct themselves in terms of making themselves available and accessible.

Brand building stages

In building a brand B2B marketers should use the five-point framework shown in Figure 15.2:

1. *Brand gap audit.* This stage is about understanding the current view of the brand, the perception of the company held by customers and business partners. Sometimes this outside view may not always align to the reality of what the business does and its goals.
2. *Positioning.* This includes a business's messaging and overall brand elements; potentially the root cause of gaps found in the brand audit may be one or more brand elements. During this phase the positioning is clearly defined.
3. *Plan for building and activation.* The plan for brand building and activation is defined; marketing vehicles and channels are selected, brand building approaches are agreed to by core stakeholders (typically the CEO or business head as well as the marketing head).

Figure 15.2 B2B brand building process

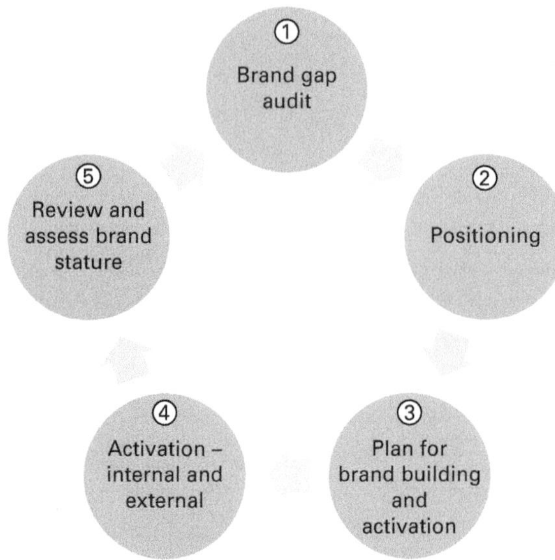

4 *Activation. Internal*: ensure all internal employees are clear about brand values and tenets, business stakeholders are re-educated with messages, the brand campaign and how branding activities support the business. *External*: expose the brand. The brand initiatives, messages and campaigns are then rolled out externally; this can be direct marketing, through third parties, agency media placement as well as through employees who articulate the new messaging and share brand campaign assets.

5 *Review and assess the brand*. During this phase various aspects are measured such as brand equity, brand loyalty and brand awareness.

1. Brand gap audit

As mentioned above the purpose of the brand audit is to understand internal and external views of the brand compared to business goals. Audits should result in understanding the performance of the brand, areas or gaps to performance, as well as the competitive brand position. Failure to track brand efforts is one of the reasons why there could be lack of buy-in: there is either a belief that it is not necessary or, if it is, there is no evidence to show where to spend the brand investment.

TIP Building a B2B brand tracker

1. *Brief creation.* Create the brief, which can be a simple document outlining the intended audience, the objective of the brand survey, timings, and expected respondent numbers.
2. *Survey creation.* The survey questions are created based on the brief.
3. *Implementation.* The survey is carried out, directly or externally by an agency or marketing services company.
4. *Collect answers.* Responses to survey are collected.
5. *Report creation.* Report against key brand metrics, showing the response rates.

In implementing B2B trackers marketers should consider several aspects. For example, with more questions the cost of the tracker will increase as it requires more time to conduct the survey; it is therefore important to carefully select questions and their number. Larger numbers of respondents will also increase costs: companies should consider what is needed or representative in terms of an audience sample. Can the questions stand the test of time and run for multiple quarters or even years? If so, this will allow companies to compare the brand tracker movements over time.

2. Positioning

This is an important step for a vendor: it is defined as creating a brand offer or presence and supports a brand in positioning value in the mind of the target customer. Brand position goals should encompass the following core elements:

- *Differentiation.* Ensure uniqueness in brand compared to alternative vendors; this can form part of the value proposition.
- *Customer focused.* Includes what customers the brand is targeting.
- *Sustainable.* Positioning statements need to be sustainable over a long period. This allows customers to relate to the brand and understand it over time.

- *Geo-agnostic.* If a brand operates across different territories, positioning activities should not be focused on one area.
- *Support organizations' business goals.* Brand positioning should serve to achieve business goals.

Taking the above into consideration, companies can use the brand positioning map shown in Figure 15.3 to understand current brand positioning against market criteria: competition and customers, customer needs, uniqueness, customer benefit and reason to buy.

Figure 15.3 B2B brand positioning map

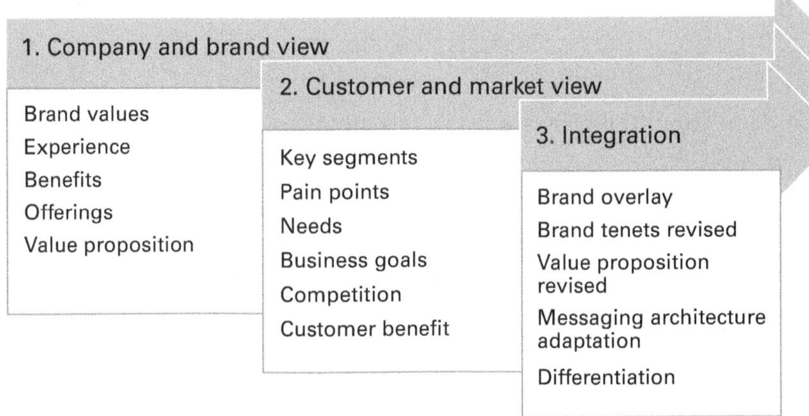

3. *Plan for building and activation*

The brand plan typically includes key goals and focus uncovered in step 1, the brand audit, positioning statements and values from step 2, and focused target audiences that may not necessarily be the current target market of the business. Also included are key messages the business wishes to deliver, the media and communication outline defining which media will be used, and across which communication vehicles.

The brand plan should include key partners that will deliver it. In B2B it's important to consider which partners will deliver the message and which marketing or business partners will be involved; partners in this sense include alliance partners, channel partners, influencer partners, associations or other organizations that the business is connected to. The partner selection and plan may indicate some gaps.

4. Activation

This stage should serve to prepare for external brand activation as well as accompany it. Similar to employee advocacy programmes for social marketing, for brand building organizations should follow the framework:

Target audience and groupings
The first step in creating a brand employee advocacy programme is defining the target audience: maybe specialists within an industry sector or a general customer-reach programme for all businesses.

Internal audience grouping
Based on the target audience, the next stage is to build internal groups; they could be general sales, specialist sales, or different business functions.

Prepare
Internal employees are trained in using social. Social-ready content is prepared, and mechanisms for internally sharing it are created. Content should be ready to share and send on.

Structured review against core KPIs
KPIs could be reach, influence, activity level or other measures.

The difference to the social employee advocacy programme is that social can be used to promote brand building, whereas the inverse is not true.

TIP Key considerations in internally activating B2B brand building

- *Ease of understanding*: sometimes the brand build initiative is not understood, so making the messaging clear is key to the success of brand advocacy initiatives.
- *Ease of access, easy to share*: organizations should make brand assets and content easy to access as well as easy to share.
- *Who messages and articulates*: internal activation success sometimes rests on internal leadership support and advocacy. Rather than leaving this to marketing, involve the CEO with public relations articles if possible; this way brand initiatives are seen as 'business' initiatives that all in the business own.

- *Who owns this*: there is a common misunderstanding that the brand is owned by marketing; in fact all employees and departments play a part in brand building. Marketing tends to own external activation and PR, and supports internal departments by providing brand messages.
- *Not only digital*: brand building, particularly in B2B, is about supporting face-to-face and non-digital engagement at events, in phone calls and meetings, and in printed material left for channel partners.
- *Communicate value of brand*: in getting campaign buy-in it's important that organizations highlight the benefit and value of the brand for their customers.

Implementing brand activities or campaigns can occur in different ways. They can be a pure media and advertising exercise or can be an all-encompassing approach including media, messaging, influencers, internal champions, digital and offline media.

Content creation and activation form part of the brand plans as well as social media activities that help amplify the brand assets and messages (see Chapters 13 and 14). In activating the brand externally B2B marketers should consider the following:

- During this phase consistency in message is key, to give strength and impact to the brand messages.
- Social in B2B has evolved rapidly in the past 10 years both in capability and usage in business. Organizations are increasingly using social platforms to rapidly reach audiences and extend the reach of brand assets.
- In B2B, business partners are important in delivering brand messages; they allow them to reach the right audience and lend messages credibility.
- Depending on history or the extent of brand activations organizations should allow time for brand activities to take effect.
- Touch rate is the rate at which marketing content (or in this case branded content) is touched and seen by customers in whatever form. The rate differs between customer type, industry sector and solution type. With digital applications as well as digital marketing, touch rate can be tracked both on- and offline.

5. *Review and assess the brand*

How do you know how customers see your brand? Is it positioned the way you want it to be? One part of the brand process is to review and assess the brand. Organizations can measure brand loyalty, awareness, health and/or perception, where brand loyalty refers to likelihood to repurchase, recommend or refer; brand awareness is awareness of the brand overall (do potential customers know about your company and what it offers); brand health highlights how values, mission, culture are communicated; and brand perception relates to how the brand is perceived against value criteria or positioning (do customers see the company as a solutions provider rather than a seller of products).

It is important to look at different types of metrics to get a full picture of the brand. Some of the key metrics are behaviour metrics, which provide insight into brand performance relating to customer expectations, competitor actions; traffic metrics which include search engine rankings, website traffic; and customer engagement metrics which include time spent viewing content, time on a website. Qualitative assessment may be of a specific area such as brand campaign or initiative reviews; see also the above section on brand tracker creation.

ACTIVITIES

Identify potential areas where customers interact with your brand directly or indirectly. How many of them can be controlled or influenced by marketing; how many of them fall outside of the marketing scope?

What metrics do you use today to measure your brand activity and which part of the brand do they measure? Brand awareness, brand health, brand consistency or brand perception?

Review current marketing materials for a given period. Are the look and feel, message and creative all consistent with one another?

Reference

Brandz (2015) Brandz top 100 most valuable global brands 2015, available at: https://www.millwardbrown.com/BrandZ/2015/Global/2015_BrandZ_Top100_Report.pdf (accessed 10 February 2017)

PART FOUR
Collaborating with channel partners

The modern B2B channel landscape 16

This chapter will give you an understanding of:

- the main B2B channel partner types
- channel partners and alignment with B2B segments
- B2B channel partner marketing
- channel marketing trends
- how to select channel partners
- differences between distribution and channel reseller marketing

B2B channel partner marketing

As most medium and large enterprises sell indirectly via channel partners and a large portion of small businesses need to engage a reseller or distributor, B2B marketers need to be equipped with skills and knowledge as to how to market indirectly. This chapter looks at B2B channel marketing and the main dynamics and trends within B2B channels. For clarity, channel partner marketing, sometimes known as 'channel marketing', is the practice of marketing indirectly via any channel partner or channel intermediary.

What is a channel partner?

Channel partners are a person or organization providing services or selling products on behalf of a vendor. They come in different forms; eg value-added resellers (VARs), distributors, online resellers and, in technology sectors, there are also managed service providers (MSPs), consultants and systems integrators (SIs).

What is B2B channel partner marketing?

B2B channel partner marketing involves channel resellers or channel partner systems oriented towards businesses; one could think of the approach as B2B2B where the channel systems serve business and where the channel partners are focused on selling to businesses. B2C channel marketing is the marketing via channels to consumers, where the channel can be retailers or online resellers.

Benefits of channel partners and channel partner marketing

B2B organizations engage channel partners to achieve different goals; some of the benefits organizations derive from using channel partners are:

- *Gaining access to a customer segment.* Where channel partners already have a legacy in doing business in a market and have built credibility with a customer segment, a vendor engaging them can immediately avail itself of this established relationship.
- *Geographical reach.* Channel partners can help businesses by providing geographical reach; this can be by working with a channel partner in the region or one that has multiple sites across different areas.
- *Entering new market sectors.* Channel partners that have established credibility within an industry sector can provide value to vendors by leveraging their contacts and relationships.
- *Solution selling and marketing.* The channel partner acts as a value-added reseller and resells combined solutions for segments, or can help assemble one vendor's products with another to create solutions.

For B2B marketers, channel partner marketing brings various benefits. Partners can raise the awareness of a product or product offering to a broader customer base or to a niche market. They can help to position a vendor's products through channel partners or influence the perception of a product where channel partners are seen to support the product and service; the vendor's products become more credible in the eyes of the customer.

Channel partner types

'Channel resellers' is the umbrella term for those channel partners reselling a vendor's products. The main channel partner types include VARs, large corporate resellers, micro-channel resellers, distributors, and online resellers:

- *Micro-resellers* are typically smaller in size; their range of products may be narrower. Often they support a set of customers based on geographic location.
- *Value-added resellers (VARs)* offer additional services to help businesses such as logistics, warehousing, stocking, credit checks, integration, advisory services and extended offerings. With changing dynamics and more services offered via the cloud, VARs need to justify their value-add even more. Some business customers still prefer to maintain their relationship with the VAR due to legacy relationships and trust in the capability of the VAR. Often a reseller will not need to be involved beyond the point of sale, enabling them to focus on generating sales and maximizing profits; the VAR takes over these efforts. Typically, a VAR helps provide exposure to new customers and the customer acquisition benefits tend to be mutual or on the side of the vendor.
- *Online and mail order resellers* are like retail stores, except they usually do not have traditional brick-and-mortar locations and so no additional expenditure on maintaining a physical location. With lower operating costs they can offer lower prices. Some resellers focus primarily on conducting business via mail order or online. Examples of online resellers selling to businesses in the UK are DABs, Insight and Ebuyer.
- *Distributors* primarily manage relationships with resellers; by managing multiple relationships with resellers they reduce time and manpower expenditure by the vendor. They typically manage relationships with smaller resellers. Where a good relationship exists, distributors may allow vendors access to their partner database for the purpose of acquiring new channel partners.

IT channel partners

More typical to the IT sector are the following channel partner types, shown in Figure 16.1:

- *Independent software vendors (ISVs)* provide software-added services and make and sell software products that run on one or more computer hardware or operating platforms; they often focus on specific vertical or niche markets.

- *System integrators* are resellers that integrate technologies into systems; they tend to offer large-scale technology solutions including consulting. These types of resellers are fewer in number, larger in size, can be very demanding, and so tend to determine elements of the relationship dynamics between the vendor and the channel partner. Within the relationship, the vendor is the party bringing customers to the table. These channels tend not to be suitable for new businesses, start-ups or companies early in their stages of growth due to the resource-intensive nature of these companies.
- *Managed service providers (MSPs)* are service providers for business and IT departments offering several offsite or cloud-based services.

Figure 16.1 Main channel routes to market: IT

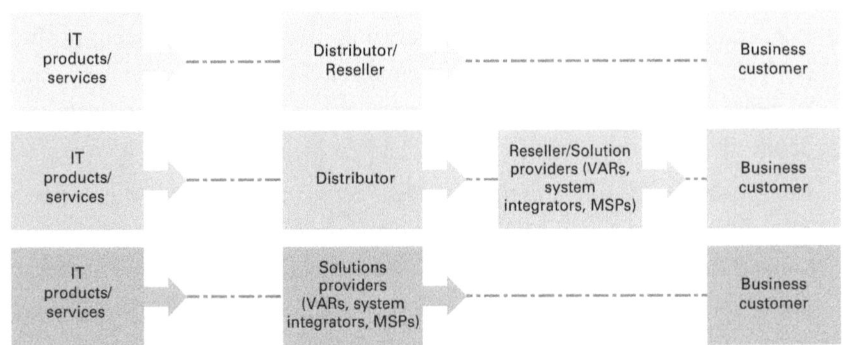

The changing channel landscape

There are a number of trends directly or indirectly impacting channel partners. Increasingly, channel resellers are building their own software and service revenue streams; vendors need to be aware of this when discussing portfolios as part of the channel partnership. For some channel partners there is an increased focus on vertical integration of their offerings, allowing them to target potential new clients and increase account penetration with a richer set of products and services, leading to increased revenue and a more successful business. In the past decade there has been a move for channel resellers to increase their presence internationally; some have achieved this through acquiring channel resellers in a different region. Messaging for channel partners will become increasingly challenging, with technologies in some areas eroding the competitive advantage of product USPs. Channel partners will come under pressure to change their messaging to businesses to meet these challenges and needs so as to sustain or gain business.

Key trends in channel partner marketing

Channel partner marketers need to consider some of the recent trends impacting marketing to and with channel partners. The shift to 'solutions marketing' thinking, as mentioned in Chapter 8, is becoming more marked for B2B marketers. One of the main areas to support this is working with channel partners to develop and market combined solutions. Combining solutions via a channel partner may be a result of some vendors being unable to offer the full suite of products or services that make up the solution, or because the channel reseller offers elements of the solution itself. This means B2B channel partner marketers need to create marketing content that can be assembled in a modular fashion so that channel resellers can incorporate assets, text, or visuals into their own creative.

B2B marketers need to think of different ways to collaborate with channel partners on marketing activities. Collaborative marketing can mean including channel partners in marketing activities and messaging such as events, webinars, online, website mentions and so on. An effective way to market is to sub-segment and create marketing that speaks to a niche or vertical market. This requires marketers to provide content tailored specifically to niche markets in collaboration with the relevant channel partners.

Channel selection

The main B2B routes to market can be subdivided into three main types: directly to business customers, indirectly via channel resellers or VARs, and indirectly via distribution and channel resellers to business customers. Below are some thoughts on when to choose each route.

When to engage channel resellers directly

- The vendor has the resources (sales, marketing, operations, etc) to engage the reseller or resellers directly.
- Channel reseller numbers are small enough to be managed by in-house resources such as sales and marketing.
- A direct engagement with the resellers is regarded as more beneficial, for example to build collaborative business, marketing or sales activities.

When to engage a distributor directly

This engagement may be in addition to or instead of engaging channel resellers directly:

- The distributor network is strong and offers the ability to access new markets.
- The distributor provides reach to smaller businesses, and the number of companies to engage or reach is so large the vendor resources are unable to manage the business directly.
- The distributor warehouse is leveraged to house, store and deliver goods; this can be the case where a business has products in another location and needs to have more timely delivering of goods to supply immediate demand.
- The distributor provides manpower and/or competence to manage reseller relationships, for example for smaller or relatively new businesses unable to commit.

When to engage a VAR directly

- The VAR offers specialized services to support a vendor.
- It offers specialized knowledge that the vendor doesn't have in-house.
- It can provide access to specialized customer target sets.
- It has its own customer relationships within a specific business segment or sector that some vendors would like to benefit from.

Marketing to or with distributors can differ greatly from marketing via channel resellers; the requirements for marketing differ depending on the channel type. Some of the main differences are shown in Table 16.1. Although distributors can offer services like marketing, branding, etc, they are normally focused on buying and selling on 'products' rather than complete offerings or solutions. Resellers tend to avoid committing to sales or revenue targets and therefore aged inventory is a risk.

Table 16.1 Distributors vs resellers

	Distributor	Reseller
Buying and selling	Buys products and sells to resellers	Buys products and sells to end customers
Managing sales to channel	Can manage sales to various resellers	NA

(continued)

Table 16.1 *(Continued)*

	Distributor	Reseller
Location	Sells to physical resellers in their territory Can have a wider area coverage than resellers	Can cover a wide area, depending on organizational size
Inventory	Large warehousing facilities to support big logistical operations Normally buys inventory	Never takes inventory of products
Margin and pricing	Often requires higher margins than a reseller	Can work with lower margins than a distributor
Merchandising promotions	Promotions widely used	Manages promotions and all other forms of marketing
Pipeline-based lead generation	Rarely follows up leads	Often will take leads, manage leads and follow up

Channel partner and marketing alignment

The marketing methods of resellers and distributors can greatly vary depending on the size or type of channel partner. Some smaller channel partners that don't have strong brand recognition may tend towards search or SEO activities while larger corporate resellers can leverage brand strength and brand budgets to generate or sustain awareness of their value proposition.

Table 16.2 shows major partners aligned to business and B2B marketing type. Before engaging channel partners, marketing departments need to consider marketing capability, competence and structure. The types of marketing are:

- *B2B transactional marketing* includes merchandising, promotional marketing, e-mail marketing, pricing and product management; typically there are strong ties between marketing and operations so as to manage product inventory.
- *B2B relationship marketing* typically includes provision of content and assets, lead generation, event marketing, webinar support, other inbound lead generation activities and account-based marketing.

- *B2B marketing enablement* is required by all channel vendors, though enablement materials will be different; see the next chapter for more information on this. Channel partner enablement is enabling channel partners to carry out any marketing on behalf of the vendor.
- *Vertical marketing* is very much like relationship marketing but oriented towards vertical market customers.

Table 16.2 Marketing and channel partners

Channel partner	Typical business vendor	B2B marketing type	Example
Distributor	All sizes depending on goals	Transactional marketing	Search, SEO, website demand generation, advertising, promotional e-mails
Large corporate reseller	Large corporates	Relationship marketing	Inbound and outbound lead generation including webinars, events, content syndication, account-based marketing
Micro reseller	Small and medium business	Transactional marketing	Search, display, SEO, e-mail
VAR	All sizes	Vertical and/ or relationship marketing	Inbound and outbound lead generation including webinars, events, content syndication, account-based marketing specific to vertical customers

(*continued*)

Table 16.2 *(Continued)*

Channel partner	Typical business vendor	B2B marketing type	Example
SI	Medium and large business	Relationship marketing	Inbound and outbound lead generation including webinars, events, content syndication, account-based marketing
Online resellers	All	Transactional marketing	Search, SEO, website demand generation, advertising, promotional e-mails

ACTIVITIES

Identify the different channel routes to customers for your industry.

Are you marketing to different channel partners today and is your marketing differentiated enough? Review marketing needs of the different channel partners by conducting brief surveys with key stakeholders within the different channel partners.

Marketing to channel partners and enabling them 17

This chapter will give you an understanding of:

- what channel partner marketing is
- channel partner marketing tactics and vehicles
- key challenges and solutions
- channel partner strategies
- digital applications

Marketing to channel partners

Vendors and suppliers can use a variety of approaches to engage and market to channel partners. The marketing mix and adoption of marketing vehicles will depend on channel partners and their ability to receive and use such marketing. The type of channel partner stakeholders can vary greatly, which means vendor marketing needs to be able to adapt accordingly.

Channel partner marketing is defined as anything intended for the channel partner and/or those working within it. Marketing to channel partners has similarities as well as differences to standard B2B marketing directly to customers. It is similar in that the channel partner in one respect should be considered a customer and recipient of marketing activities and messages. The differences lie in the scope or context of the working relationship where the channel partner plays the role of partner as well as customer. Marketing needs to take these two approaches into account when working with channel partners.

Marketing to channel partners covers five main elements (see Figure 17.1):

1 Clear and effective communication.

2 Provision of content and information in the right format across the communication channels.

3 Tools to use the information and content, which could be marketing campaign creation tools or content creation tools such as templates.

4 Training to support channel partners in effectively using the tools.

5 Marketing communities: some vendors have built forums or communities for marketers.

Figure 17.1 Marketing to channel partners (key areas)

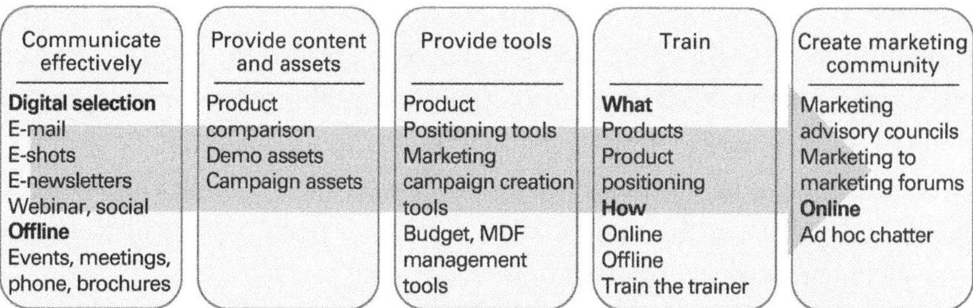

Channel partners often have a selection of providers and suppliers to work with. Almost like marketing to customers, vendors need to capture channel partners' attention and win them over through channel marketing. Channel marketing helps to arm the channel partner with all the right materials and information so that they can in turn market a vendor's products and services.

Digital communication

The main marketing vehicles used to communicate to the channel partners are increasingly digital and online. Table 17.1 is a summary of the main communication vehicles split into digital and offline.

Table 17.1 Digital and offline marketing vehicles

Digital	Offline
E-mail	F2F
E-shots	Events
E-newsletters	Magazines, brochures
Own website	Onsite demonstrations
Webinars	Onsite trainings
Webcasts	Direct mail
Portals	
Social	

E-mail marketing

In terms of e-mail marketing to channel partners, the principles are like e-mailing directly to customers. The main difference is that the receivers of e-mails at channel partners tend to be sales rather than purchasing departments.

E-mail and information management needs to be structured in terms of contact people, number of e-mails in a given period and overall number of e-mails from the brand if it has different parts of the organization communicating with the same channel partner. For example, as some channel resellers will have multiple stakeholders or sales people to engage, getting the names of the right contact people may be necessary to ensure messages reach their intended audiences or to drive accountability for forwarding and re-distributing e-mails within a channel reseller.

As with e-mailing customers it's important to make e-mails easy to read, short, and with a call-to-action. With a channel partner the call-to-action may include follow-up accountabilities.

E-shots can be a form of e-mail and can be used to announce new products and services or promote offers or events. E-shots are designed to deliver clear and concise messages and are a good way of supporting other marketing activities or reaching a broad audience at low cost.

E-newsletters are used to include a selection of pieces of news and serve to provide the intended stakeholders with several pieces of information. It's important to ensure the e-newsletter is easy to read rather than coming across like a lengthy e-mail. Images are important to engage the audience.

The choice between e-shots, e-mails and e-newsletters depends on different audiences, bandwidth and resource of the vendors.

Website-vendor website

The website is important for housing information as well as providing access for channel partners to separate portals. The main website is also there for the public and business to view and serves as a great opportunity for vendors to redirect customers to channel resellers' own websites or other useful points of information supporting the business through channel partners.

Vendor portals for channel partners

Portals in this case are specific for the channel partner rather than a general website intended for anyone. Portals should be there as the hub for channel communication and all communication should drive traffic to them. They need to be easy to access and contain information in a structured manner.

Portals provide information only for the eyes of channel partners; some vendors segment content according to channel partner type. Types of information to provide are product information sheets, marketing campaign information, assets to support channel partners' marketing in creating their own campaigns, training, information on rebates and bids budget, the ability to purchase directly for more sophisticated websites, and customer opportunity assessment tools.

Webinars

Webinars can be a great way to update more complex or important information for channel partners. Some channel resellers or partners may have their operations some distance from the vendor, making physical contact impractical; webinars allow vendors to educate, update or even provide virtual events with interactive possibilities.

Offline communication

Offline ways to market or communicate to channel partners include events, face-to-face communication, phone calls and printed brochures or leaflets.

Events

Events can be used for updates on the latest product offerings, and allow a vendor to promote itself. Depending on the size of channel partner and relationships, events can be exclusive to one channel partner or to multiple channel partners. The benefits of events marketing include having a forum where it is possible to engage and answer questions and be more interactive. Events are also a great way to build better relationships between vendors and channel partners. For more complex solutions or technical products events are an ideal way to get across their value and benefits to a lot of people.

Printed brochures and catalogues

Brands can use educational or promotional brochures to communicate product offerings to channel partners. Printed materials are also a great way for vendors to be top of mind if they're placed on site at channel partner locations and can also be used by sales people as reference material.

Selecting channel marketing communications

The purpose behind marketing to channel partners will determine the communication vehicle used; see Table 17.2. Is it to educate, to inform, to provide any necessary tools, or to help sell?

Having established the purpose, the next main criterion is the channel partner audience. For example, if the audience is sales specialists it is likely that more specialized information is required with more time to explain complex products. E-mails may not be the best means to communicate in this case; webinars, printed brochures and follow-up e-newsletters may be more appropriate.

Beyond the purpose and audience, the budget available would determine the communication possibilities. Where the vendor has a limited budget or resource, 'pure' digital approaches are probably more appropriate: e-mails, e-shots, website promotions and possibly webinars. For dispersed offices, digital marketing using webinars or webcasts is best suited for educating and engaging channel marketing audiences.

Table 17.2 Audience and communication/content type

Channel partner audience	Communication channel	Content type
All	E-mail, E-newsletter	E-newsletter
Sales	Webinar, social media	SlideShare, digital brochure, digital product, demonstration
Sales specialist	Webinar, online portals, website	Technical, solutions-oriented, SlideShare, digital brochure, digital product demonstration
Marketing	E-mail, online portal access	All types
Senior management	E-newsletter, event, meeting	Informative meeting or event

Channel partner enablement

Channel partner enablement has become an increasing trend in recent years due to the changing role of channel partners and greater demands on channel partners to sell solutions and value rather than simply products. This shift requires help from vendors in providing different sets of content, tools and training. Channel partner enablement is essentially enabling the channel partner to perform effectively on behalf of the vendor; it is normally mentioned in conjunction with marketing where the channel partner is equipped by the vendor to carry out marketing activities.

Scope

The vendors' role can be challenging as multiple stakeholders need to be enabled to perform marketing. Examples of stakeholders may include marketers, sales and some senior executives. The four main areas of channel partner marketing enablement are:

1. *Tools*: access to tools and instructions on how to use them, eg tools to help identify and size customer opportunities.
2. *Content*: access to content, information, resendable or forwarding-friendly communication.
3. *Training*: product/portfolio benefits; information to help argue and position against the competition.
4. *Insights*: tips on customers and behavioural information that supports the sales process.

TIP How to enable channel partners

Content

Content for channel partner enablement is usually not intended for end customers. Types of content can be comparison sheets, product positioning data, demonstration software, and printed brochures highlighting the portfolio. Other assets can be product details or case material for channel partners to assemble into a campaign themselves.

Tools

These can include product positioning tools, marketing campaign creation tools, customer assessment tools that marketing roll out, planning tools, and access to online applications that allow both channel partner and vendor marketing to track marketing performance. Tools can also extend to budget, market development fund (MDF) and planning.

Training

Training can be very structured leading to certification. It can be carried out on- or offline, though with more sophisticated products or solutions it is better to conduct face-to-face training. Training can include how to use content and marketing tools, how to position products, and demonstration training of products.

Insights

Finally, insights used in partner enablement can be based on market or customer trends that the vendor has researched. These insights show how to better market or engage customers through marketing and convert them to sales.

Measuring enablement

In enabling channel partner marketing, the channel partner needs to ensure the right sales stakeholders are using the right tools and information and attending any enablement event or activity. Channel partner enablement can be measured in different ways:

Attendance
Where the enablement activity is onsite training, a webinar or a face-to-face event, attendance numbers can be used as a measure.

Channel partner portal sign-in and frequency
Where enablement is content and information in an online partner portal, the total number of people using the tool can be one indicator. The frequency of use in each period per stakeholder as well as time on site can be used to understand how well the online portal is used. It can also provide insights back to the vendor on whether the content or tool is effective. Where frequency of usage is low this may point to the online tool not being easy to access or use and adaption or further training is required.

Completion of training
Where training covers more than one activity or module, completion of the training set can be another way to assess sales readiness.

New approaches: social for marketing to channel partners

Social is increasingly used in B2B and it's not different for channel partner marketing. The main platforms used are Twitter, LinkedIn, Facebook and YouTube.

For marketing to channel partners social can be used in different ways. The main objectives are to keep the channel partner network updated with the latest information, in educating channel partners about new products and services, in reinforcing communities between vendor and channel partners, and to improve the relationships between the channel partner and vendor.

For vendors and channel partners to use social effectively it's important that both understand how to use it. The rules of engagement should be established in advance and social media sub-groups may need to be set up, based on subject matter expertise or a focused theme, to improve sharing.

EXAMPLES

Users of social forums with channel partners include Dell and Channel. Dell Channel Europe communicates the latest pieces of news to its channel partners as well as to the channel marketing community. HP Partner Ready is on Twitter to provide the latest news.

Marketing to channel partners: challenges and solutions

Challenges

Whether the vendor is a small or large business, marketing to channel partners can be challenging for the following reasons:

- *Too many stakeholders – no accountability*: for vendors one challenge can be reaching multiple stakeholders and gaining mindshare. Where the vendor's marketing department communicates with many stakeholders within one channel partner this may lead to stakeholders' apathy in receiving or reading such e-mails.
- *Resource*: smaller businesses typically have fewer resources and therefore may not have the capacity to communicate to multiple channel partners.
- *Channel partner organizational structure*: the structure may mean that there are too few marketing resources to deal with the many channel vendors that need to be engaged.
- *Over-communicating*: vendors can use too many market communication forms; this may lead to channel go-to people becoming numbed by the communication and not reading or digesting it.
- *Over-reliance on one vehicle*: e-mails or e-shots can become over-used leading to channel partner recipients not leveraging or responding to them.
- *Stakeholder relevance*: where a message is intended for a marketer but written for sales this may mean it is not followed up or acted upon.

Solutions

Marketers need to see how they optimize communication with the channel partner sales and marketing. Some of the ways to address the challenges include clearly defining marketing go-to people and agreeing with the channel partner on who they are and who is accountable for any follow-up. Vendors could check with channel partners to capture any changes in personnel to ensure contact data is up to date.

Sending e-mails to fewer stakeholders can reduce the perception of over-communicating as well as supporting accountability measures for those go-to people at the channel partners. In addition, by selecting communication and better frequency management the number of e-mails can be controlled. E-mail should be easy to re-use or send on, allowing for sharing of information by channel partner stakeholders.

Having the vendor's CMO involved can sometimes help increase the level of reading and responding to e-mails by the partner. Where the channel partner is a premium or very strategic one, and the budget allows, some companies opt for having someone on site to support messaging, sales, marketing and training.

TIP Solving communication challenges through one point of access

One way around trying to message multiple channel stakeholders while reducing traffic sent to their inboxes is using a single hub of information. Many larger companies are doing this but it can also work for smaller ones. Making the portal easily accessible and having a home page with all the information allows users to easily access it without any website navigation problems. Rather than worry about sending e-mails to multiple stakeholders, businesses can create forums on Twitter or LinkedIn to message updates or additions about the information hub.

Digital applications

One solution to managing communication to channel partners can be using channel partner content syndication. One of the top challenges in campaign management is coordinating communications across multiple channel partners.

Channel content syndication replicates and customizes digital content across external web properties, ie to channel partner websites. Different types of content syndication can include social media, e-mail or asset syndication. The benefit is that channel partners, including all forms of resellers, have up-to-date information and content.

Creating one marketing team: vendor and channel partner

One additional approach is to facilitate marketers in engaging and sharing information between vendors and channel partners. Such marketing forums or communities can be created either in a structured way by setting up forums or sub-groups on social media, by having an online space to share information not housed on a social platform, or by an offline engagement through meetings. The benefits of such forums are that the vendor can facilitate sharing of ideas and information to stimulate a team atmosphere and to motivate individuals through being part of a community.

ACTIVITIES

Review with a channel partner the e-mails sent to their stakeholders in a given period for quantity, relevance and whether they're used. Identify improvements in communicating.

Review channel partner marketing needs and whether current vendor marketing efforts support those needs. For any challenges in channel partner marketing, review current digital applications.

Marketing through channel partners 18

This chapter will give you an understanding of:

- goals of marketing through channel partners
- types of marketing through channel partners
- criteria for selecting activities
- main solutions for marketing through channel partners
- lead generation
- gaining mindshare

Definition

Marketing through or with channel partners aims to engage existing or potential business customers; the marketing flows can happen in three ways (see Figure 18.1):

1. *Directly by the vendor*, ie vendor directly markets to the customer and directs the customers to the channel partner, for example through links on their website, or in redirecting to channel partner sales (B).
2. *Indirectly*, ie via the channel partner to the business customer where the channel partner markets on behalf of the vendor (A).
3. *With the channel partner* to the business customer, where the vendor collaborates with the channel partner to engage the customer as a joint marketing activity (C).

Figure 18.1 Marketing through channel partners

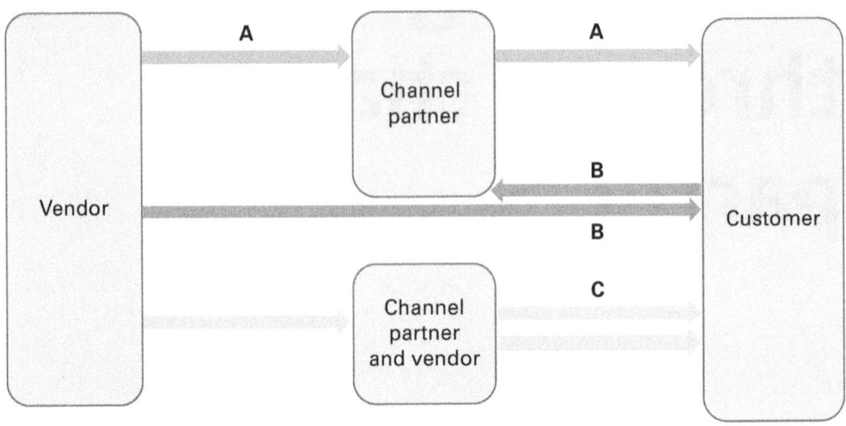

Why market to a customer if channel partner marketing is used?

If a vendor has engaged a channel partner to reach and engage customers, why would the vendor use its own resources to market to customers? The reason could be the initial agreement between the vendor/supplier and channel partner regarding the purpose of the relationship, for example where the partnership was set up for logistical reasons or for customer reach. Other reasons could be that the vendor believes the core messages that the channel partner needs to deliver are not strong enough and that more direct messages to the target market are required, or that the channel partner's use of marketing communication doesn't cover certain aspects, for example if the channel partner relies on newsletter and e-shots and it's felt that other forms of marketing should be used.

Types of marketing through channel partners

The type of marketing will depend on customer audience, channel partner type as well as the marketing flow. Where the marketing is directly to the customer, the marketing can come in three forms, shown in Table 18.1. The first is awareness-based marketing such as PR, e-shots, social and co-branding; advertising aims to create awareness for the vendor's brand and to direct customers or traffic to its channel partners. The second is lead generation, where vendor marketing invests in generating leads through content syndication, outbound telesales or other to capture leads and pass

Table 18.1 Digital and offline marketing vehicles

Awareness tactics	Lead generation tactics	Demand generation tactics
PR E-shots Newsletters Social Branding Advertising	E-shots Social lead generation Content syndication	Promotions Incentives Seed units

these on to channel partners. The third, demand generation, is about directing traffic to the channel partner's website or sales through incentives, promotions or direct response marketing.

Where a channel partner markets on behalf of the vendor the channel partner typically does less marketing than the vendor would. It would do little awareness-based marketing as this is the vendor's role. Lead generation may occur where the partner has such an approach in place and where the vendor has a market development fund (MDF) or other budget. Channel partner and vendor marketing collaboration examples can span all the types of marketing shown in Table 18.1; examples are collaborative PR, advertorials, testimonials, and lead generation marketing such as content syndication where the channel partner participates.

Types according to channel partner type

Types of B2B marketing can vary depending on the type of channel partner; a supplier/distributor relationship may be based more on demand generation, lead generation and associated marketing vehicles.

With large value-added resellers the forms of marketing may be more relationship based; eg launch events or webinars with channel partners, combined online advertising, combined lead generation/content syndication, and outbound marketing forms. This type of marketing is looking at generating larger sales volumes from fewer sales transactions.

Selecting and sharing marketing

So how are marketing activities selected between a channel and vendor? What are the selection criteria? How are the responsibilities divided up?

One approach is to split responsibilities based on budget level, ie the amount of budget made available from the vendor that the channel partner can commit to a set of marketing activities on its behalf. The channel's type of business dictates the effectiveness and forms of marketing, eg a distributor will focus marketing on promotions or driving demand rather than driving leads which have a longer conversion time. Cost will dictate that phone calls may be too expensive and time-consuming to engage a huge volume of small business customers; on the flip side the cost to serve a large corporation may justify more elaborate means of marketing. Finally, the stage of relationship between channel partner and vendor will have a bearing on what role they play in supporting the business for each other: in the early phase there may be less marketing investment as the channel partner is testing and piloting the new vendor's products as well as marketing them.

TIP Process for selecting and sharing activities

This should follow the below TMAR framework:

1. *Targets defined and co-defined*: vendor channel marketing and channel partners should agree on business targets for marketing activities; this can be unit volumes, website traffic or phone traffic to generate leads, opportunities and pipeline, and time for delivery of marketing activities.
2. *Marketing mix defined*: which customer solutions to include in portfolio, which themes or campaigns to focus on, which communication vehicles, which content, etc.
3. *Activity split and focus defined*: may already be set out based on existing marketing but may need redefining for incremental or larger-scale marketing activity. Key questions concern who invests and implements which activities; eg does the vendor set up the event or the channel partner or both?
4. *Roll-out and review*: marketing enablement assets are provided for activities the channel partner owns. Activities are implemented and then reviewed together in terms of achievement of KPIs.

Marketing through channel partners: lead generation

Enterprise or relationship marketing (see Chapter 1) will tend to rely a lot on lead generation activities. Lead generation without a channel partner in the mix can be challenging in terms of tracking leads, ensuring follow-up, conversion, etc, and using multiple channel partners and their sales can bring additional challenges.

The first challenge is about accountability and ownership: who owns the lead and which stages of the lead generation process they are accountable for. Aside from ownership, how is the follow-up handled between vendor and channel partner or between a third party that generated the initial lead? How does the vendor ensure the leads are kept as warm as possible and don't go cold? With different entities covering different stages of the lead journey, how are leads tracked? Finally, how are leads assigned if there are multiple channel partners working with the vendor?

Managing lead generation with channel partners

Here are some ways to manage lead generation with channel partners.

Stakeholder management

Clearly define steps in lead generation from marketing-ready lead through sales-ready lead to follow-up, opportunity identification, pipeline detection and closure. For each step define who owns the step: who is responsible for generating the lead, for nurturing the lead, for qualifying it.

Assigning leads to channel partners

1. Create assignment rules for types of leads so they are automatically directed; rules may be based on customer location, specialist based, type of lead, product based.
2. Agree on business rules for leads: volume of leads, type of lead, timing, etc, for channel partner.
3. Review the effect of business rules: check timing and volume of leads meet expectations.
4. Maintain consistency of rules through lead assignment.
5. Optimize lead allocation by removing or adding channel partners where needed, eg where the channel partner doesn't execute or decides not to take further part.

Ensuring lead execution

1. Agree on follow-up timelines. Some companies apply zero tolerance beyond 24 hours for lead follow-up; ie no lead is left unfollowed beyond 24 hours. Others will agree to longer follow-up times.

2 Follow-up and execution. Define champions or accountable people within the channel partner who enforce a discipline on lead follow-up and conversion.
3 Quality of execution. Ensure that diligence is applied to qualifying the lead if this is the channel partner's responsibility, and applied to nurturing the lead and following up; this will all mean better ROI for the channel partner and vendor.
4 Visible and transparent executive support. Get senior level support from the channel partner and make it visible; this in turn will mean sales are more bought-in to the process.

How to track leads via channel partners

Tracking of leads can be cumbersome but there are ways to support this across different channel partners, outlined in Table 18.2.

Table 18.2 Leads tracking via channel partners

Lead tracking option	Detail
Channel partner CRM	The channel partner uses its own CRM system to track and manage leads and provides the vendor with access to the CRM system for purposes of reviewing performance
Vendor CRM	The channel partner uses the vendor's cloud-based CRM systems and inputs and tracks leads performance
Marketing automation platform (MAP)	The vendor uses a marketing automation platform that can integrate multiple CRM systems, providing access across channel partners
Manual	Reporting of leads is manually captured by channel partners and vendors and tracked through reporting devices such as Excel

Lead handover

Lead handover refers to leads being passed from one party to the next; usually handover aims to improve conversion. An example is where a telemarketing agency passes on leads to channel partners; another is where leads are handed over by the vendor sales. Handover typically occurs with help from a marketing automation or CRM system.

Gaining channel partner mindshare

One of the challenges of marketing through channel partners is gaining mindshare. A partner needs to maximize its share of the marketing space that channel partners devote to their vendors, whether directly or indirectly competing or just taking up marketing communications space.

Even if agreements and structures are in place a business and its marketing department need to go a few steps further in motivating channel partners and gaining mindshare. The competition are doing the same so doing the bare minimum means the vendor will lose out. Having maximum mindshare and support from channel partners will in turn mean greater probability of achieving targets. There are a number of ways vendors can increase mindshare and support from channel partners:

- *Sales incentives* help to motivate sales to promote products; some vendors believe that having a contract and agreement in place is enough but if other vendors use channel incentives (and they often do) then attention will be drawn away from a vendor's products.
- *Great content*: if the vendor can provide some compelling content, sales people are more likely to read and forward the content to colleagues and partners.
- *Lead generation*: providing high quality leads to channel partners.
- *MDF*: a larger contribution of marketing development fund from one vendor over the other will mean the channel partner invests more in communicating and marketing and therefore customers and sales have greater exposure.
- *Onsite sales activities*: onsite activity from vendors can be focus days or burst focus sessions.
- *Partner programmes*: partners participate in a vendor programme and receive rewards for achieving specified levels of sales.
- *Awards schemes*: partners can take part in a competition with other channel partners and thus will have increased focus and push for a vendor's products; this can be effective in driving sales where the vendor has multiple channel partners.

According to a 2014 Canalys press release about its survey of 130 partners, on average partners rated the importance of programmes to their vendor relationships as 8 on a 10-point scale (Canalys, 2014). The results of the survey also highlighted the benefits of a partner programme in order of importance: rebates, deal registration, lead generation, account management and front-end discounts. Twenty-six per cent of partners said back-end rebates were the most important benefit, while 66 per cent of partners selected lead generation as a top-five benefit.

EXAMPLE The Oracle channel marketing handbook

Oracle has developed a handbook specifically for channel partners covering a broad range of marketing services. Channel partners' marketing stakeholders can use different marketing services such as 'campaign as a service', events, marketing automation support, sales velocity days and other resources. Through this comprehensive handbook channel partner marketers are able to access everything in one document.

Partner programmes

Partner programmes are a great way to gain mindshare and lock in channel partners. Most IT vendors operating via channels use them. They are typically segmented across three or four types of partner as follows:

Level 1. The highest level, where the channel partners are regarded as premium accounts that generate high revenues; they are typically account managed, sometimes exclusively by one account manager. These channel partners will usually have their own in-house marketing resources.

Level 2. Mid-level channel partners may or may not share an account manager; they may be managed via phone instead of a face-to-face arrangement. These channel partners may be reselling some products but not a wide or full portfolio.

Level 3. These may not be account managed but still have access to some vendor marketing resources.

Level 4. May be an additional tier of newly acquired channel partners.

Marketing support to these channel partner levels would differ:

1 Assignment of leads from vendor would typically only go to level 1 channel partners.
2 MDF would be provided to those channel partners actively marketing the vendor's products and investing so level 3 and 4 probably would not receive it.
3 Type of content may differ: premium partners would receive richer content.
4 Marketing campaigns may only be provided to level 1 and 2 accounts, where channel partners are specifically included.

Social media and channel partner marketing

The channel partner's role in using social media as part of collaborative marketing may take different forms:

- *Co-marketing awareness activities*: channel partner and vendor support awareness of a new initiative through social presence. Social media can help in supporting thought leadership activities.
- *Lead generation*: the vendor generates leads via a social platform that are then handed over to the channel partner.
- *Vehicle-assisted*: a channel partner integrates use of social to promote an event and engage customers at or after the event.
- *Co-marketing employee-assisted*: employees of the channel partner use content and information and promote this through their own channels.
- *Combined social forums*: the channel partner and vendor agree to host a combined social group or discussion via a social platform.

Through-partner marketing applications

Through-partner marketing applications are starting to grow, which is great for large businesses wanting to streamline efforts and drive efficiencies as well as for smaller or medium-sized businesses that need help with activities that are too resource intensive. Through-partner marketing applications include social syndication through channel partners, channel content syndication, and marketing automation platforms designed to work across multiple partners and automate efforts to track and nurture leads.

EXAMPLE EIMS Channel Energizer programme

EIMS is a global sales and marketing agency founded in 1996 by IT industry professionals who still run the business; it has consistently grown 25 per cent year on year. One of its specialisms is to build and enable a channel, feeding the partners with high quality leads to optimize channel value. One of the services in EIMS's channel portfolio is called 'Channel Energizer'.

The purpose of the EIMS Channel Energizer is to increase channel productivity and deliver high growth in a way that is cost-effective; through insights and data a tailored programme is created to target specific opportunities. In many cases, the programme enables vendors to reach more effectively into their channel, boosting the revenues of partners that have not enjoyed the benefit of high-touch account management and transforming the relationships with some partners that had previously not delivered significant revenue.

The EIMS method starts with analysis and planning, a study to identify the characteristics displayed by successful partners to really understand how to achieve agreed business goals. To assess potential, EIMS understands the partner's business mix including other solutions and relationships that may be competitive or complimentary to that of the vendor.

Driving growth through increasing the productivity of existing partners is often the shortest route to success, but the initial analysis and assessment may conclude that to deliver aggressive revenue goals, especially in new markets, new partners may need to be recruited. The identified characteristics of successful partners informs targeting of potential new partners. The resulting shortlist of new and existing partners is engaged, typically by tele conference, to assess their levels of motivation for long-term success and alignment to the vendor's goals. The EIMS approach is to then engage with the principal decision maker to evaluate the business ambition to grow with the vendor and understand alignment of strategic direction. As a result, the shortlist is further refined to create a final 'hot' target group of high propensity partners ready to enrol in the Channel Energizer programme.

EIMS has a unique technology platform to ensure optimal process and consistent partner experience; it includes a storefront allowing vendors to offer services to their channel from their own marketing teams and a multitude of preselected and approved external providers. Partners can self-select, guided by a concierge service where required, to ensure an optimal use of marketing development funds. This enables delivery of approved partner plays across a large partner base in a hassle free and a highly scalable way. Partner engagement and activity outcome is completely transparent and reportable and the partners can stay one step ahead of their competition.

This proven approach has helped many organizations drive accelerated growth in the channel while increasing the number of transacting partners. Vendor and partner engagement is enriched as each delivers more value to the other, supporting sustainable and predictable long-term success. For some customers this programme has allowed them to break into new international markets; for other customers it delivered incremental pipeline of around $19 million.

Reference

Canalys (2014) Partner programs prove key to channel relationships, Canalys press release, 2014/060, 8 September, available at: https://www.canalys.com/static/press_release/2014/canalys-press-release-20140908-partner-programs-prove-key-channel-relationships.pdf (accessed 10 February 2017)

Channel marketing strategy and control 19

This chapter will give you an understanding of:

- types of channel partner marketing strategies
- channel partner lifecycle marketing
- channel partner acquisition marketing
- channel planning and control
- channel partner marketing – measuring and planning

Channel marketing strategy

Channel partner marketing strategy, called 'channel marketing strategy' for the purposes of this chapter, refers to the different approaches to marketing via channel partners or intermediaries to customers. Channel selection, management and strategy are important business decisions typically encountered by organizations' business leaders and senior executives in sales, marketing, operations and financial departments.

In most organizations the marketing departments have insights into the market and market structure including the channel structure; the role of marketing regarding the channel partner marketing strategy is to support and guide business leaders in assessing optimal routes to customers, and in defining the optimal mix of channel types. Marketing can also help the business by providing an overview of the full channel partner universe, highlighting all the channel partners and intermediaries in a given region.

Based on the goals and agreed route(s) to market, the marketing department needs a structure that best supports the business and channel type. For example, some channel resellers require a high-touch sales process and marketing departments will focus resources on supporting distribution channel partners.

B2B channel marketing goals and objectives

In defining channel marketing strategies and channel strategies it's important to first determine the goals; below are some of the main ones influencing channel partner marketing strategy selection (see also Table 19.1):

Market coverage. Where a company's goal is to cover a particular geographic area, channel selection would be based on location.

Customer reach. Where a company is unable to reach customers with its own resources, a channel partner that helps in reaching customers would be selected.

Provision of end-to-end solutions. Channel resellers can complement the brand's offering to provide a complete solution.

Accelerate growth. Collaborating with a channel partner could help the firm grow its business faster.

Vertical growth. A vertically aligned channel partner strategy may be well suited to achieve such growth.

Credibility. Where a new brand or a brand in a new market needs to gain credibility, channel partners with established relationships in that given market can help organizations promote their products to the new audience.

Table 19.1 Goal and channel partners

Goal	Channel marketing strategy type
New market coverage	Channel partner acquisition
New customer reach	Channel partner acquisition
Provide end-to-end solutions	Channel partner integration marketing Partner enablement
Accelerate growth	1. Expansion marketing via channel partner through demand generation and lead generation 2. Channel partner acquisition
Brand and market presence building	Collaborative channel marketing Channel partner enablement
Improve execution	Channel marketing operations

Here are some of the main types of channel marketing strategies aligned to the above goals:

Expansion channel partner marketing. Where a vendor works with an existing channel partner to increase business with existing customers by marketing and selling more of the portfolio.

Channel partner acquisition. This involves adding new channel partners to support business goals such as market coverage, customer reach, or vertical market access.

Customer acquisition via channel partners. This is about working with channel partners to focus on specific customers to acquire.

Integration marketing. This hinges on collaborative marketing and integrating marketing messages across the channel partner and vendor's portfolio to highlight end-to-end solutions.

Brand and market presence building. Marketing together with the channel partner intensifies brand building efforts; this may be a combined new solution both parties will benefit from, or where investment in co-branding is expected to reap returns through additional business.

Alliance channel marketing. Vendor and channel partner work together to promote the vendor's product portfolio, for example where a technology vendor can contribute a lot of value to the relationship through thought leadership, budget or other aspects.

Marketing operations. This can be where digital applications are adopted or processes are optimized to support smoother marketing operations and execution. An example can be a new marketing automation system.

EXAMPLE Alliance channel marketing

In 2000 Datapipe and Equinix established a customer and vendor relationship which by 2016 developed into a real channel alliance partnership. Their two business complemented each other well: Datapipe acted as a managed hosting and cloud services provider needing to expand its business across multiple geographies while Equinix, an industry leading data centre company with global footprint, was also growing at a rapid rate. In 2016 they used a joint marketing approach with Datapipe and Equinix co-sponsoring marketing and industry events, as well as mutually investing in co-marketing material, success stories and lead generation.

Channel partner lifecycle marketing

One approach to channel marketing is to manage and support the lifecycle of the partner through business- and marketing-aligned activities. Figure 19.1 shows the main stages of the partner lifecycle with the appropriately aligned marketing activities:

- *Acquisition.* A channel partner is identified, targeted, engaged and then added to the list of a vendor's channel resellers.
- *Onboarding.* A channel intermediary becomes a channel partner for the vendor. The role of vendor marketing is to support the new channel partner in becoming familiar with the vendor's products through introductory training, value propositions per product/solution and product positioning information.
- *Enabling.* Following onboarding the partner is enabled through provision of tools, systems, training, roadmaps, demo units and access to people who support channel partner marketing personnel.
- *Demand creation.* Once enabled the partner should be able to create demand on behalf of the vendor through marketing resources, advertising, marketing development funds and, in some cases, additional marketing budget.
- *Grow and expand.* During this phase the partner and vendor tend to work more closely together; the channel partner acts as an extension to the vendor business and vendor marketing can make available budget and additional resources to support lead generation and marketing development activities.
- *Retain and integrate.* The final stage is in retaining the channel partner and integrating some existing vendor practices; marketing activities could include marketing forums and co-partner communications.

Figure 19.1 Channel partner lifecycle

Onboarding	Partner enablement	Demand generation	Partner business development	Integration
• Product positioning • Value proposition sharing • Sales profile registration • Self-service portal for provision of product assets	• Provision of business, marketing tools • Provision of assets, market communication information • Training • Market development fund (MDF)	• Advertising through and with channel partners • Insights on • Alignment on target customer • Marketing resources to create demand • MDF	• Leads handover • Leads management • Customer lifecycle strategies	• Partner promotion • Partner communication integration • Partner case studies • Improved incentives • Co-marketing • Advisory boards

Acquisition channel partner marketing

Channel partner acquisition marketing can occur via two routes: directly from the vendor targeting, selecting, engaging and onboarding the channel partner, or the vendor and distributor work together to acquire a reseller. To understand marketing's role in channel partner acquisition we need to first understand the typical steps in the overall process. Here is a simple six-step process (see also Figure 19.2):

1. Define target market, target customers and number of customers per territory or region. This information will help you later in selecting the most appropriate channel partner type and to understand if a region is under- or over-served.
2. Define offerings to meet target market needs. The needs of a certain target market may not be met by the existing portfolio and additional products or services are needed for a more complete offering. In this case the selection criterion is whether the channel partner can assemble its own products with those of the vendor to meet the customer's needs. Sometimes a customer's needs may be so specific that a specialized channel partner needs to be acquired.
3. Review current GTM approach, coverage for market. During this step, you look at existing channel partner coverage and structure to understand whether the established business and channel partners are sufficient. It may be that you don't need to acquire more channel partners but rather to work better with existing partners.
4. Identify gaps between intended target market and current GTM model to create a channel partner checklist by, for example, geography, channel partner type and customer segment.
5. Evaluate and select channel partner based on a set of criteria that could include location, specialism, appetite to engage new vendor or ease of engagement.
6. Initiate acquisition process directly or indirectly. The vendor may decide to use a distributor to start acquiring channel partners. In some cases, the distributor may already have the intended channel partner in its established list of partners; in other cases, the distributor's reputation may allow it to engage and acquire the channel partner more easily.

Figure 19.2 Channel partner acquisition process

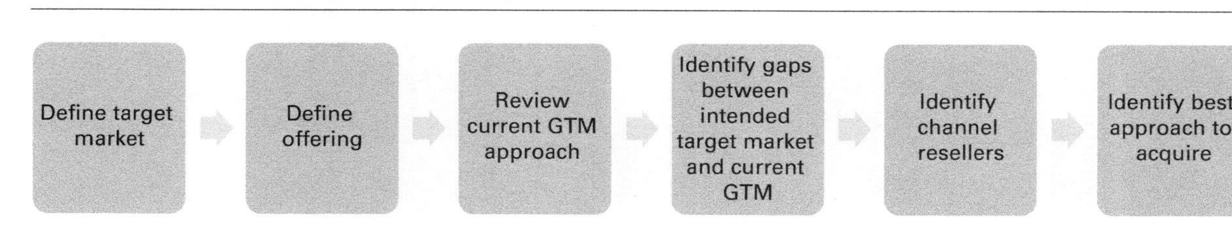

Channel partner for customer acquisition

Acquiring customers via channel partners can follow a similar process to the one outlined in Chapter 5, although there are several differences that make it worthwhile for vendors to consider the channel partner marketing route. Figure 19.3 shows the different routes to acquiring customers via channel partners.

Figure 19.3 Customer acquisition through channel

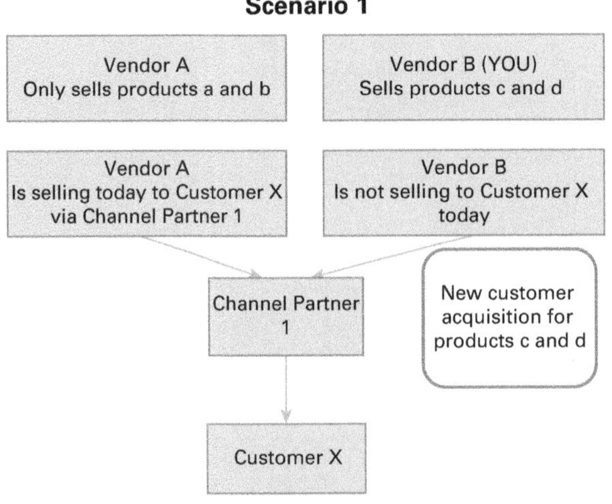

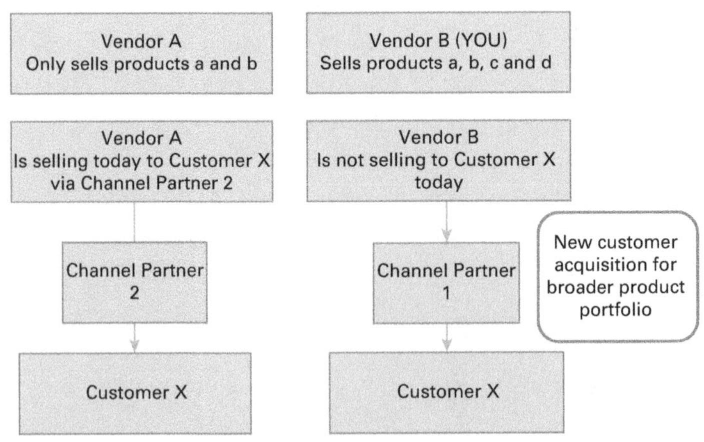

In scenario 1 the prospect is already a customer of the channel partner but only buys certain products from another vendor. This could be because the vendor only offers those products, or the customer prefers to buy only those products from the other vendor. The prospect is still interesting for both you and the channel partner to sell additional products and services not currently bought by the other vendor, if there is no conflict. The channel partner has an existing relationship or reputation that carries credibility with the target customers, and the buying process can occur faster than a vendor trying to acquire the customer directly. As the channel partner already has an established business relationship with the customers, social media can be a powerful tool to engage the customers through forums, YouTube and social networks to share information about additional products and services. The channel partner could follow up by inviting the customer to webinars or face-to-face events to explain and engage further.

In scenario 2 the prospect is a customer purchasing products/services through another channel partner (channel partner 2); in this respect the intended customer is a prospect for both you and channel partner 1. As there is no potential conflict of interest, ie the vendor is not a supplier of channel partner 1, the full products/services can be offered through channel partner 1 to the new customer. The benefits of this approach can be that channel partner 1 has a strong reputation in the market, sector or region, which improves the possibility of acquiring new customers rather than the vendor going directly. Vendor B and channel partner 1 can agree on how to create an initial market plan for educating and informing customers through a mix of advertising, social media, online and other media.

Integration marketing

Integration marketing can occur in different ways, for example in integrating products to form solutions, integrating messages, or integrating channel partners further into scope of vendor's business. Marketing's role in these can be either to ensure messaging is delivered clearly to channel partners in the form of assets as well as integrated into the channel partner marketing tactics. In terms of channel reseller integrating within the business, marketing can support through extending lead generation activities to include the channel partner and also pass on opportunities to the partner. Other aspects are onsite enablement and sales activities supported by marketing to train and motivate the channel partner sales.

Channel contact strategy

Effectiveness in marketing to, with and through channel partners can be heavily influenced by having a contact strategy. A contact strategy for channel partners is about creating different sub-segments of channel partners for the different business and marketing activities and aligning the marketing contact or engagement approaches accordingly. These channel sub-segments can be split into retention marketing, expansion/growth marketing, marketing based on acquiring channel partners and marketing based on promoting and further integrating the channel partner. Other aspects include improving efficiencies in selecting and engaging channel partners, in messaging to and through them, and in intensifying relationships through tailored channel marketing.

Possible activities supporting a promotion strategy could be to leverage social media channels to promote types of content, to include the channel partner in new online forums, or in reworking a communication strategy to add or remove contact people to distribution lists (see Figure 19.4).

EXAMPLE SAP – Our Business Runs Better

In 2011 SAP launched a marketing programme to improve its presence and visibility within the SME segment, called 'Our Business Runs Better' (OBRB). It approached this by demonstrating to an experienced network of channel partners who knew and understood the business challenges pertaining to SMEs, as well as demonstrating solutions to those pain points. Through co-marketing planning and provision of assets such as images, e-mail, landing pages and online banners it could develop new engagement opportunities with its network of channel partners across the EMEA territories. This resulted in over 1,000 leads and sales revenue of over €15 million and €30 million for 2011 and 2012 respectively.

Channel planning and control

The vendor and the channel partner need to establish a discipline for sharing plans, activities, resources and marketing schedules. There should also be budget and marketing development funds provision. The difference between

Figure 19.4 Channel partner contact strategy

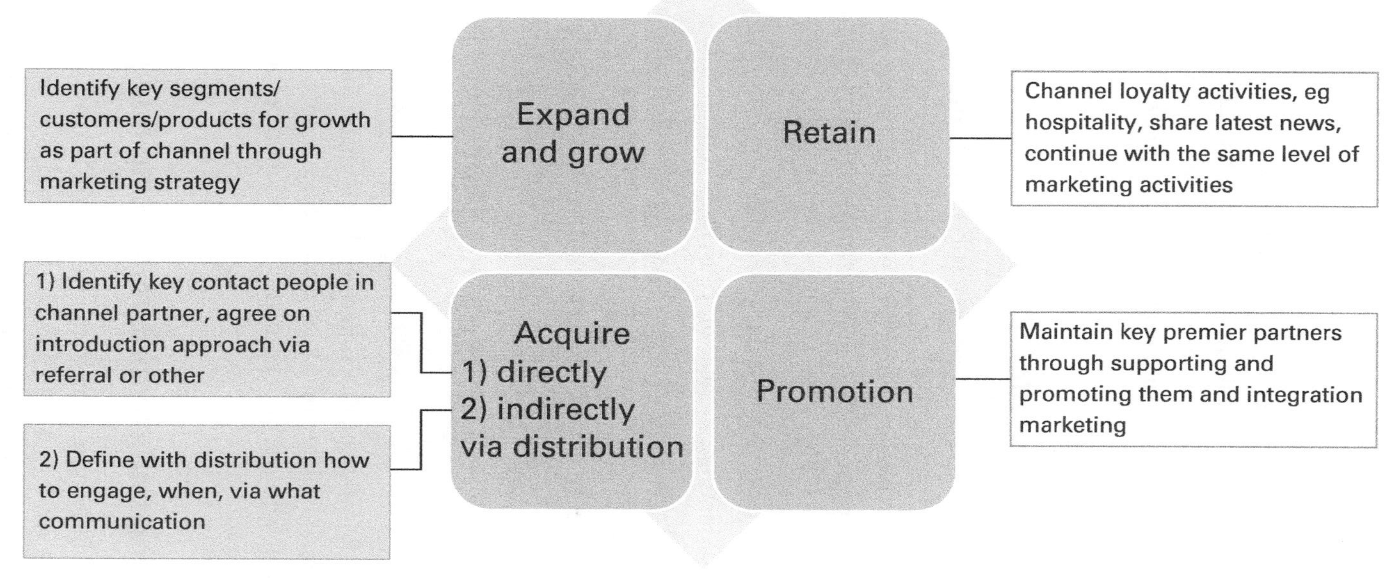

standard and channel marketing planning is that the channel partner will normally need to plan with multiple vendors, so it's important the vendor maximizes its use of the partner's resources and market communications vehicles.

In planning with partners, channel marketers have additional alignment challenges: they not only need to align internally with their stakeholders on priorities and budget spend but also with channel partner stakeholders. There need to be measurement systems in place to track activities, review them and optimize.

Measuring and planning

The channel marketing measurements or KPIs are dependent on the type of marketing activity. In dealing with channel partners and potentially offsite remote measurement systems it's important to keep KPIs simple and relevant. Here are some ways to measure different types of channel marketing activities:

- overall marketing: pipeline, revenue;
- lead generation: number of leads, leads converted to opportunities;
- demand generation: channel partner website traffic and conversion to leads;
- marketing enablement: quotes on the day, attendee level.

Channel marketing budgets

Managing channel marketing budgets includes several aspects such as budget allocation methods, partner development fund management, budget tracking and budget review. If these elements are badly managed there can be budget wastage, poor execution and friction between the channel partner and vendor.

Building and creating marketing budgets

Marketing budgets can be sourced from different areas. The main ones are from the vendor's own resources, from suppliers that have a vested interest in the vendor's sales, and from investment companies.

TIP How do you source additional budget?

Vendors may have hidden or undiscovered opportunities to find new sources of marketing budget. For example, Intel and Microsoft, which are both component and software vendors, provide additional marketing budget to IT companies through partner development programmes. Outside of the IT industry sources of additional funds can be suppliers, additional channel affiliates, or services companies that could benefit from collaboration. If you're struggling to find budget, you may discover hidden opportunities with your suppliers or partners who have a vested interest in your business's growth.

Channel budgeting process

Here is a typical process for marketing budgeting for channel partners:

1. The channel marketing budget is defined for a given time.
2. Marketing budget is allocated according to business goals.
3. Marketing budget is then allocated for specific channel partner marketing activities.
4. Channel marketing budget allocation can be based on these criteria: premium channel partner status, legacy marketing activities where vendor channel marketing ring-fences budget in advance; potential growth in given period; seasonal business peaks.
5. Budgets are reviewed based on ROI.
6. Budget are optimized based on return, through changing the marketing mix or allocating more budget to those channel partners performing the strongest.

Justifying your channel marketing budget

Where channel partners only require budget to train and enable sales, there are more challenges for marketing to justify its budget: proving the link between final sale and marketing budget may be difficult as the activity is further removed from the sale. In such situations it's important that the value and measurement of training to sales is better articulated, for example the metric for enabling or training sales could be attendance at a training event, or how often sales accessed an online marketing training tool.

PART FIVE
Optimizing marketing execution

Sales and marketing alignment

20

This chapter will give you an understanding of:

- importance of alignment
- benefits of alignment
- obstacles to sales and marketing alignment
- how to identify misalignment
- steps to establishing alignment
- integration best practice

The importance of alignment

Sales cultures within organizations can in themselves be obstacles for marketing to engage or to build relationships. Some organizations have very complex sales structures, further complicating the marketing task in achieving alignment with sales.

Alignment is important as it highlights the value each party delivers for a goal. In an aligned situation, sales will get what they need to support the business and marketing achieve their goals through delivering to the right customers. The right messages are sent via the right sales structure and physical and communication channels. In B2B marketing the success of marketing often hinges on sales alignment, for example in lead handover, or in participating in an activity. Alignment is less of an issue in B2C marketing.

Changing sales role

The modern buyer is digitally driven, socially connected, mobile and empowered, with virtually unlimited access to information and people. The role of sales has shifted according to changes in organizational buying behaviour and this means that sales need different support from marketing in the form of sales enablement, information and content tailored to buyer stages. On the flip-side marketing needs sales to adapt their role to understand and embrace how to educate customers indirectly and how to embrace new communications channels such as social media.

Benefits of sales and marketing alignment

Research suggests that business productivity is greater and targets more easily achieved when sales and marketing are aligned and engaged. Recent reports have produced the following insights:

- Companies with dynamic, adaptable sales and marketing processes achieved an average of 32 per cent annual revenue growth while less aligned companies reported an average 7 per cent decline in revenue (Aberdeen Group Study, 2011).
- Organizations with tightly aligned sales and marketing operations achieved 24 per cent faster growth and 27 per cent faster profit growth over a three-year period (Setty, 2013).
- Organizations with tightly-aligned sales and marketing had 36 per cent higher customer retention rates and achieved 38 per cent higher sales win rates (MarketingProfs, 2015).

Overall the main benefits can be summarized as:

- *Increased sales conversion rates.* Sales convert more leads as marketing deliver leads that sales need and desire.
- *Faster sales conversion.* With tighter engagement between sales and marketing, leads are handed over to sales more efficiently and sales follow up in a more timely fashion.
- *Transparency on pipeline improves.* As marketing understands how pipeline builds and sales understands what is being delivered from marketing, there is a greater visibility to the pipeline progression.

- *Less leakage of leads.* Where leads are not followed up this can be rectified earlier and they can be reassigned to a different sales group or further nurtured by marketing.
- *Optimization of marketing budgets.* As there is greater input and direction from sales, marketing budgets are optimized for lead quality and conversion.

Organizational obstacles to alignment

There are often several reasons why sales and marketing departments aren't well aligned:

Culture
Sales cultures and marketing cultures tend to be very different. They use different terminology, value different things, work differently and have different behaviours. Some business cultures can be heavily sales focused, have silo departments, or emphasize the importance of sales over marketing. Cultures within sales and marketing can be based on legacy leaders, teams, etc. These cultural aspects can maintain divisions between sales and marketing departments.

Targets
Sales teams are set targets and incentivized differently to marketers. Sales targets can be based on pure pipeline and revenue whereas marketing looks at website traffic and quality of content. Where targets are set separately for marketing teams and sales teams this will lead to a lack of alignment.

Lack of focus
Organizations may simply not focus on marketing efforts, which can frustrate marketing teams who feel undervalued. This lack of focus can be due to seasonal business peaks where sales need to focus on opportunities to close rather than working on leads earlier on in the customer buying cycle.

Multiple sales teams and priorities
Where the organization has different sales teams, this can lead to different or conflicting requests; eg an internal sales team may prioritize leads whereas an external sales team may prioritize enablement tools and materials to support more customer-facing activities.

Leadership

Leadership is required to correct misalignment, not only from marketing but also from the overall business lead. Leaders can help unite different departments around common goals.

Establishing sales and marketing alignment

For alignment to be established organizations should follow this four-step process:

1. *Recognize misalignment.* During this step the organization agrees and recognizes that there is a misalignment between sales and marketing, and acknowledges the need to address it. Stakeholders are identified, ideally representatives from sales and marketing, to take the lead in the process for alignment.
2. *Identify and audit.* Obstacles and contributors to sales and marketing alignment are identified. This is carried out by reviewing structures, cultures, KPIs, etc. This will typically be a qualitative exercise involving outsiders as well as key stakeholders from sales and marketing. Marketing or sales investigate and listen to feedback to understand the factors behind the misalignment. The results can then be plotted in a radar diagram like the one shown in Figure 20.1 to help plot the impact of each misalignment factor.
3. *Agree on fixes, priorities and timelines.* The organization and sales and marketing leaders agree on where to start and the priorities to address to solve the misalignment. As part of this process marketing may relook

Figure 20.1 Alignment radar

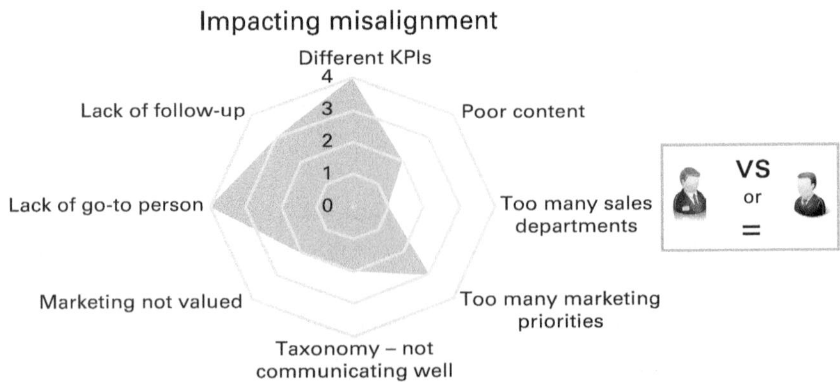

at business goals, challenges and opportunities as well as more granular behaviour and process aspects. These can be through service level agreements (SLAs) between sales and marketing teams holding both parties accountable for what they deliver; they can be extremely formal or less formal allowing for change where needed.

4 *Implement and review.* The steps and activities to resolve the misalignment are implemented and progress checked through regular reviews.

Alignment areas

Define marketing's role in the organization

The role of marketing in midsize or larger organizations may stretch across multiple types of marketing. Where marketing resources are limited this means the department may not be able to deliver across all the marketing areas that the business and sales are asking for. The main types of marketing are:

- *Sales enablement.* The focus is on preparing and supporting sales through training and provision of marketing materials and assets that support the sales cycle.
- *Marketing communications and content.* Marketing's focus is on managing the marketing communication channels and the content across those channels.
- *Brand building and awareness.* The focus is on building the brand and investing in activities that promote the company and its value proposition.
- *Demand and lead generation.* Marketing focuses on generating demand and leads and investing in activities to maximize traffic for the business.

To improve marketing effectiveness there needs to be an agreement within the executive team on the core priorities of marketing; this doesn't preclude marketing from doing something in all areas but helps provide a core focus for marketing to deliver on.

Target customer

It's important to define the type of customer to target: whether existing or new and, if new, which sector. Other aspects to stipulate are size of business, geographical focus, key target stakeholders and department. Having customers defined in a granular way will help when planning the right marketing mix and materials and in supporting sales in the right and relevant way.

Activity alignment

Once customers have been defined the next stage is for sales and marketing to agree on activities. Some activities will involve both or either sales and marketing; for example what type of content will be used to engage customers directly from marketing or via external parties, and which content is sales expected to use to engage customers themselves? What messages will be used to generate leads and who is responsible for nurturing and to what stage in the lead development process?

Communication structure/governance

A communication policy should cover the following:

- *Forms of communication to use.* It should be agreed how sales want to receive updates from marketing and how marketing expect to be updated by sales. Is this through e-mail, phone conferences or face-to-face meetings?
- *Frequency.* Both parties need to agree on how frequently the updates will occur.
- *Timing.* Timing of reporting is key to allow for sales to address or correct their performance if it is not on plan.

Shared KPIs

Both parties should agree on KPIs relevant to each other and this should form a two-way SLA. For example marketing's commitment to sales could be on number and quality of leads in a given period, pipeline or revenue. Sales commitment to marketing could be time to follow up leads. Marketing and sales goals should both be aligned to the same business targets to ensure both departments speak the same KPI language.

Alignment initiative: sales integration

One effective way for marketing and sales to align is to work together on common projects and for marketing to include or integrate sales within marketing initiatives. This could be at an activity level such as 1) co-

Figure 20.2 Key areas of alignment

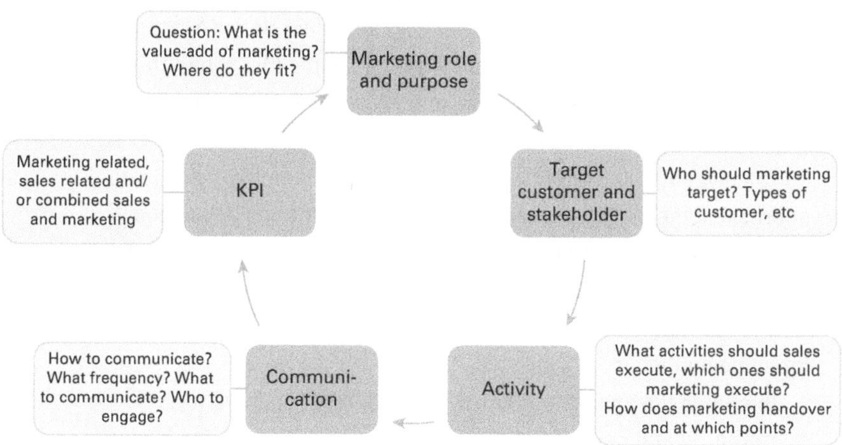

creating content, 2) co-designing campaign focus, 3) in execution process or design, or 4) in promoting and marketing. In co-creating content or designing marketing campaigns, the focus can be in providing customer input indirectly from sales to support more relevant messaging, as well as using customer language.

Regarding 4) promotion and marketing, some organizations include sales people who are also specialists and/or influencers in the market. Other ways are to integrate sales in advocacy programmes for social marketing and brand building or, at a marketing vehicle level, by inviting sales to participate in an event, either as speakers or to support customer networking.

Having sales acting as part of the marketing team helps marketing through additional support as well as gaining further buy-in to other departments. Sales gains more understanding and appreciation of marketing efforts and can influence marketing to optimize their activities to improve impact and ROI.

EXAMPLE Atos

In February 2014, Catherine Howard stepped into the role as Atos UK Marketing Director. It was quickly apparent that there was a lack of alignment between marketing and business stakeholders and a lack of buy-in to marketing and its deliverables.

The process for turning around the marketing department kicked off with reviewing attitudes towards marketing and past delivery of marketing;

this was captured through various research and surveys: one-to-one meetings with key business stakeholders including United Kingdom and Ireland board members, client facing team meetings, one-to-one meetings with the marketing team, and an online survey across the wider organization.

The investigation surfaced underlying issues which needed to be addressed; the marketing department led by Catherine developed a business-led marketing strategy focused on three core areas all supporting the objective of externally delivering business value. The plan was presented to the board and marketing secured an increased budget for implementing it.

To enable the implementation, the new marketing team was restructured and people and activities were better aligned to business and objectives. The new structure provided each key business stakeholder with marketing contacts; and behind the scenes stakeholder plans were developed to ensure each marketing team member was engaged with his or her respective business stakeholders in a regular and appropriate fashion. This new approach improved accountability and response rates within marketing and helped establish a new team collaborative culture between marketing and the rest of the business. Accompanying the team reinvigoration were daily guidance from the marketing leader, improved communications in the form of weekly calls, regular one-to-one meetings, pay realignment, as well as celebration of marketing successes both at an individual and team level.

Following the implementation, the marketing culture was transformed and team morale issues addressed and improved; additionally, new process and business leading programmes were introduced to support the business. The marketing team could deliver a much-improved return on investment and demonstrate a contribution to Atos's business growth; the marketing team also received consistent praise from key business stakeholders.

ACTIVITIES

Based on the different types of marketing – sales enablement, brand building and lead generation – what percentage of time do you or your marketing department spend on each type of marketing? Is the allocation of time aligned to business requirements?

Conduct a mini survey with sales to understand their perception of marketing. Where do they see value-add and where do they see a need for improvement?

References and further reading

Aberdeen Study Group (2011) Introduction to integrated marketing, Aberdeen Study Group, available at: http://docplayer.net/7387863-Sales-and-marketing-alignment.html (accessed 10 February 2017)

Alterra Group (2011) Account-based marketing: an approach on the rise in professional services – initial survey results, available at: http://alterra-aroup.com/wp-content/uploads/2011/04/AlterraGroupABMTopLevelResults.pdf (accessed 10 February 2017)

MarketingProfs (2015) In search of sales and marketing alignment, The Marketing Advisory Network, available at: http://marketingadvisorynetwork.com/2016/03/31/4173/ (accessed 10 February 2017)

Setty, R (2013) How to get started on marketing and sales alignment, Sirius Decisions, available at: https://www.salesforce.com/blog/2013/10/align-marketing-sales.html (accessed 10 February 2017)

Account-based marketing

21

This chapter will give you an understanding of:

- the importance of account-based marketing (ABM)
- types of ABM programmes
- ABM process
- preparing for ABM
- challenges and pitfalls in ABM
- ABM technologies
- measuring ABM

Definition

Account-based marketing (ABM), originally known as 'key account marketing', is a very strategic approach to marketing to companies. The philosophy of ABM is to treat an organization as a set of key individuals and decision makers to market to in a targeted fashion, rather than marketing to organizations as a whole hoping the right message will reach the right stakeholders. ABM is about targeting specific accounts with a company's value proposition and relies on the vendor aligning its processes, resources and departments with those specific accounts.

ABM has been around since the mid-1990s and was mainly used by larger companies. It was originally part of a high-touch process by organizations' sales teams to focus on accounts rather than generic marketing. HP and Xerox were notable early adopters. Today, thanks to new marketing technologies, ABM can be used by almost any size of business; smaller companies with very limited business and technical resources can target, assign and manage hundreds, even thousands, of prospective accounts and customers. They can keep track of their customers, segment lists and target accounts with personalized content for e-mail nurture campaigns or for generating new interest.

Benefits of ABM

ABM is popular because it drives higher response rates; it is also a great way to bring together sales and marketing and for creating alignment between them. Fundamentally ABM focuses on the customer and means a business customizes its approach and messages to customers as it improves relevancy of sales.

Some insights from recent research have shown that 97 per cent achieved higher or much higher ROI with ABM than with other initiatives (Alterra Group, 2011), and 84 per cent found ABM provided significant benefits to retaining and expanding existing client relationships (Newman, 2016).

ABM types

There are five distinct types of ABM:

1. *Strategic ABM.* A form of ABM that is usually reserved for strategic accounts and/or large accounts, and typically includes one-to-one marketing. It can involve a dedicated marketer and a dedicated customer account manager. Performance metrics and ROI are typically focused over the long term due to the nature of the account and type of marketing activity associated with it, for example hospitality, collaboration events and co-marketing are typically associated with large, strategic accounts.
2. *Segment-based ABM.* This is aligned to customer segments or customer sub-segments, eg targeting mid-market accounts per criteria of purchasing power, behaviour, or potential.
3. *Vertical account ABM.* Oriented towards public or private verticals; for example, where a company is looking to target senior clinicians for healthcare-related products.
4. *Campaign-based ABM.* Sometimes called programmatic ABM. Campaigns including messaging and themes oriented towards a set of accounts established through research; may involve some in-depth research that uncovers new insights into customer concerns. Campaign-based ABM usually has a set of content and vehicles behind it.
5. *Product/solution ABM.* Related to buying decisions; can sometimes be referred to as lifecycle as it's based on the purchase lifecycle of customers. Examples could be previous product purchase and associated purchase behaviours centred on a group of accounts.

The ABM process

The following framework, also shown in Figure 21.1, will allow organizations to effectively set up and implement ABM. Figure 21.2 shows the process and key applications.

1 *Strategic alignment.* During this step it's important that business objectives are understood in terms of growth areas and customer focus, as well as marketing's role in supporting such goals.
2 *Account analysis and identification.* The next stage is to build customer intelligence and profiles and use insights from sales about existing customers related to target customer segments. Target accounts are identified, working closely with sales based on a combination of sales input and third-party databases; predictive analytics may be used to determine the specific accounts most likely to buy.
3 *Define scope.* Scope of activities and size of accounts are defined and account lists are created. The scope will depend on sales force size, sales objectives, and ability of marketing to support sales with, for example, content.
4 *Asset and activity preparation.* Marketing builds assets and information for account-based initiatives; examples are qualification scripts, white papers, associated infographics and associated promotions.

Figure 21.1 ABM process

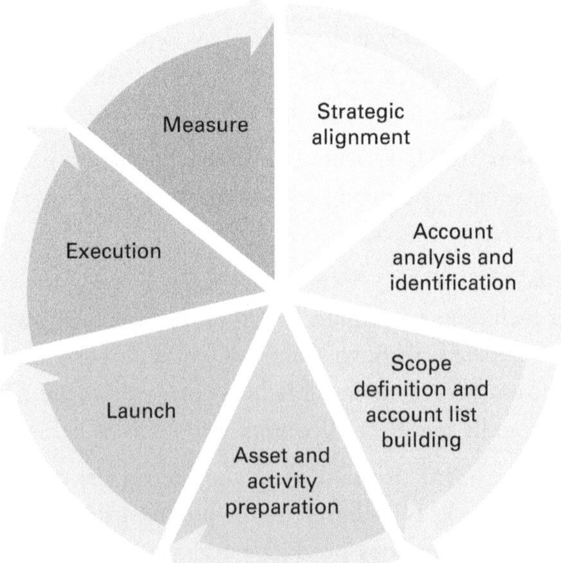

Figure 21.2 The ABM process and key applications

Step	Strategic alignment, account data analysis Steps 1 and 2	Account scope Step 3	Content and activity preparation Step 4	Launch and execute ABM Steps 5 and 6	Measurement Step 7
Description	Source account information, understand relevant accounts. Gather insights	Identify and prioritize accounts	Create account-specific content and messaging	Manage 1:1 account specific interactions and associated marketing channel activity	Demonstrate results of ABM, coverage, awareness, reach
Applications to support step	D&B, LinkedIn, Agent, Hoovers	Lattice, Leadspace, Everstring	Various B2B sources, use content management systems	Data management platforms, various marketing automation platforms	Marketing automation platforms

5 *Launch ABM*. Account data is loaded, typically into a CRM application. The ABM activity is launched according to scheduled timings. Coaching or training accompanies this step to support sales in using marketing assets and tools.

6 *Execution*. During this phase sales follow up on leads or make outbound calls for the pre-defined set of accounts.

7 *Measure and review*. KPIs are reviewed for each of the activities according to the accounts targeted. Corrective actions are taken where KPIs are not achieved; eg where follow-up is behind plan sales executives may act to ensure greater focus during a given period.

ABM methods

- Outbound ABM is most commonly used by larger businesses in relationship marketing; it is about leveraging marketing tactics such as e-mail, phone, direct mail and events to engage a target set of accounts for specific messages and content.
- Display-based ABM involves lining up ads so they only appear to people at specific companies. Some account-based advertising networks go one step further in targeting by role or title.
- Social is a great way to optimize ABM activities. By using social listening programmes, companies can gain insights into target account needs and pain points. Leveraging such insights, companies can post relevant content on social media sites, answering directly those customer needs. Using LinkedIn and Facebook, organizations can run very targeted adverts, down to named individuals of companies. LinkedIn allows for targeting adverts to people in companies according to role or job title.

TIP Where do you find account information for ABM?

One core success factor for ABM is correctly targeted accounts based on analysis and insights and can be drawn from different areas:

- *Past purchase and portfolio gaps.* These can be drawn from previous purchase history and can highlight purchase gaps, eg where only a few of the products/services are being purchased from a larger product portfolio.

- *Account propensity modelling.* A more sophisticated approach is to take multiple criteria such as sector, size of company and past purchase history, and use them to create a more accurate set of accounts based on richer detail. The idea is that a vendor can identify accounts with a higher propensity for purchasing its products or services.
- *Account plans.* Account manager input can help with customer insights and highlight likely prospects for targeting with additional products or services.
- Other sources of information include external telemarketing and data research companies.

Here are some key success factors drawn from companies that have demonstrated best practice:

- *Sales inclusion.* Co-leading or involving sales in the ABM process up-front can help with improved selection of customer accounts and improved focus in follow-up.
- *Insight-led.* Having some level of insights clearly helps in the identification process; although sales should provide help, this should be focused on criteria used for selection and informed rather than ad hoc input.
- *Business focused.* Having ABM programmes aligned to the business can help have the broader organization aligned to making ABM a success.
- *Programme design.* Programmes should be designed as a response to specific business challenges or need and thus add value. Content should be provided at different touch points for the intended target, off- and online.
- *Technology enabled.* Marketing integrating with CRM will help with reporting and tracking performance on a regular basis. Digital audience applications and social media applications can further complement ABM.
- *Communications.* How ABM is communicated to sales makes a difference; the purpose behind the activities needs to be emphasized.

Challenges with ABM

Despite the benefits of ABM, there are challenges that can hinder its effectiveness. These include lack of sales buy-in where sales are not fully aligned to the ABM activity; this could be due to poor communication or lack of agreement on target customer and type. Other factors can be resource based; for instance the number of accounts delivered to the business can exceed the capacity of specific sales people to cope with the volumes assigned to them.

Is ABM right for you?

ABM is suited to companies that have either relatively few accounts they wish to target or where they have a target group of accounts with similar characteristics. The latter could be an industry sector or a department within a company from a specific customer segment. Organizations should have some form of tracking and monitoring to carry out ABM effectively; this means having a form of CRM in-house or help from third-party companies.

ABM is not right for companies that are looking to market to a wider or mass audience or where the audience is so broad no segment or characteristics can be drawn. ABM relies on the ability to target so platforms that have targeting capabilities should be used. For example, LinkedIn can target customers by size, type and stakeholder.

The success of ABM lies in the personalized experience it can offer to customers, allowing the creation of relevant content according to buyer stages. ABM is a powerful tool for serving the right message and content to the right customer at the right time. Figure 21.3 shows how ABM leverages content and content marketing to engage customers.

Measuring ABM

ABM can be measured according to one or more of these categories:

- *Awareness*. Based on serving display adverts to targeted named people at the account, or monitoring according to named people's web or digital engagement. This allows the vendor to understand which themes are important to the account and potentially allows sales and marketing to improve their efforts.
- *Consideration/evaluation*. Based on the middle of the purchase journey and the evaluation stage the account may be in, this could be response rates or feedback on different tactics, eg e-mail response or white paper activity.
- *Account purchase activity*. This is the frequency and scale of purchase, and what was purchased.

Figure 21.3 ABM and the buying cycle

	Goal	Activities	Content	ABM KPIs
Early buying cycle	Transition from leads to qualified accounts	• Campaigns • Inbound • Outbound	• Blogs • Infographic • White paper	• Marketing-ready leads • Contact activities • Number of appointments
Late buying cycle	Convert opportunities to customers	• New opportunity • Evaluation • Negotiation	• Video testimonial • Case studies • 'How to' resources	• Lead conversion • CTR • Sales-ready leads
Portfolio expansion	Increase share-of-wallet	• New products • Outbound • Upgrades	• Case study • Video testimonial	• Net, new sales • Revenue per account • Deal size

- *Account penetration.* A measure of the extent to which the vendor is engaged in the customer account, the pipeline the customer delivers and the percentage share-of-wallet it has with the customer account.

ABM measurement ensures every campaign or activity scoped against the account is tied to the account in measuring and monitoring.

EXAMPLE Business success through ABM – RingCentral

RingCentral, a leading provider of software as a service (SaaS) for business communications, recently found great success through implementing an ABM strategy. The challenge was that around a third of its inbound leads were missing key fields or had inaccurate data and thus could not be aligned to sales teams; also, 20 per cent of inbound leads couldn't be matched to accounts. By using Leadspace Enrichment, RingCentral was able to add 80 new types of data in real time to leads, which in turn allowed it to qualify and route leads to sales. The results were an increased opportunity for conversion by over three times and the average sales price per customer rose by around 7.2 per cent. An associated benefit was a reduction in sales time to qualify leads.

References and further reading

Alterra Group (2011) Account-based Marketing: An approach on the rise in professional services, available at: http://alterra-group.com/wp-content/uploads/2011/04/AlterraGroupABMTopLevelResults.pdf (accessed 10 February 2017)

Event Marketer (2016) Event Track 2016 Content Edition – experiential marketing content benchmarking report, EventMarketer.com, available at: http://www.eventmarketer.com/wp-content/uploads/2016/05/2016EventTrackExecSummary.pdf (accessed 10 February 2017)

Newman, D (2016) Why B2B CMOs Need to Know About Account Based Marketing, *Forbes*, 29 April, available at: https://www.forbes.com/sites/danielnewman/2016/04/29/why-b2b-cmos-need-to-know-about-account-based-marketing/#26b58e465ab9 (accessed 10 February 2017)

Lead generation 22

This chapter will give you an understanding of:

- lead generation challenges
- types of leads
- leads and the buying cycle
- lead generation process
- lead generation tactics and strategies
- lead nurturing approaches

Introduction

Lead generation is the bread and butter of any B2B marketer and the challenge as always is extracting better leads and getting better value from them. Lead generation includes anything that constitutes an opportunity to sell to a customer, whether in the short or long term. They can be described as outbound or inbound; early buying cycle, mid or late buying cycle leads; as well as top, mid or bottom of funnel.

Difference between demand generation and lead generation

Sometimes lead generation is confused with demand generation. Demand generation covers all marketing activities that create awareness about an offering, company or industry and includes a mix of inbound and outbound marketing. Lead generation is a subset of demand generation. Demand generation is a marketing operation that serves to create a demand for or interest in your product. Lead generation, on the other hand, is used to collect specific information about potential clients, turning them into sales leads.

Trends in lead generation

During the 1990s and earlier, B2B marketers used to rely on outbound telemarketing for generating leads. These leads were typically internal or external third-party sales with accompanying scripts for calling a list of customer contact names. Today, companies doing well with lead generation are leveraging digital a lot more: they are connecting both off- and online and incorporating new automation platforms to better track leads.

Lead generation has recently been influenced by changes in buyers' journeys, by changes in how customers access and use information, and due to the increased availability of information. To be successful with lead generation today it's important for marketers to take on board such changes as well as to capitalize on the breadth of lead generation vehicles and content formats that can be used across the customer decision journey. Five years ago social media was rarely cited as a means of generating leads; it has now matured in such a way that it can be very effective in helping marketers identify and capture new business.

Challenges impacting lead generation

Below are the main challenges marketers and sales need to deal with regarding lead generation:

Getting the right quality of leads
Where the lead quality is not meeting sales requirements and leads are handed over before being ready for sales, this can lead to poor follow-up or impact sales productivity as sales are taking more time than they should in qualifying and nurturing the lead.

Time to load
If the time between lead capture and loading the lead for sales to follow up becomes unacceptably long, the chances are that the lead will be no longer viable.

Late sales follow-up
Where a lead is loaded on time but sales don't follow up in a reasonable amount of time, the lead can go cold.

Lack of a lead nurture process
Not having a specific process in place to engage, qualify, follow up and move the prospect further through the funnel can mean that good potential leads can amount to nothing.

Misaligned sales expectations
If sales expectations regarding leads are not set correctly, for example on volume, timing or type of leads, this can quickly result in misalignment of lead execution and opportunity detection.

Resourcing
If marketing has misaligned leads and sales resources this can mean poor lead execution. For example, where lots of leads are loaded at any given time and sales are not equipped to follow up, a high percentage of leads could be abandoned.

Types of leads

Leads can be categorized in many ways. In B2B the language used in defining leads is critical for talking the same language to internal and external parties. Here are the main categories of leads:

- *Marketing-ready leads (MRL)* are leads ready for marketing; unless it has been agreed to do so they should not be released to sales teams.
- *Marketing accepted leads (MAL)* can be the same as an MRL but are defined as those leads accepted by marketing; there can be a filter system only allowing through leads that adhere to a set of criteria.
- *Sales-ready leads (SRL)* are deemed ready for sales and for sales follow-up; depending on company's internal policies they can be the same as BANT leads.
- *BANT qualified leads* are ready to be passed to sales per the BANT set of criteria (see below).

BANT criteria are used for assessing the quality of prospects and tracking them through the sales qualification process:

B: Budgeted, where the leads have been budgeted.

A: Authority, where the lead is tagged with contact name, details.

N: Need based, where need and requirements are associated with the lead.

T: Timescale, regarding the lead in terms of the opportunity.

Lead generation and the customer buying cycle

In simple terms, we can think of lead type and status according to the marketing funnel; more appropriately should be mapped to the customer buying cycle.

The first are leads that relate to the initial stages of the buyer journey; they can be regarded as early buying cycle leads (EBL). Customers in this stage are aware but not yet in the evaluation phase. The next set of leads relate to customers who are aware of the company or need and are now evaluating a potential vendor; this should be thought of as mid buying cycle leads or MBL. During this phase customers have probably engaged with the vendor through some form of interaction with the vendor's content, directly or indirectly. The final stage is almost at the point of purchase or late buying cycle..Internal organization approaches to lead management, handover and lead nurture will determine whether these stages can be managed by sales or marketing, internally or externally (see Figure 22.1).

The lead generation process

The end-to-end lead generation process is summarized in the following main steps, mapped to customer buying cycle and typical marketing/sales process:

Enquiries	early part of buying cycle	marketing driven
Lead capture	mid buying cycle	marketing
Lead pre-sales qualification	mid buying cycle	marketing
Lead handover	mid to close	sales and marketing
Lead sales qualification	close of buying cycle	sales
Sale	close of buying cycle	sales

Enquiries are customers in the early stage of the buying cycle; they could be quantifying their need or evaluating vendors and alternatives. As business customers tend not to engage vendors directly, this stage of lead generation is typically led by marketing or third parties through content distribution.

Figure 22.1 Leads and the buying cycle

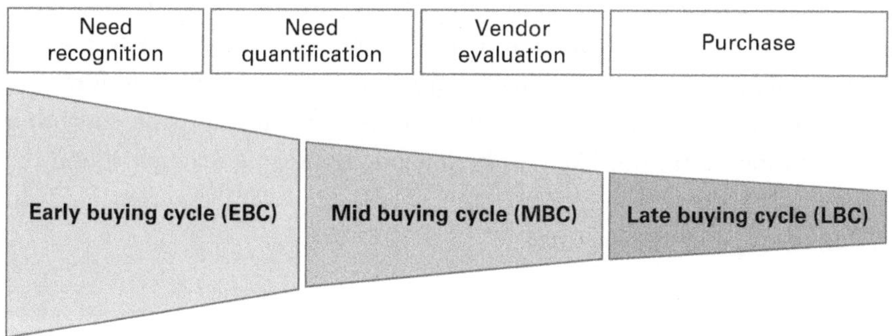

Lead capture. Can be through multiple lead generation vehicles; eg events, content syndication, download of content.

Lead pre-sales qualification. Can be through third-party telemarketing agencies, internal market/pre-sales teams in nurturing, or through marketing automation.

Lead handover. During this step the lead is handed over to sales, who are responsible for carrying out the remaining stages of further qualification (if required), opportunity conversion and ultimately closing the sale.

Lead sales qualification. During this stage sales qualify and progress the lead.

Sale. This is the final stage where the customers make the purchase.

Lead capture

Lead capture can occur through multiple different marketing vehicles or a combination of them; the main ones are door openers, webinars, e-mail with call-to-actions, events, outbound calls and content syndication. Content downloads are in the form of infographics, access to information, white papers or other, SEO, paid search, PR, social, direct e-mail, advertising, mobile and print advertising.

Multiple sources and lead quality

As customers will use multiple pieces of content across different channels before engaging a vendor it's important to consider the mix of lead generation tactics by campaign or customer type. Touch points are where customers interact with a vendor directly or indirectly. Multiple sources will tend to lead to a better output in terms of customer and lead capture.

Gated content and engagement

Lots of companies still ask interested parties to share their details prior to sharing content; it's common in B2B marketing. The risk with making content 'gated' is that a customer is not prepared to fill in long forms to get something in which he or she has a passing interest. Customers with a definite interest are not likely to be put off. Companies can get round the problem by either asking for very few details or providing automated field filling to speed up the process.

Lead qualification, handover and scoring

A lead is usually qualified against a set of criteria, according to marketing or sales requirements. The quality of these leads can be very different.

The sales handover within the lead generation process is important and lead management disciplines need to be adhered to. On average, less than a quarter of the leads on a company's website are ready for sales representatives to follow up; that's why lead scoring approaches are great, followed by lead nurturing. This allows relationships to be built with qualified prospects who may not be ready to speak with sales. The lead scoring systems allow the marketing department to understand which are the right leads to handover.

Handover can occur in different ways, according to the type of sales person and whether the customer is early or later in the buying cycle. The type of sales person can impact how leads are received; this is not about competence or ability but aligning the right lead with the right sales person. Additionally, where a lead requires a sales specialist but is handed to a generalist, this can quickly kill it off. It's therefore important to categorize leads by richer details and according to different sales types.

It's important not to pass leads on too early. If the marketing department feels pressurized to deliver on volume and not quality this can lead to poor quality leads being passed to sales. This can backfire on the business in terms of wasted effort, budget and time for both sales and marketing.

Figure 22.2 shows different views on lead scoring.On the left is scoring leads according to cold, warm and hot, which is about capturing and logging leads according to the stage of the buying cycle. Cold leads are very early leads and hot leads are late in the buying cycle, ready to be handed over to sales. In the box on the right, leads are categorized by propensity to purchase and stage in the buying cycle. The hottest leads are A1, A2 and B1.

Figure 22.2 Lead scoring

Lead type	Cold	Warm	Hot
Stage in buying cycle	Early buying cycle (EBC)	Mid buying cycle (MBC)	Late buying cycle (LBC)
Ranking	0–2	3–6	7–12
Lead level	NA	Marketing-ready lead	Sales-ready lead
Action	Target with content	Nurture further	Handover to sales

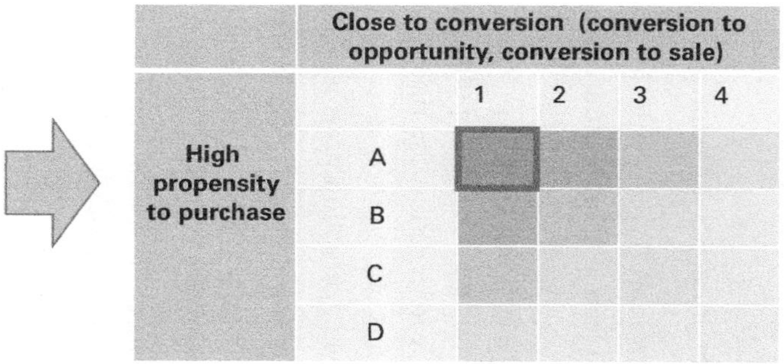

		Close to conversion (conversion to opportunity, conversion to sale)			
		1	2	3	4
High propensity to purchase	A				
	B				
	C				
	D				

Lead generation tactics and strategies

Here are some of the main tactics and strategies used in lead generation:

- *Sales handover adaptation.* Typically the lead generation process involves passing leads from a lead generation source, eg a telemarketing agency or content syndication company, to marketing and then to sales who may pass them to a different department of sales. This process can quickly expand to having multiple handover points, which prolongs the time it takes to progress a lead and runs the risk of the lead growing cold. One approach to improving effectiveness is to reduce the number of handover points during the lead generation process.
- *Funnel focus.* Depending on marketing department objectives there may be a focus on improving leads according to different areas of the funnel.
- *Website capture improvement.* Optimizing website pages for receiving leads through aligning content to buyer journeys as well as offering information or content alternatives for customers can help them along their buyer journey.
- *Lead nurture alternatives.* Rather than focus on one method, businesses can develop different ways to nurture different campaign leads through a mix of telemarketing, in-house nurturing, automated nurturing or media-based nurturing.
- *Reducing the cost per lead.* This can be achieved by putting out lead generation to tender, requesting more competitive quotes.

Lead generation agencies

Lead generation agencies come with greatly varying competencies. If the marketing department isn't responsible for the agency relationship, it's important to review lead quality through conversion and close ties with sales.

How do you select and manage a lead generation agency?

In selecting a lead generation agency the marketing department is now the potential customer. Ways to understand and select lead generation agencies can be through forums, word-of-mouth from contacts in similar roles in the industry, referral from a different type of agency, and from online searches.

Lead generation agencies should be managed on the basis of a clear briefing. The briefing should clearly communicate needs, expected quality and quantity of leads, expected cost per lead and contingency arrangements, for example where lead quality doesn't meet desired level. Outputs from lead generation agencies can then be monitored against this brief. Pipeline may be a difficult measurement, as the agency won't know the level or scale of opportunity in terms of revenue before taking on the role.

TIP How to manage and correct poor lead conversion

One of the recurring and frequent complaints from marketing departments is the conversion levels of leads. Below are some key steps that have been effective in resolving the issue of lead conversion and improving the quality of conversion:

1. *Map out the process in detail.* The current process that has led to poor results should be mapped out from lead capture through lead qualification and opportunity identification to deal closure. Each point in the process should be labelled accordingly.
2. *Look at conversion points* in the process to understand which metric is underperforming. Lead volume, marketing to sales accepted lead, sales lead to opportunity, pipeline creation or deal closure are all conversion points but it may be that only one of them is underperforming.
3. *Analyse further the conversion point* not meeting its KPIs; eg if the opportunity conversion rate is low, it could be that the quality of the lead is poor.
4. *Find the root cause of the impact.* For example, if opportunity conversion is the issue, is the cause a sales person or group not converting enough? Are they distracted with other demands? Opportunity conversion can also be impacted by timing of handover, type of lead, type of sales person, or experience of sales person.
5. *Assess* possible corrective actions and implement the most appropriate.
6. *Review* corrective action, based on implementation and new metrics.

Lead nurturing

Lead nurturing is the process of developing relationships with buyers at each stage of the sales process and the buyers' journey. It can be conducted in a variety of ways, depending on type of customer and customer segment. There are four main mechanisms to lead nurturing, shown in Figure 22.3:

The telemarketing agency's role can be to qualify leads and nurture to a stage in the buyer's journey. The competence of the agency and how marketing and sales expect to receive opportunities will determine to what stage a lead is nurtured. The benefit of this approach is that organizational resources are not tied up with lead nurturing.

In-house team. An organization may assign a person or people the task of qualifying leads or may establish a different team to nurture leads. This approach may be useful where the product or solution in question is complex and thus requires in-house expertise and investment in training. The costs for lead nurture are only the salaries of the in-house team members; another benefit is control over the lead's progress.

Media agencies capture leads and can nurture them through retargeting; such leads may still be passed to telemarketing agencies but be managed by media agencies.

In-house automation is managed by businesses that may decide to take captured leads and pass them through a marketing automation technology application such as Eloqua or Marketo to nurture them further.

EXAMPLE Crowe Horwath lead nurturing

One example of a lead nurturing programme is that of Crowe Horwath, an accountancy firm, which developed a programme covering a 12–18-month sales cycle. It involved targeting C-suite executives of large financial institutions. The programme included 48 pieces of content aligned to the customer decision cycle, intended for 4,000 executives. Executives were sent monthly e-mails offering free content and including them in a nurture programme. Based on the downloading of three pieces of content or one piece of content towards the end of the decision journey, the leads were regarded as sales-ready. This programme resulted in 33 per cent of invited executives entering the programmes and up to 80 per cent open rate for nurtured e-mails.

Figure 22.3 Lead nurture mechanics

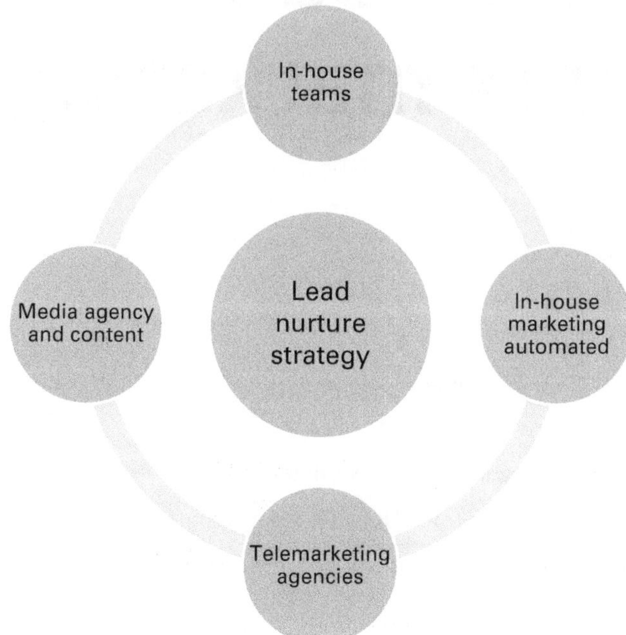

Further reading

Kirkpatrick, D (2015) Lead nurturing via e-mail series and content marketing, B2B lead blog, available at: http://www.B2Bleadblog.com/2015/01/lead-nurturing-via-email.html (accessed 8 February 2017)

Modern B2B events marketing 23

This chapter will give you an understanding of:

- B2B events types and segmentation
- events objectives and events selection
- event marketing and business buying stages
- key success factors for B2B events marketing
- event marketing and performance optimization
- social media and events

B2B events marketing

A marketing event in B2B is an activity revolving around a themed display or presentation leveraging people engagement, either virtually (via webinars) or physically. Events can occur on- or offline and can be participated in, hosted, or sponsored.

What are the benefits of using events?

Events can take a lot of time to organize, and are often more costly than other marketing vehicles. They involve a lot of effort in collaborating with agencies, third parties and other functions in a business.

However, they are extremely effective in marketing and ultimately selling a company's products and services. Where a businesses' portfolio is broad or complex and requires more than a few minutes to pitch, events can be an effective means of explaining more complex solutions. When done well events are also great incentives for potential customers, whether it's down to the opportunity to network and meet peers or discover new information. Events also help businesses stand out from the competition.

With more and more information accessible online for business customers during all phases of the buying cycle, events hold the opportunity and advantage of being a different communication channel that offers a more powerful engagement approach than online forums. Events also allow business vendors to engage customers via third-party conferences, collaborative events through sponsorship opportunities as well as market stall type events where vendors can pitch their portfolio to a large throughput of people. Webinars allow vendors to engage customers digitally, again through third parties if early in the buying cycle or directly later in the cycle where customers require more information in the evaluation phase.

Companies that run their own events have the advantage of greater control and influence over the event's scope, agenda and communication. Participating in a third-party event means a company can engage with customers at a lower cost. According to a study by the Event Marketing Institute (2016), 98 per cent of the respondents said that assuming the product or service promoted was one they were interested in, participating at the event or experience made them more inclined to purchase.

B2B event types and segmentation

Events come in numerous forms so it makes sense to segment them. They can be divided into virtual events (via the internet), face-to-face (in person) and voice-to-voice (using telephone and screens). They can also be segmented into company's own and third party, and customer orientation: by vertical, stakeholder or sector segment. In this case third-party events are run by a separate organization that subsequently invites different organizations to participate, rather than being appointed by one particular company. Voice-to-voice or webinars can be great ways to achieve customer reach, eg where customers are dispersed across a geography. The main types of events are as follows:

- Physical trade shows or trade fairs are exhibitions organized around a specific industry and allow companies from that sector to showcase their latest products and services. They tend to be large and include a range of businesses involved in the sector whether suppliers, customers, partners or channel partners.
- Seminars are usually educational in nature and focused on specific topics or themes; they are usually for groups of less than 50 and there to update and educate audiences. Companies sometimes use seminar-type events to engage new customers and to talk about topics related to their service offering.

- Product launch events are geared exclusively to the launch of a new product or service.
- Networking events are set up to allow business people to network with one another; event owners can engage and connect with people.
- Webinars are presentations, lectures, workshops or seminars transmitted over the web using video conferencing software. A key feature of a webinar is its interactive elements: the ability to give, receive and discuss information in real time.
- Workshops are like seminars but much more interactive; they involve audience participation.
- Networking dinners and lunches are designed to bring a small number of people together; they are typically there to allow vendors to engage more intensively with potential customers. They can also serve the purpose of retaining customers and help build or reinforce relationships.

EXAMPLE SPE Offshore Europe

One great example of a third-party vertical event is the SPE Offshore Europe, recognized as one of Europe's leading events covering the oil and gas industry. It takes place once a year in Aberdeen. In 2015 it attracted over 56,000 customers, over 1,500 exhibitors and at the event over 100 countries were represented. The event is the main go-to place for business professionals to learn the latest about oil- and gas-related trends, products and services. From a marketing perspective there were over 60 media association supporters who attended, more than 90,000 database contacts captured, and over 17,000 social media followers. Based on a survey of the 2015 events, over a third of exhibitors said they received orders worth between £50,000 and more than £10 million as a result of the event; at the event over 120,000 leads were generated and 24,000 leads were generated online.

Events marketing goals

There are multiple goals for events. A goal can be to introduce a company to new potential customers set up by a third party. Events can also serve to introduce existing customers to new portfolios, ie where a company gives the customers the opportunity to see new products or solutions first-hand or for organizations to be able to present and pitch new solutions more effectively.

A goal could be to deepen engagement with existing customers. Events are a great way to demonstrate an extended portfolio and discuss ways to improve business with customers. The events will vary, depending on existing customer relationships, the nature of the business and the number of customers. Events can be used as opportunities to surface and resolve any final questions or queries customers have before they purchase. They may be a way to draw customers away from alternative vendors and convert customers while they are in the consideration phase.

Physical events can help vendors reach customers in a particular location, or can span multiple regions. Vertical trade shows or conferences may be more appropriate for engaging potential customers from a vertical sector; annual sector-specific conferences or exhibitions can be an effective way to engage all involved in that sector.

Events marketing and business buying stages

Events can support a business throughout a customer's buying cycle in different ways; they can help customers move from one stage to the next. Some of the types of events and event implementations, shown in Figure 23.1, are:

Need recognition. Customers and organizations can stay in touch through themed events and trade shows; business can reach a mass of customers some of which use events to keep themselves up to date. Events also allow customers to discover new ways of doing business and optimizing their business and therefore recognize different needs.

Need quantification. Webinars and informal events allow customers to engage and further discuss a challenge, providing them with the necessary tools and information to quantify a need internally.

Vendor evaluation. In the vendor evaluation phase, vendors may indirectly target a type of customer through sponsoring or participating in events.

Vendor selection. Between consideration and purchase, organizations can take advantage of events by inviting customers who may have downloaded white papers or other content or made contact by phone. The

Figure 23.1 Events and the buyer journey

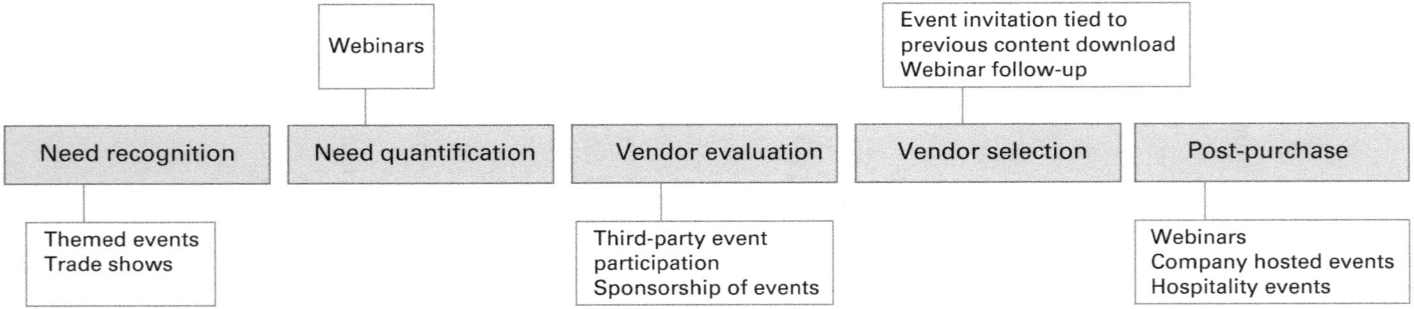

Webinars

Event invitation tied to
previous content download
Webinar follow-up

Need recognition

Need quantification

Vendor evaluation

Vendor selection

Post-purchase

Themed events
Trade shows

Third-party event
participation
Sponsorship of events

Webinars
Company hosted events
Hospitality events

event invitation and attendance gives the vendor the opportunity to promote its offering and value-add.

Post-purchase. Events or webinars in different forms can be used to reinforce relationships with customers as well as continue to communicate value propositions; hospitality post-event allows businesses to stay in touch with customers and build stronger relationships.

Events marketing problems and success factors

Problems

Events marketing performance can be affected by multiple aspects. An event agency may not capture all leads and contacts due to insufficient event staff being in place, or missed opportunities at the point of entry. If the event agency doesn't hand over contacts or leads in a timely fashion, the leads can go cold before the vendor has a chance to follow up.

A company can quickly change priorities or marketing change their priorities or focus; where this is the case captured leads may be neglected. Where event leads are not assigned correctly, the quality of follow-up can be adversely affected. Finally, the customer opportunity may not be correctly captured, resulting in a poor sales follow-up.

Key success factors

Below are some of the main factors that contribute to the success of events marketing:

Data capture. Ensure that information can be captured and is captured about customers before, during and after the event.

Plan. Allow time to set up and implement; with short lead-times companies can falter by finding ideal venues booked up for the best dates.

Allow for customers' timelines and schedules. Plan in advance to allow for potential attendees having calendars booked up months in advance. Notifying customers a few weeks prior to the event won't work.

Know the events market. Avoid setting up events on dates where competing industry or trade events are taking place.

Set realistic attendee targets. A number of customers will drop off between the registration stage and the date of the event; industry standard drop-off rates are around 50 per cent.

Venue selection. The venue needs to suit the type of event, audience, audience location, etc. The right venue can have a major impact on the success of the event and therefore its goals.

Follow-up. Provide customer contact information and leads from events within a few days of the event.

Capturing data prior to the event applies to customers that are more likely to attend. Where the event is intended to be split by region, the data can be used to understand customer location and invite according to a maximum distance to the event. Attendee details can be gathered along with comments and opinions on presentations, content and speakers. Audience ratings of the event overall will provide feedback as to what can be changed or adapted should the event be repeated.

TIP How to engage customers before and after events

The mistake some companies make is to view an event as a single activity and opportunity to engage customers, thereby missing out on potential opportunities to connect with customers before and after the event. Look at the pre- and post-event activities in Figure 23.2. Organizations can use events to inform, educate and interact with customers, through surveys, through Q&A, through sharing pieces of content or research. This can be done on the company website, social media platforms or through advertising.

Following the event, organizations can connect and follow up with customers by sharing related pieces of research or content, or by helping them in their evaluation of current challenges. Post-event, companies can use this interaction to acquire, retain or grow business with the customer or prospect.

TIP How to maximize attendance and reduce 'no-shows'

Organizations can maximize attendance by sending event invitations well in advance, helping customers to plan better around the event. Before sending the invitation organizations or agencies can contact the customer directly to explain more about the event; this is easier where the intended audience is

(*continued*)

Figure 23.2 Events pre- and post-engaging the customer

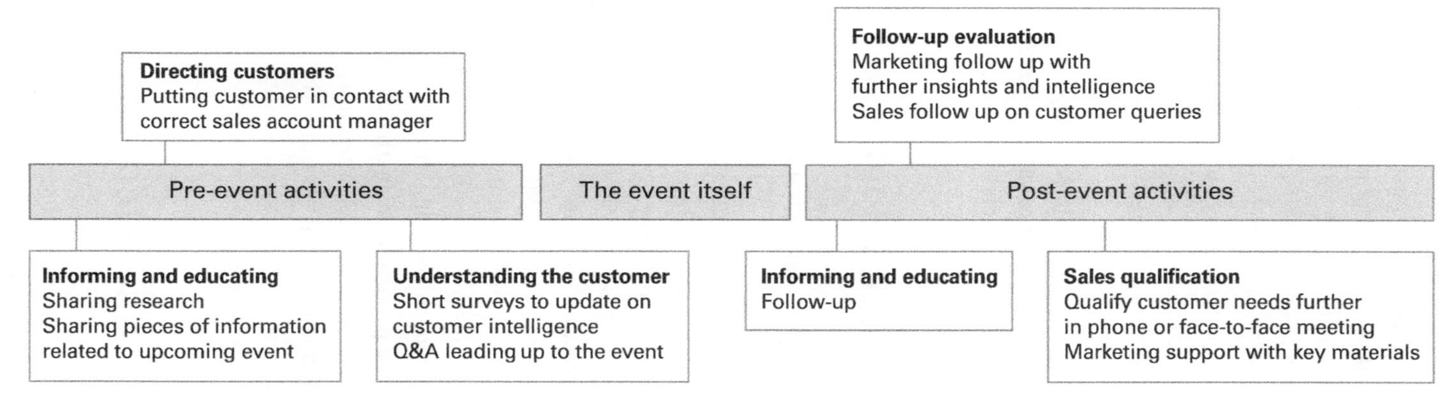

(*Continued*)

existing customers or where the organization has some form of relationship with them. Reminder e-mails help prompt the customer, though organizations need to be careful not to send too many reminder e-mails too often.

There are two different views on charging event fees; on the one hand they help lock in the audience and therefore they are less likely to not show up; on the other hand, it can put off attendees as they feel the event shouldn't be charged for.

Some vendors involve customers in the event whether providing a stand or booth or as part of the presentation.

Events can be promoted in different ways to increase exposure or targeting; some of the ways are to use telemarketing agencies, PR and the company's own websites and social media sites.

New events technologies

New events technologies and digital applications can help B2B marketers maximize and optimize events. With the help of near field communication (NFC), event organizers can make their events much more interactive. NFC-enabled devices come in different forms such as smartphones, barcode readers or tablets. NFC technology can be activated by chips in attendees' wristbands or badges. Terminals with NFC readers could encourage attendees to take a picture and automatically share it on social networks, for example. NFC devices are perfect voting and rating tools and could be used to determine the most desired product at trade fairs.

Virtual event platforms allow for virtual participation so customers can attend events without leaving their desk. Webinar platforms allow businesses to provide presentations with one-, two- or three-way communication, eg vendor to customers, customer interaction or between customers. Registration platforms can help you quickly set up a webpage and then invite attendees; set-up can be done in minutes, and the platform can help with reminder e-mails. Some platforms are free.

Social media and events marketing

Social has become a powerful tool for B2B marketing in the past decade. For events marketing purposes social can be used to maximize the event before, during and after (see Table 23.1):

Before the event

Twitter can be used to promote events and to increase exposure through likes, shares regarding the event and related topics. LinkedIn and Facebook can also be used to highlight an event.

During the event

The most commonly used social platform is Twitter. By creating a Twitter handle or address linked to the event, information and comments can be provided and shared in real time. It's important to build Twitter lists and for vendors to promote sharing by providing regular updates through the event to encourage usage and participation.

After the event

After the event LinkedIn and Facebook can be used to share stories or longer articles related to the event. Twitter can be used to direct people to LinkedIn and Facebook or other website landing pages.

Table 23.1 Social media and events

	Before	During	After
Twitter	Great for spreading news, can be good to promote to Twitter groups or specific members	Most interesting as Twitter is more for real-time occurrences at event, photos	Great to talk generally about event
Facebook	Nice way to promote through graphics		Share stories about event
LinkedIn	Great for advertising and promoting Via InMail most targeted way	Not easy to use in real time	Reports and overviews can be shared on forums, company LinkedIn pages, etc

Maximizing event lead capture

Twenty years ago event leads capture was conducted manually, writing on paper and/or collecting business cards. Nowadays leads capture includes badge or barcode scanning during and after the event at exits and entrances. The main ways companies can capture event leads are:

- *Badges with barcode and barcode scanning*. Event personnel use barcode scanners, usually at the entrance to the event.

- *Use of PCs or tablets.* Tablets are used to log in audience details, usually at event entrances or reception.
- *Business card collection and scanning electronically.* Business cards are collected manually and then scanned in or manually inputted into a database.
- *Surveys.* These can help host companies get feedback and at the same time understand attendance, providing a hard copy back to attendees.

There are three considerations when selecting the best way to capture leads:

1. *Number of customers.* Where there are few customers it might be better to collect business cards and manually input them rather than invest in using technology.
2. *Speed and ease of registration for visitors.* Visitors may find data capture a lengthy process and be put off.
3. *Data protection.* The form and process of lead capture must comply with data protection legislation.

ACTIVITIES

Review your current marketing activities in engaging customers face-to-face (physical events) or voice-to-voice (webinars). How are you using events to support customers during the buying journey and where are there gaps?

Look at the key success factor list in this chapter and look at where there is potential for optimization.

Reference and further reading

Event Marketing Institute (2016) Event track 2016 content edition – experiential marketing content benchmarking report, eventmarketer.com, available at: http://www.eventmarketer.com/wp-content/uploads/2016/05/2016EventTrackExecSummary.pdf (accessed 10 February 2017)

SPE Offshore Europe (2015) Post show review (conference and exhibition), SPE Offshore Europe, available at: http://www.offshore-europe.co.uk/RXUK/RXUK_Offshore-Europe/documents/RXOE8255 per cent 20Post per cent20Show_V6_final.pdf (accessed 10 February 2017)

Modern marketing operations

24

This chapter will give you an understanding of:

- marketing data management
- marketing budget management
- marketing reporting and measurement
- metrics – overview and model

Marketing operations

Marketing operations serves marketing and the business. It covers a set of activities that support efficiencies within marketing departments in their delivery of value to the business and in demonstrating that value. Marketing operations is the backbone behind marketing departments that allows it to function to its maximum capacity. It also acts as a control group to assess how marketing is performing and to identify areas to correct. The main areas it covers are:

- managing a set of activities that support demand generation;
- managing marketing infrastructure;
- budgeting and planning; financial governance and reporting;
- campaign analysis and reporting;
- customer, market, competitive intelligence, research and insights;
- data management;
- technology, automation and pipeline management.

In large organizations, these may be covered by entire departments and teams, usually centralized to avoid duplication of resources. In smaller companies this can be part of someone's role or subcontracted to an external company, depending on budget and the scale of work involved.

Figure 24.1 MPM areas

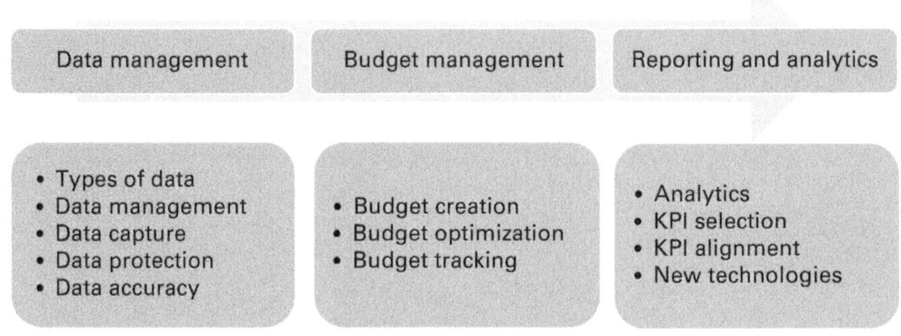

Marketing data management

Data for any marketer is critical in allowing them serve the business, in marketing, in tracking marketing performance and reviewing effectiveness of marketing. Marketing data can be split into three main areas.

1. *Customer data.* Customer data helps profile customers, identify buying behaviours and understand how to engage them, eg by phone, e-mail or other forms.
2. *Marketing campaign data.* This refers to the tracking of leads by activity and campaign, and helps marketers demonstrate value-add to the business; it can also help track effectiveness of budget spend.
3. *Market data.* Includes market trends, segments, growth, size and competition.

Data can also be split according to the source of the data, for example:

- *First-party data.* Data from proprietary assets or contained in enterprise systems.
- *Second-party data.* Someone else's first-party data, often shared with another company in a mutually beneficial relationship.
- *Third-party data.* Consolidated from websites and platforms other than own data.

Capturing data

Capturing data or insights is often seen by a business as one of the great value-adds of a marketing department; the department provides a view of markets, customers, competition and other macro dynamics that may not be seen or captured from ongoing business activities or conversations with existing customers. Marketers need to be able to look at different capture mechanisms, understand how to track data, and monitor, manage and present it.

Customer data can come from different sources such as sales account plans, including customer needs, challenges, upcoming projects, and anything related to the account; account plans can also help marketers understand which messages to deliver to address the latest needs. Sales account plans can be loaded to CRM applications where they may be more readily accessible. Surveys are a great way for marketing departments to reach out to potential customers to capture interest. Marketing events and webinars are useful to capture input through networking with customers, as are surveys carried out at events.

From digital traffic, eg customers downloading documents from the company website or syndicated content, information can also be captured. Customer preferences regarding topics and themes can also be tracked through website analytics highlighting most-clicked topics on website pages. Finally, customer data can be purchased from different companies such as Dunn and Bradstreet, Equifax and Experian.

TIP The new digital applications for tracking customer behaviours

Social monitoring or analytical tools can help monitor conversations and key words; they can aid marketers in assessing what people think about products, customer service experiences and corporate developments. These tools can also help to monitor competitors, to identify pain points or trends based on chatter themes, and identify influencers. There are many social listening tools; examples are Hootsuite, Radian6, Alterian, Sysomos and Hubspot.

Data management platforms (DMPs) are being increasingly used by B2B marketers; they draw data from internal and external resources and help in personalizing online channels and content for customers. DMPs can be used to drive website and mobile personalization, display targeting, content targeting, e-mail and direct e-mail campaigns and can determine where targeted or frequency of messages drives higher response rates. Examples of DMPs include Bluekai, Mediamath and Turn.

Marketing campaign data can be captured through automation platforms to track response rates on tactics, to track marketing performance, and content click-throughs. Alternative approaches are to use CRM applications to track lead-based marketing activities that eventually require sales follow-up and separately use web-based analytics programs to track digital and online marketing activities.

Market data such as trends and segments can be purchased from market research companies. Alternatively, companies can use their own market research methods such as surveys, forums, and focus groups that potentially leverage sales.

Data accuracy and data integrity

Marketers constantly wrestle with maintaining accurate data. Data describing companies can become obsolete if they have undergone mergers or acquisitions, or where a company experiences growth moving it from a small business to being categorized as a medium one. At a stakeholder level within customers or prospects, data can be impacted as individuals either change roles within the company or move outside the company.

For small business data accuracy can be maintained by using data houses whose responsibility it is to maintain that accuracy. Smaller organizations can insist that account managers ensure data and profiles are kept up to date. Larger companies can look to sales operations to ensure all existing data is maintained in its CRM systems and via marketing complement data through external data sources. Additionally, software can be used to merge data or capture inaccuracies within it.

'According to one survey, 55 per cent of respondents had been sent information about an irrelevant product by a business in the previous 12 months,' says Nigel Turner, VP of information management strategy at Trillium Software (Wickey, 2016). A large proportion of customers are annoyed when businesses get their personal information wrong. This is the consequence of bad data; vendors can lose credibility if they use the wrong names, titles, etc.

Data protection and marketing solutions

Over the past decade, marketing and data privacy laws have been implemented such that customers now can opt out of e-mails or other forms of communication and thus control what you send to them. This means that marketers need to think more about tailoring content to customers' needs.

E-mail marketing and data

The term 'soft opt-in' is sometimes used to describe the rule about existing customers. The idea is that if someone bought something recently and provided their details but didn't request opting out of marketing messages, they are probably happy to receive such messages about similar products. This doesn't apply to prospective customers: organizations need to provide the customer with the opportunity to opt out of e-mails.

TIP How to you improve your contact strategy despite data protection restrictions

Where data protection influences contact strategy to such an extent, organizations can employ different options to engage customers:

- *Use different channels.* Where e-mail is no longer an option, organizations can look to social to engage the same target customers.
- *Request to opt in again.* Using a different route, an organization can offer a customer the chance to opt in to e-mails but based on selected topics or preferred themes.
- *Different contact route.* Where the contact person isn't receptive, an organization can employ a different contact route through a different department or person.

Marketing budget management

Many B2B marketers at some point experience the challenge of doing more marketing with the same or lower budget. As a result marketers need to be able to justify every part of their budget while optimizing and improving ROI, as well as looking for creative ways to further optimize their marketing activities.

Marketing budgeting trends

Some recent trends impacting marketing budgets are the increasing spend on digital marketing. As a result of changing customer behaviours and how they use and access information, allocation of spend to digital channels is increasing.

Programmatic spend is on the increase, is growing more efficient and becoming more focused; it will help maketers target, retarget and engage customers. With increased competition, B2B marketers are looking not only for lead generation but also to position the brand and communicate its value proposition. Sales are demanding better and higher quality leads from marketing. Marketing are being asked to provide nurtured or more qualified leads.

With the need to pre-empt buyers in self-informing and deciding to go for a different vendor, organizations are looking to marketing to invest more in social platforms, social communications and content, so as to capture customers earlier in their buyer journey.

Defining the marketing budget

There are different ways to calculate the marketing budget and budgets can vary according to the type of marketing, ie consumer or B2B. Typically, consumer marketing budgets can be substantially bigger than those of business marketing. Many businesses allocate a percentage of revenue for marketing, sometimes called the reinvestment rate – the amount of spend the business reinvests in marketing.

Allocation of budget will depend on a number of factors: size of business, growth stage, profit and margins a business is making. Other factors include industry type: in some sectors, B2B marketing is more about sales enablement and support. Marketing-led environments, as in B2C, rely on marketing to do the lion's share of communicating to customers. Marketing will be expected to support a new strategic focus, for example if the business is to open up new channels or to maximize a product or solutions launch; to meet the temporary peak in marketing activity, budgets may be increased for a while.

Marketing budget process

Once the level and size of budget have been set, marketers should plan their budget:

1 *Translate business objectives into marketing objectives.* Assuming the business objectives for the upcoming period are already in place, the next step is to define those objectives in marketing terms. If the business objectives are: a) to go for incremental growth, and b) positioning a new product or solution, the marketing objectives could be supporting messaging and communication of a new solution or product, and generating leads for the business.

Figure 24.2 Budgeting process

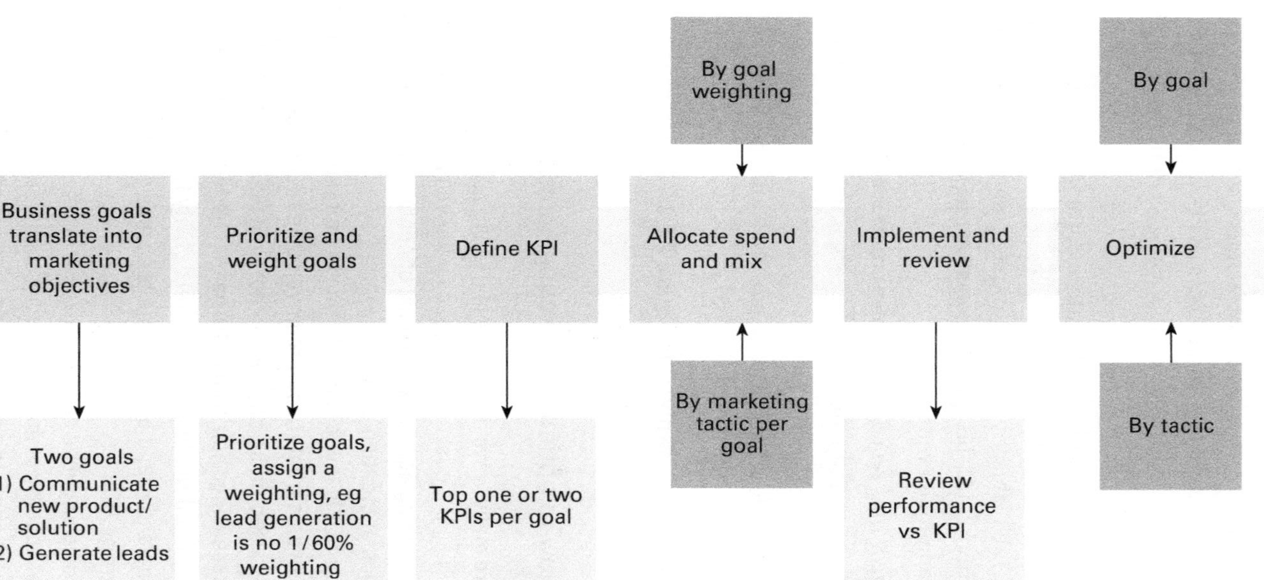

2 *Prioritize and weight objectives.* Assuming the weighting and importance of a and b above is equal, the budget should be split between the two core areas. If this is not the case, it's important to prioritize one over the other and agree in principle on a weighting.

3 *Define KPIs by marketing objectives.* Whether for internal briefing purposes or external with agencies, KPIs should be defined. They could be number of opportunities and leads; or objectives linked to customer reach or impressions.

4 *Allocate spend and mix.* Allocate according to priority and weighting of goals and then by marketing vehicle or tactics, considering key tactics to achieve each objective. For example, communication of a new product or solution could be split by social media, PR, advertising, banner, and maybe a launch event.

5 *Implement and review.* Implementation then occurs with time to review. The KPIs in step 3 can be used to see if marketing activity is performing as planned.

6 *Optimize budget.* Depending on ROI and performance against KPIs, budgets can be optimized by goal or tactic.

The budget process is shown in Figure 24.2.

TIP How to optimize marketing budgets

There are many ways to optimize marketing budgets. Costs can be reduced by reviewing the cost of agency fees if the company is using marcom, PR, or telemarketing agencies. The cost of content can be looked at in terms of production or creation cost.

Where ROI is low or contribution to marketing goals is not regarded as effective, marketers can remove some tactics or activities. Marketers should be cautious in defining which activities to remove and in assessing their true performance in terms of relevant KPIs. They may need to allow time for an activity to take effect – acquisition marketing and brand building can take time to implement and demonstrate ROI.

Reducing priorities and objectives is another way to optimize budgets. Marketers can try to do many things, supporting many objectives, and end up with multiple priorities. Reducing priorities, improving focus and aligning marketing resources can lead to improved ROI.

Another possibility is to increase/reallocate the budget. For instance, regional marketing can request more budget from a central marketing function; or the regional marketing department can engage a local partner that will provide additional funding.

Changing the marketing mix to shift from high cost marketing tactics to lower cost ones can help. For example, where a B2B marketing programme contains a lot of video content that eats up a disproportionate amount of the budget, a marketer could consider moving to lower cost marketing channels. Marketing could also look at reducing the number of pieces of content per buying stage or reusing content over a longer period.

Reporting and analytics

Marketing reporting and analytics provide a consistent way to measure and track business as well as different views of marketing performance. They facilitate marketing in improving performance as well as the business in justifying marketing investment decisions.

Applications for reporting and analytics

In reporting and tracking performance two main types of applications are available to marketers: marketing automation platforms and CRM systems. Marketing automation platforms are still only used by a minority of marketers according to the Lead Generation Benchmark Report (Demand Metric, 2014), while half use CRM systems.

Difference between marketing automation and CRM

Marketing automation allows companies to streamline, automate and measure marketing tasks and workflows. It allows marketing departments to increase operational efficiency.

Marketing automation spans several marketing areas including e-mail marketing, campaign management, lead generation, social marketing and much more; it can cover almost every marketing activity and can even integrate elements of CRM.

CRM can be defined as an application for managing all of a business's interactions with current and prospective customers. Although very much a tool more used by sales, it's also used by marketing to better track opportunities.

What to measure

Marketing measurement systems depend on the type of customer segment, business model and marketing. For example, where marketing is supporting a high-touch sales model, measurement may include outbound metrics, use of content by customer journey, number of attendees at events, etc. Where marketing supports a low-touch sales model but high-digital-touch model the measurement may be purely based on digital KPIs.

Marketing measurement systems may also be heavily focused on the bottom of the marketing funnel where marketing's main role is to support marketing execution, or weighted more to the top of the funnel where the main role is in positioning the brand and communicating its value proposition. In other cases, the marketing role may be a mix of awareness, consideration and purchase-based activities. Table 24.1 shows a summary of the types of marketing and relevant KPIs.

Table 24.1 KPI alignment and goals

	Type of marketing	Example KPI descriptors
Hi-touch sales model	1. Enablement 2. Outbound 3. Offline 4. Digital	1. a) Sales participation, b) sales engagement 2. a) Account follow-up, b) opportunity, c) pipeline 3. a) Event leads, b) event opportunities 4. a) Website traffic, b) online downloads, c) online queries, d) digital leads from content syndication
Digital intensive	1. Website 2. E-mail 3. Video 4. Other	1. Website traffic, engagement, time on site 2. E-mail click-through rate, click-to-open rate 3. Video download, engagement 4. Digital leads, sales-ready leads, opportunities
Top of funnel	Awareness Brand building	1. PR circulation 2. Online traffic 3. Content engagement 4. Other brand KPIs
Execution intensive	Marketing execution – bottom of funnel	1. Sales-ready lead volume 2. Opportunity volume and conversion 3. Pipeline 4. Revenue
Blended	Awareness Consideration Execution (purchase)	Blended mix of the above selecting maximum of one or two key KPIs from each of the areas of the marketing funnel

EXAMPLE Thomson Reuters – marketing automation

Thomson Reuters is a professional services company and is an example of a business that uses marketing automation to improve its targeted messaging. Thomson Reuters relied heavily on e-mail marketing to produce leads, though the quality of the leads wasn't always high, leading to sales conducting their own lead generation activities.

Through marketing automation, Thomson Reuters could bring together sales and marketing while improving segmentation, targeting and overall lead scoring. This led to 23 per cent more leads provided to sales, and a 17.5 per cent increase in revenue attribution to marketing leads.

ACTIVITIES

Review current marketing performance. What top three KPIs are being used to communicate with the business?

Are all current KPIs relevant to communicate to the business? Which ones need to be removed and which ones need to be added?

Is the current measurement system reflecting the work that marketing delivers for the business or are certain marketing efforts being ignored? Why?

References and further reading

Demand Metric (2014) Lead generation: fueling the revenue engine, available at: https://www.salesfusion360.com/uploads/1/Kayla/Docs/Demand%20Metric%20-%20lead_generation_benchmark_report.pdf (accessed 8 February 2017)

Oracle (2016) Thomson Reuters uses content to start conversations that boost conversions, Oracle Marketing Cloud, available at: https://www.oracle.com/marketingcloud/content/documents/casestudies/thomson-reuters-customer-success-oracle.pdf (accessed 8 February 2017)

Wickey, W (2016) Why data is the (not so) secret ingredient to marketing and sales alignment, available at: http://www.business2community.com/b2b-marketing/data-not-secret-ingredient-marketing-sales-alignment-01716196 (accessed 8 February 2017)

INDEX